The Muse of the Revolution

The Muse

of the

Revolution

The Secret Pen of Mercy Otis Warren
and the Founding of a Nation

NANCY RUBIN STUART

BEACON PRESS, BOSTON

Beacon Press
25 Beacon Street
Boston, Massachusetts 02108-2892
www.beacon.org

Beacon Press books
are published under the auspices of
the Unitarian Universalist Association of Congregations.

11 10 09 08   8 7 6 5 4 3 2 1

This book is printed on acid-free paper that meets the uncoated paper
ANSI/NISO specifications for permanence as revised in 1992.

Text design and composition by Susan E. Kelly
at Wilsted & Taylor Publishing Services

Frontispiece: Portrait of Mercy Otis Warren by John Singleton Copley.
Photograph © 2008 Museum of Fine Arts, Boston.

Rubin Stuart, Nancy
    The muse of the revolution : the secret pen of Mercy Otis Warren and the found-
ing of a nation / Nancy Rubin Stuart.
        p. cm.
    Includes bibliographical references and index.
    ISBN 978-0-8070-5516-8 (acid-free paper)   1. Warren, Mercy Otis, 1728–1814.
2. United States—History—Revolution, 1775–1783—Women.   3. Women historians—United States—Biography.   I. Title.
    PS858.W8Z89 2008
    973.3'092—dc22
    [B]   2007038365

To Bill,
first friend of my heart

CONTENTS

Preface *xi*

PART I *Daughter of Liberty*

1   A Pen As Explosive As Gunpowder *3*
2   Fires, Civil and Domestic *19*
3   "Neither the pen nor the tongue of a lawyer" *33*
4   The Patriots' Secret Pen *45*
5   "No one has at stake a larger share of
     domestic felicity" *57*
6   "Perhaps the whole land be involved in blood" *69*

PART II *Conscience of the Revolution*

7   Reporter of Revolutionary Events *83*
8   A Still Calm Within, Violent Concussions Without *97*
9   "Ladies are the greatest politicians" *109*
10   "The hand often shrunk back from the task" *121*
11   "War has ever been unfriendly to virtue" *133*

PART III *The Patriot Historian*

12   Views from Neponset Hill *147*
13   Hope Is an Airy Queen *159*
14   The Public Is a Monster Seldom Guided
     by Reason *171*
15   "The fair fabric of a free, strong and
     national republic" *183*
16   "Too federal to talk freely" *195*

PART IV   *Penwoman to Posterity*

17   "A sister's hand may wrest a female pen"   *209*
18   "Alas, humiliated America!"   *221*
19   A Sea Change in Party Politics   *233*
20   "In the spirit of friendship"   *245*
21   "Blessed are the peacemakers!"   *257*

Acknowledgments   *269*

Notes   *273*

Bibliography   *287*

Index   *299*

WHEN I BEGAN RESEARCHING this biography of Mercy Otis Warren, friends often wondered about her identity. I explained that John Adams considered her the "most accomplished woman in America"[1] whose literary works he thought "incontestable instances of genius." His wife, Abigail, who was one of Mrs. Warren's closest friends, "loved the characters"[2] drawn by her pen. To Thomas Jefferson, Mrs. Warren was brilliance itself. George Washington praised her literary merits. Diplomat Arthur Lee claimed he knew no woman "whose conversation pleased him more than Mrs. Warren's."[3]

During the Revolutionary era, Mrs. Warren's propaganda plays appeared on the front page of the *Massachusetts Spy* and the *Boston Gazette*. A dozen years later, her widely distributed pamphlet "Observations on the New Constitution" influenced the Bill of Rights. By 1805 her three-volume publication of *The History of the Rise, Progress and Termination of the American Revolution* became the sole Antifederalist, or Jeffersonian republican, interpretation of that extraordinary event.

Mrs. Warren's words still have a contemporary ring. Americans, she reminded readers of her *History*, must never forget that "the elective franchise is in their own hands; that it ought not to be abused, either for personal gratifications, or the indulgence of partisan acrimony. The principles of revolution ought ever to be the pole-star of the statesman, respected by the rising generation."[4]

To most people, Mercy Otis Warren, nevertheless, remains a forgotten Founding Mother. While occasionally cited in books about the Founding Fathers, studies of her life are usually confined to college seminars, academic biographies, and the rare-book rooms of libraries.

It was not my intention to focus upon the theoretical aspects of Mrs. Warren's long life, but rather to paint an intimate picture of her life for the general reader. Through excerpted selections from her correspondence,

Mercy Otis Warren reveals herself as a perceptive, strong, and deeply caring individual, sometimes foolishly driven by emotions, at other times guided by cool rationality, alternately witty and vitriolic, but ultimately human in her flaws and virtues.

The reasons for Mrs. Warren's obscurity are complex, a result of the eighteenth-century bias against learned women and her commitment to the unpopular republican values of the early Revolution.

Relatively few biographies have consequently appeared on Mercy Otis Warren. The first, in Eizabeth Elett's 1848 series, *The Women of the American Revolution*, hailed her as "perhaps the most remarkable woman who lived at the time of the Revolution."[5] Forty years later, Elizabeth Cady Stanton, Susan B. Anthony, and Matilda Joslyn Gage's *History of Woman Suffrage* reminded readers that Mrs. Warren advocated "not to the freedom of man alone, but to that of her own sex also."[6] By 1896, playwright Alice Brown had obtained copies of her letters and wrote the first documented account of her life. In the mid-twentieth century, Katharine Anthony's biography reminded modern readers of Mrs. Warren's existence, followed in 1995 by Rosemarie Zagarri and Jeffrey Richard's two analytical studies of her life and work.

Mercy Otis Warren would probably have applauded those efforts, especially since her correspondence often lamented women's second-class status. Repeatedly, in her plays and poems, she portrayed female weakness and dependence upon their men, implicitly urging readers to behave courageously in the face of ongoing civil strife.

When "Betsy," one of the young women Mrs. Warren counseled later in life, asked why women were often ignorant or silly, the author maintained that their "deficiency" was less related to the "interior contexture of female intellect" than the "different education bestowed on the sexes." A complete education for women, she insisted, would make them "rational companions to men" and "distinguished for their economy" in the home.[7]

Highly educated herself, Mrs. Warren enjoyed the full measure of a womanly life. Happily married to Massachusetts merchant-farmer and politician James Warren, the mother of five sons, a skilled homemaker, needle worker, and gardener, her life epitomized the advice she once gave a niece. If a woman had a kind husband, a pleasant home, a decent income, and good children, she had "all that the world could bestow."[8]

Proof of Mrs. Warren's belief in that formula appears in her letters, revealing her own traditional dependency upon men for emotional support—especially from her husband, James, her mentor, John Adams, and in old age, from her sons Henry and James, Jr.

By the late twentieth century, feminist scholars observed that regardless of Mrs. Warren's support for women's educational equality, her published work never specifically addressed that issue unlike other, slightly younger writers like Judith Sargent Murray, Catharine Macaulay, and Mary Wollstonecraft. Feminist historians also ponder why Mrs. Warren failed to respond to Abigail Adams's 1776 "petition" in reaction to her husband John's rejection of her plea to "Remember the ladies."[9]

No less ironic to me were the occasions when, in spite of Mrs. Warren's patriotic fervor, she balked when her husband, James, was offered important Revolutionary posts that required long absences from Massachusetts. As I have indicated in the pages below, her traditional dependence upon James often intruded, and indeed, precluded, the full achievement of the Warrens' fervently expressed patriotic goals. In her defense, the high-strung Mrs. Warren was approaching fifty at the time of the Revolution, having spent most of her adult life as a conventional wife and mother.

Her literary bent, her paternal family's participation in the politics of Massachusetts Colony, and her brother James "the Patriot's" role as spark to the Revolution nevertheless inspired her to compose inflammatory plays, poems, and essays. Another factor was the Revolution itself, which transformed her, Abigail Adams, and their friends into "war widows," who clung to one another for comfort and expressed their patriotism by raising loyal citizens in what contemporary historian Linda Kerber famously termed "Republican Motherhood." Other contemporary scholars, such as Mary Beth Norton and Nancy Cott, traced that generation's rising awareness of female strength as antecedents to the nineteenth-century suffrage movement.

To portray Mrs. Warren's life, I drew upon primary sources from her correspondence and those of her contemporaries. Among them were the unpublished *Warren Family Letters and Papers, 1763–1814* housed at the Archives of Pilgrim Hall Museum, the Mercy Otis Warren Papers at the Massachusetts Historical Society, and the published collections of her correspondence in the *Warren-Adams Letters, The Correspondence of John Adams and Mercy Otis Warren,* the *Adams Family Correspondence,* and *A Study in Dissent: The Warren-Gerry Correspondence 1776–1792.*

Mrs. Warren once told John Adams she believed the reader should never "suffer from fatigue when listening to the humiliating story of human conduct." In that spirit, I have modernized the spelling and capitalization of original sources.

Mercy Otis Warren's life as wife, mother, homemaker, patriot, and author remains exceptional even by the standards by which we judge women's lives today. While often anonymously published, her work, the caricatures in her popular propaganda plays—the first written by an American woman—her forthright plea for a Bill of Rights, her poetry, and her three-volume *History* immortalize Mrs. Warren as the muse of the American Revolution.

PART I

Daughter of Liberty

1

A Pen As Explosive As Gunpowder

INITIALLY, MERCY OTIS WARREN was overwhelmed by the invitation, which arrived in Plymouth on a chill, snowy day in late December 1773, written in the familiar hand of John Adams.

The letter, addressed to Mercy's husband, James, merchant-farmer and high sheriff of Plymouth County, included a special message for her: "Make my compliments to Mrs. Warren and tell her that I want a poetical genius —to describe a late frolic among the sea nymphs and goddesses. I wish to see a late glorious event, celebrated by a certain poetical pen, which has no equal . . . in this country."[1]

John's mention of a "late glorious event" was that moonless night of December 16, 1773, when a dozen citizens disguised as Mohawk Indians boarded three British ships and dumped ninety thousand pounds of tea into Boston Harbor. The next morning, Bostonians congregated at an enormous elm known as the Liberty Tree, celebrating what would later be called the Boston Tea Party.

Grim repercussions would follow, but relations with the Crown were already brittle. At issue was a long list of grievances—above all, the collection of nonrepresentative taxes. In May 1773, years after the repeal of the despised Stamp Act, Parliament had passed the Tea Act, creating a monopoly for the sale of tea from the British-owned East India Company over tea sold by American merchants.

It was an outrage, the citizens grumbled, still another Parliamentary scheme to stifle the rights of the colonists. Tea, imported in ships from Great Britain's Indian colony and transported across the Atlantic to Boston's seaport, the busiest in North America, was a staple of the colonial hearth and home.

A decade earlier, a cadre of colonial protestors, led by Samuel and John Adams, Mercy's brother Jemmy, her husband, James, and other Sons of Liberty, had organized protests against Britain, splitting Boston into two camps.

Since then, the rebels, or Whigs, had seethed over British-controlled cargo taxed at Boston's wharves and the chink of hard currency paid at the exchange, which was sent overseas and swallowed in Britain's voracious maw.

Pitted against the Whigs were those later known as Tories, men who easily accepted the rewards for British rule—fine furniture, fabrics, silk, sugar, and molasses—deeming them more important than arguments over citizen rights. Repeatedly, since the 1760s, those political differences had exploded into angry confrontations, stirring animosities in taverns, coffee houses, the silken drawing rooms of Beacon Hill, and the Massachusetts Assembly.

Throughout the colony, the Whigs and Tories clashed over the concept of their right to self-government—conflict stirred north of Boston, in port towns such as Salem and Marblehead; in its western agricultural centers of Springfield and Worcester; and on Boston's South Shore, in communities such as Braintree and Plymouth, where the Adamses and Warrens lived.

As the wife of James Warren, the wiry, dark-eyed Mercy had witnessed the seeds of that dissension at close hand. Rarely a month passed in Plymouth without the arrival of John or Sam Adams or other Sons of Liberty plotting their next move against British authority, while partaking of what Abigail Adams once described as "Colonel Warren's famed hospitality."[2]

The source of that hospitality, the Warrens' gambrel-roofed house with large windows and a central chimney on the corner of North and Main streets, was a stone's throw from old Plymouth Rock. Before the fireside in the Warrens' front parlor, Mercy served as hostess, witness, and confidante. It was there that John Adams came to know her, to warm to her intelligence and literary abilities.

By January 1774, Mercy felt obliged nevertheless to reject Adams's proposal for a poem on the dumping of the tea. While she had already published two satirical, anti-British plays, the idea for a poem, as Mercy reminded Abigail on January 19, had originated with John. Therefore, it was best if he applied "his own genius for the completion."[3]

John never responded to her message. A shrewd judge of character, he knew he had stirred Mercy's literary appetites. Within a few weeks, she composed a whimsical fantasy about the Boston Tea Party that John published anonymously on March 21 in the patriotic *Boston Gazette*. Years later, Mercy would reprint that work as "The Squabble of the Sea Nymphs; or the Sacrifice of the Tuscararoes" in her collected works.

The satire was not only better than John's original "clumsy, undigested"[4] idea, he later observed, but "one of the incontestable evidences of real genius."[5] Warren's wife was brilliant, an exception to most other women, much like his own beloved wife, Abigail.

Mercy came by her radical ideas naturally, for her family, the Otises of West Barnstable, had long clashed with British authorities. The instigator was her eldest and favorite brother, James "the Patriot" Otis, an attorney, who, in 1761, protested to the Massachusetts Superior Court that "taxation without representation"[6] was unconstitutional. It was then, observed young attorney John Adams, that "the child of independence was born."[7]

During the turbulent years that followed, Mercy realized that her words could also be as explosive as gunpowder. While they might not ignite muskets and cannons, they might stoke smoldering civic resentments into an open flame.

By the time hostilities exploded at Lexington and Concord, Mercy had evolved into the secret pen of the American Revolution. Yet she had done so only haltingly, for women, who were seldom educated as well as men, were discouraged from politics. Their knowledge, consequently, as Mercy once ruefully reminded John, "is circumscribed within such narrow limits, and the sex too often forbidden to taste the golden fruit."[8]

The best colonial women could do was prepare that fruit for their men in their capacity as wives, mothers, and aunts, as spinners, embroiderers, cooks, and nurses. Theirs were the worn hands that guided the creaking wheel of eighteenth-century family life.

Mercy was no exception. To outward appearances, she was a model wife to James Warren—petite, elegant, gracious, the mother of five sons. At the time that Mercy's "The Squabble of the Sea Nymphs" appeared on the front page of the March 21, 1774, *Boston Gazette*, most of her forty-six years had been spent raising sons, spinning, sewing garments, and stocking her larder, pantry, and root cellar for the arrival of unexpected guests and the inevitable chill of a New England winter.

In 1763, eleven years before the Boston Tea Party, native Bostonian John Singleton Copley painted the Warrens. James appeared as an amiable, gentleman-farmer wielding a walking stick. Mercy is pictured more vibrantly, as a slight, warm, but plain-featured woman in a blue ruffled gown, staring intently ahead, her hands hovering over a nasturtium.

Copley's flower may have been more than mere artistic convention, for during the 1760s Mercy was writing nature poetry, a seemingly innocuous pastime for the wife of a country squire.

But by 1773, the docile matron was transformed. No longer would she remain mute about British efforts to "prove the people the property of arbitrary and distant lords."[9] Over the next thirty-five years, Mercy secured her role as the nation's first eyewitness recorder of events; she produced political poems, satirical plays, an essay advocating a Bill of Rights, and the three-volume *History of the Rise, Progress and Termination of the American Revolution*. Her strong beliefs, captured in print, made her the muse of the Revolution.

In late summer, when sprays of purple loosestrife, goldenrod, and ripening cranberries burst into color along the old road cutting through the Great Marsh of West Barnstable on Cape Cod, the air vibrated with the drumbeat of cicadas, the caws of seagulls and geese. To the north of Old King's Highway stood the Otis homestead, a spacious three-dormered mansion.

There, just after the autumn equinox on September 14, 1728 (by the Old Style calendar, and September 25 by the modern one), in the "borning room" near the kitchen fireplace, Mercy Otis first opened her eyes. The infant was the third child and first daughter of Mary Allyne Otis and James Otis, a merchant, attorney, and local judge, famous for his hospitality and fondness for ideas.

Mercy's parents probably met in Wethersfield, Connecticut, where Mary

Allyne's father, Joseph, a sloop owner, relocated the family from Plymouth during her girlhood. In 1724, twenty-two-year-old Mary met and married young James Otis and moved into his family's home in West Barnstable, Massachusetts.

Over the next two decades, the couple produced thirteen children, seven of whom survived. No details are preserved beyond the date of Mercy's birth, for as a colonial female, her life was expected to be as anonymous as the era's needlework. Preceding Mercy were two brothers, the restless, dark-eyed James, Jr., nearly three years her senior, and Joseph, born in March 1726.

Their mother, Mary Allyne, a descendant of Pilgrim stock, had strict religious inclinations. Her great-grandfather was Edward Dotey, an indentured servant who attempted mutiny on the *Mayflower*, but, after a duel, became a peaceful citizen of Plymouth Plantation.

Little is known about Mercy's relationship to Mary Allyne. Copley's portrait of 1760 depicts her as a sturdy, practical-looking matron, uncomfortably stuffed into a corset and dark silks. A bible sat on the adjacent table, possibly representing Mary Allyne's ability to read and instruct her children.

Mercy, who often memorialized her loved ones in poems, never wrote about her mother. Years after Mary Allyne's death in 1767, the author described her to a young woman simply as a "mother in whom was concentered every excellent quality that could endear her to her family and secure her...many friends."[10]

In a letter to Janet Montgomery, the widow of the Revolutionary War hero Richard Montgomery, Mercy recalled that her mother always had some "instructive precept"[11] for her children. Even considering the New England tendency for understatement, Mercy's words seem more dutiful than affectionate. Scholarly theory suggests that Mary Allyne's childbearing years, punctured so tragically with six infant deaths, made her a moody, remote, and possibly even depressed, parent.

Mercy's father, James, was altogether different. An affable man whose great-grandfather came from Devonshire, England, in 1621, James had increased his father's farmlands in Barnstable and his retail shop with supplies

Portrait of James Otis, Sr., by John Singleton Copley.
The Roland P. Murdock Collection, Wichita Art Museum, Wichita, Kansas.

Portrait of Mary Allyne Otis by John Singleton Copley.
The Roland P. Murdock Collection, Wichita Art Museum, Wichita, Kansas.

of pickled fish, West Indian rum, and British silks, wools, and ribbons. A self-taught lawyer and member of Barnstable's local militia, James was a judge of the district court.

In 1727, after James's father, John Otis III, died, he inherited the Otis homestead, the spacious fields bisected by Old King's Highway—today's Route 6A—as well as the barn, hayfield, and orchard facing Sandy Creek near the Great Marsh. For all his wealth, stature, and loyalty to the English Crown, James had a lively Whiggish, or democratic, spirit, a man who litigated the petty crimes and homicides of Barnstable's poor whites and indentured servants as well as the property disputes of more prosperous citizens.

That James lacked a formal education mattered little to his admiring clientele. "I'll give you double for coming,"[12] an Eastham resident promised James if he took his case. A plaintiff from Dartmouth begged him to desist from litigation. A third, a Harvard man and capable attorney himself, pleaded with James to defend his Taunton client.

To expand his practice, James rode the court circuit along the dusty roads of the Cape as far east as Chatham and as far west as Scituate. By 1734, Mercy's father had met James Warren, Sr., high sheriff of Plymouth County and fellow merchant-farmer, who occasionally witnessed his legal papers.

The Otis farm was supervised by a foreman and manned by a staff of laborers and indentured servants, several of them American Indians and at least one an African American slave. At the noon dinner hour, the field workers, in accordance with rural tradition, ate either in the kitchen or with the family in the dining room.

That daily contact with Barnstable's working class gave Mercy an appreciation of ordinary people. While independence from British rule became a "plant of later growth,"[13] as she wrote in her *History of the Rise, Progress and Termination of the American Revolution*, Mercy's childhood had already introduced her to the frustrations of the disempowered.

Enhancing the close relations between the Otises and other residents of West Barnstable was the location of their homestead near the village center. Across the road, near some of their own fields, stood the home and farm of their neighbors the Hinckleys. A gristmill and tavern lay to the west, where mail, carried by travelers from Boston and Plymouth, was left for local residents.

Central to the life of that quiet seaside hamlet was the West Barnstable Meeting House, a stark two-storied white clapboard building with a sixty-foot bell tower and a rooster weathervane. Built in 1719 for community meetings and used as a church on Sundays, it remains one of the few such structures still standing in New England.

Further east on the old county road lay the burial ground of the community's earliest white settlers, who had arrived there from Scituate in 1639. To the north, opposite Barnstable harbor, was a seven-mile stretch of beach known as Sandy Neck, where wigwams housed the Wampanoag.

Most handsome of all the West Barnstable residences was the Otises' triple-dormer wood-framed "mansion," admired for its grand stairway and wainscoted walls. In summer, the home was shaded by enormous buttonwood trees; in winter, it was heated by large fireplaces burning more than fifty cords of wood.

Richly furnished with mahogany cabinets, chests, gilded mirrors, damask-covered tables, and fine plate, the homestead also contained a tall case clock, the first in Barnstable County. The cellar was stocked with barrels of West Indian rum, pipes of Madeira, and fine European wines. At dinner, the table groaned with standing ribs, mutton chops, cranberries, apples, pears, and vegetables harvested from the Otises' fields, as well as cod and oysters from nearby shores. Once the day's business was done, James invited visitors to his sitting room or for supper with his family.

According to young John Adams, who once rode circuit court with Mercy's father from Taunton to Milton, James Otis, Sr., was "vastly easy and steady in his temper . . . good-humored and sociable and sensible." Yet beneath James's affability and prominence lurked discontent—in contrast to his brothers, Mercy's father lacked a formal education, and this embarrassed him as an adult.

His more erudite colleagues apparently agreed. "Learned he is not,"[14] as John Adams diplomatically noted.

To compensate, Mercy's father decided that his sons must be well educated—especially his two eldest, James, Jr.—or Jemmy, as he was known

—and Joseph. The lads would profit from the education their father never had by attending Harvard College or the college at Cambridge.

Neither the local dame school where little children, including girls like Mercy, were sent, nor the Barnstable grammar school for older boys, would suffice. By the time Jemmy and Joseph were seven or eight, they crossed Old King's Highway and walked down Hinckley Lane to the parsonage where James's brother-in-law Rev. John Russell, pastor of the West Barnstable church, tutored them.

Kin relations were not the only reason why Mercy's father chose Rev. Russell. A graduate of Yale College, the minister was learned as well as respected for his piety. In recompense, Mercy's father provided him with the wheat, vegetables, and fruit grown on the Otis farm.

During the eighteenth century, even well-born girls like Mercy were expected to assist with maintenance of the home. By the age of four, a girl knew how to sew clothes and knit a pair of stockings; by five or six, she learned needlework and embroidery. Colonial girls helped with other household duties as well. Among these was the preparation of meals in heavy pots or on spits in the open-hearth fireplace, baking in Dutch ovens, churning butter, boiling clothes with lye and bleach, and stirring hot vats of grease for soap.

Prosperous matrons like Mary Allyne Otis supervised such tasks and often pitched in themselves. That was not always possible for Mercy's mother. By 1730, with three youngsters under the age of six, she birthed a second daughter, Mary, followed in 1732 by a third, Hannah. By the time Mercy was eleven, her mother had delivered three more—Nathaniel, Martha, and Abigail. The first two died as infants.

Mary Allyne's relentless childbearing and burying cycle suggests that Mercy, as the Otises' eldest daughter, was probably responsible for many domestic duties. That chain of sibling deaths also left Mercy feeling guilty and wondering if she had been spared for a higher purpose. A believer in a benevolent, if mysterious Creator, Mercy showed appreciation for her survival in a poem. One of its stanzas expressed thanks that the Almighty had "preserv'd my early youth" and "In the midst of death's relentless power/I yet among the living stand."[15]

Mercy, nevertheless, disapproved of the "irksome methods of sever-ity"[16] with which she was raised, the Calvinistic principles of her parents that expected youngsters to atone for every sin. As an adult, Mercy, like other women of the Revolutionary era, became more tolerant, believing, as she once wrote to Abigail Adams, that children were to be nurtured like "tender plants."[17]

The only documented respite Mercy had from household duties were the books that her brothers Jemmy and Joseph read at Uncle Russell's house. So insistently did she plead to join her brothers that her father finally agreed. Just why has perplexed scholars for decades.

The most popular theory is that James allowed her to study to compen-sate for his disappointment in his second son, Joseph, who, like him as a teenager, rejected higher education. After quitting his studies, the youth was sent to work on the ledgers in his father's store and soon afterward mar-ried. In the wake of Joseph's defection, James agreed that young Mercy could take his place in Pastor Russell's study.

Years later, writing to Ann Gerry, the invalid wife of Massachusetts gov-ernor Elbridge Gerry, Mercy observed that reading often furnished people with intellectual escape since "the powers of the soul are apt to languish un-der a continual sameness of place or company."[18]

As one of Barnstable County's best-educated men, Pastor Russell pro-vided Mercy with that escape through his instruction in Shakespeare, Mil-ton, Pope, and Dryden. "Great advantages are often attended with great inconvenience,"[19] as Mercy later reminded Abigail Adams. Education was one of those "great advantages" acquired along with the "inconvenience" of being the eldest Otis daughter.

From her uncle, Mercy learned to write, absorbing the rhythms, ca-dences, and phrasing of his Sunday sermons, which were later echoed in her writing. While prevented from studying Latin and Greek, Mercy de-voured Pope and Dryden's translations of Virgil and Homer. With equal enthusiasm she also read Raleigh's *History of the World*, a work that, com-bined with her knowledge of the classics, led her to realize that the rel-atively peaceful years of the Great Britain of her childhood were an aberration.

As Mercy later wrote in her *History*, "the inhabitants of the American colonies lived" during the first half of the eighteenth century "perhaps as near the point of felicity as the condition of human nature will admit."[20]

In the spring of 1739, Mercy's brother Jemmy was admitted to Harvard College. His father was thrilled, knowing it augured "fine prospects," for the youth to enter Boston society and become "useful to himself and family and the world."[21]

As Reverend John Russell anticipated, the Harvard curriculum demanded mastery of Latin, Greek, and Hebrew, as well as rhetoric, logic, natural philosophy, geography, ethics, divinity, and mathematics. Trained to formal debate and imbued with a sense of moral outrage, young Jemmy soon made it his cause célèbre to protest all instances of absolute power. By his senior year, having defended a fellow student dismissed for contempt toward college authorities, Jemmy grumbled that the Harvard administration was a "miserable, despicable, and arbitrary government."[22]

At the time, James Otis, Sr., probably regarded Jemmy's complaints as typically youthful, little dreaming that his son's sense of justice would strike the spark that founded a new nation.

Mercy, who was only eleven when Jemmy entered Harvard in 1739, spent most of that year assisting her mother, who delivered a new baby, Elizabeth, followed in 1740 by Samuel Allyne. Nor could she have had much respite from household duties when, two years later, Mary Allyne birthed Sarah, then another boy named Nathaniel in 1743, and in 1744, an unnamed baby girl. None of that trio survived.

Whenever Jemmy returned from Cambridge, he shared his books—and political views—with Mercy. Particularly striking was his excitement over the theories of John Locke, whose *Two Treatises on Government* claimed man's right to "perfect freedom" and "the rights and privileges of the law of nature."[23]

But for all of Jemmy's brilliance and charisma, he had an odd streak. High-spirited and witty one minute, he could become moody and incommunicative the next.

Legend has it that once Mercy and her teenage friends planned a dance at the Otis homestead, and Jemmy agreed to play the violin. Suddenly, in the midst of the merriment, he stopped playing, waved his violin above his

Engraving of James "the Patriot" Otis by Oliver Pelton.
Library of Congress (LC-USZ62-102561).

head, and shouted, "So Orpheus fiddled and so danced the brutes!"[24] Without another word, Jemmy ran out of the house and disappeared into the garden.

Later in life he repeated those strange outbursts. "Your brother Jem dined with us yesterday, behaved well till dinner was almost done, and then in the old way got up and went off where I know not,"[25] Mercy's husband, James, wrote from Watertown in 1775.

In the 1740s she nevertheless deeply admired Jemmy, whose lofty ambitions she never expected to emulate.

Like other colonial young women, Mercy aspired instead to marriage and children. To win a fine mate, she was expected to be accomplished in domestic skills, epitomized in early adulthood by the completion of a chimneypiece, a framed needlepoint picture displayed over a fireplace mantel.

Traditionally, the subject was a bucolic representation of colonial life copied from French or English engravings. By 1750, Mercy's twenty-year-old-sister, Hannah, having received instruction in a Boston needlework school, completed a chimneypiece of an idealized Boston Common, at whose edge loomed shipping mogul Thomas Hancock's mansion and the steeple of West Church. Three year later, their younger cousin Eunice Bourne finished another chimneypiece on courting couples. Both are still displayed at Boston's Museum of Fine Arts.

While Mercy may also have attended that needlework school with Hannah, her chimneypiece has not survived. What remains is a still more impressive needlework screen of cards, flowers, and filigree that covered a mahogany card table. Extraordinary in design, color, and workmanship, a testimony to Mercy's deft hand, the screen not only reflected the Otises' worldly fondness for the whistlike game of loo, or lanterloo, but symbolized Mercy's expectations for a prosperous future. All that was needed was a man to appreciate it.

By the mid- or late 1740s, Mercy had probably identified James Warren. Virtually nothing is known about the details of her first meeting with the fair-haired, handsome young man from Plymouth. Historical scholars suspect that they became acquainted either through her father's legal business with his father, James Warren, Sr., high sheriff of Plymouth County, or through Jemmy's June 1743 commencement from Harvard. During the graduation picnic in Harvard Yard that followed the commencement, Mercy met Jemmy's friends, among whom was young James Warren, then about to enter his third year at college.

Between 1743 and 1746, Jemmy returned to West Barnstable, where he "read" literature for his master's degree. However, James Otis, Sr., announced that his son, instead of devoting his life to the classics, must study law, which, he maintained, was the surest route to power and influence. The older man's life had already exemplified that. In 1744, Mercy's father had become a selectman in Barnstable. The following year he became a delegate to the Massachusetts House of Representatives and, within another four years, a leader of several important committees. During that same period, James Otis, Sr., also became colonel of the Barnstable militia.

Such honors, he confided to Jemmy, were only prelude to joining the Governor's Council and perhaps, since he was a favorite of Governor William Shirley, even to the Superior Court.

An added incentive for Jemmy's future was the offer of an apprenticeship from Boston's leading lawyer, Jeremiah Gridley. Ultimately Mercy's brother assented, and after two years of "poring over ... black letter"[26] in Gridley's office, passed the bar.

Initially, Jemmy opened an office on North Street in Plymouth, halfway between Boston and West Barnstable, to assist with the overflow from his father's law practice.

In contrast, Mercy's life during the 1740s was uneventful, subsumed in the stitching and silence expected of young colonial women, interwoven, according to legend, with occasional visits to Jemmy in Plymouth, where she became better acquainted with his friend James Warren.

2

Fires, Civil and Domestic

ON NOVEMBER 14, 1754, Mercy Otis and James Warren exchanged wedding vows in a civil ceremony.

The slender bride was twenty-six, the affable groom, twenty-eight. Afterward, the guests enjoyed a meal at the Otis homestead, or so historians believe, based upon the discovery of Mercy's "second-day" dress of white watered white silk. Today a fragment of that garment is preserved as a pincushion at the Plymouth Antiquarian Society.

Little is known about Mercy's dowry, except that her father valued it at £438, 4 pence. Included within his calculations was the cost of the mahogany card table. Mercy's relatively late age as a bride was probably connected to her unusual education. A young woman's ability to read beyond the bible had little practical value. "Girls, mark my words: and know, For men of sense / Your strongest charms are native innocence,"[1] as Benjamin Franklin reminded readers in *Poor Richard's Almanack*.

Modesty of mind and body were crucial feminine traits, as Cotton Mather, New England's prominent Puritan minister, insisted in his 1692 *Ornaments for the Daughters of Zion*—a book still in print in Mercy's youth. By the mid-eighteenth century, warnings against intellectually accomplished women had become even shriller. "A witty [well educated] woman is a scourge to her husband...her children...Elated by the sublimity of her genius, she scorns to stoop to the duties of a woman,"[2] warned the French Enlightenment philosopher Jean Jacques Rousseau in his 1762 novel, *Émile*.

To that and earlier colonial expressions of misogyny Mercy's bride-groom, James Warren, paid little attention, praising her later in life for her "mind possessed of masculine genius well stocked with learning."[3]

The day after their wedding, the young couple rode, or perhaps sailed, twenty-three miles west to Plymouth, the waterfront town of their common Pilgrim ancestor, Edward Dotey. Like most colonial newlyweds, the Warrens had no honeymoon.

Practicality rather than passion, it is conjectured, prompted the marriage, a result of the couple's fathers desires to strengthen their mutual mercantile interests. One of Mercy's letters, however, contradicted that. James, she tenderly observed in a letter years later, was "the center of my early wishes, and the star which attracts my attention."[4]

Nor for all the Calvinistic self-denial of Mercy's upbringing did she seem reticent about acknowledging physical pleasure. "If the mental faculties of the female are not improved, it may be concealed in the obscure retreats of the bedchamber,"[5] she coyly wrote Abigail Adams.

Years later, when her son Henry wed, Mercy bluntly reminded his wife that "many of our thoughtless sex as soon as the connubial knot is tied, neglect continual attention . . . to keep the sacred flame of love alive."[6]

Nine years into Mercy's marriage, that flame still burned bright. "I again tell you that on your happiness depends mine," James wrote Mercy when they were apart in May 1763. "I am uneasy without you . . . wish for the time that I am to return . . . everything appears so different without you."[7]

During the Revolution, the couple's letters revealed the strength of their bond. "I want nothing to keep up my spirits . . . but seeing you in [good] spirits,"[8] James penned in April 1775 from Concord.

Several months later, he declared, "No husband ever loved and respected a wife more."[9] Still later, James wrote his political ally Elbridge Gerry, "I wish you every possible happiness, and among others, a very good wife, which I can assure you is the greatest in this life."[10]

Mercy expressed her love for James with equal fervor. Her letters are sprinkled with tenderness about him as the "first friend of my heart,"[11] the "dear companion of my life,"[12] and "my dearest friend."[13]

In September 1775, during one of the Revolution's darkest moments,

Mercy confessed that while "grieved at the advantages gained by our ene-mies... my little heart is more affected with what gives pain or endangers you than with everything else."[14]

A week later, when James explained he planned to visit Plymouth, Mercy canceled a trip to West Barnstable, explaining, "I shall give up that and ev-ery other pleasure... for the superior pleasure of your company."[15]

Mercy and James's first home was the Warren saltbox-style home in Plym-outh, surrounded by forty acres of farmland near the Eel River. Of proud Old Colony stock, the Warrens descended from two Plymouth settlers, *Mayflower* passengers Edward Dotey and Richard Warren.

In May 1627, the pilgrim Richard Warren built a home on a ridge above the Eel River; his descendants replaced the home in 1700 with a second house, which still stands in the Chiltonville section of Plymouth. From the home's south and west windows are picturesque views of the Eel River, threading its way to Cape Cod Bay. To the north and east are dazzling views of Plymouth Bay.

In spring and summer, tawny stalks of rye rippled upon nearby the hills, which Mercy drolly dubbed the "Mountains of the Eel River."[16] Upon them were fruit orchards, surrounded by rolling pastures with grazing sheep. To Mercy, the Warren homestead seemed as bucolic as a colonial chimney-piece. "Beneath the shady forest of the Eel River... my best friend has walked towards the fertile plain, to survey the reapers, or perhaps ascends the rugged hills to view the... flocks,"[17] she once lyrically wrote to Abigail.

The newlyweds shared the Warren homestead with Mercy's father-in-law, James, and his unmarried daughter, Sarah, until her marriage to William Sever the following year. Mercy depended upon Ann, a childhood servant who accompanied her from West Barnstable, to help with domestic chores. Additional assistance probably came from the Warren servants, some of whom worked as farmhands or at the docks loading sacks of grain onto the family's small fleet of boats.

As early as 1756, change was already shifting the direction of those sails as the health of Mercy's father-in-law declined and her husband assumed his post as high sheriff of Plymouth County.

Simultaneously, Mercy's brother Jemmy was also rising in the world. Six months after her wedding, Jemmy, who had established a law practice in Boston with prominent clients like John Hancock, married Ruth Cunningham, the beautiful daughter of a wealthy merchant. That alliance, combined with Jemmy's influential clientele, made him one of the city's most prominent young attorneys.

A shrewd negotiator, Jemmy healed a rift between his father and the new Massachusetts governor, Thomas Pownall, and was rewarded with a post as advocate general of the Vice Admiralty Court, which supervised the colony's busy maritime trade.

In contrast, Mercy led a quiet life, the one notable event of 1757 being her first pregnancy. During that period, she often claimed that providence had treated her kindly: "When I participate [in] the family happiness" Mercy later wrote Abigail, "I flatter myself it is an emanation of benevolence."[18]

Inevitably that "emanation" posed challenges. The first, on July 2, 1757, was the death of Mercy's father-in-law, James Warren, Sr. Subsequently, her husband inherited the Warren homestead, farm, fleet, and the mercantile business, responsibilities that, when combined with James's duties as Plymouth County sheriff, meant long hours away from the farm. With a baby on the way, the Warrens consequently purchased a home in Plymouth center owned by James's maternal relatives, the Winslows.

Being inordinately fond of Clifford Farm, the young couple retained it as their summer house. By 1759, Mercy's poem "On Winter" reflected her annual return to Clifford—as she called the farm—after "the hills of snow" melted and "buds expand... and [produced] plenteous fields of ripening grain."[19]

The new Warren home, a spacious two-and-a-half-story building with wainscoted walls and nine large windows, on the corner of North and what is now called Main Street, was known as the Winslow House after its first owner, Edward Winslow, an early governor of Plymouth Colony. His descendant and the home's seller was the fifty-three-year-old, newly retired general John Winslow.

The general had already moved to a grander house in seaside Marshfield, purchased during the French and Indian War after he had relocated twelve thousand Acadians from Grand-Pré, Nova Scotia, to the American colonies. With great reluctance, John Winslow herded them onto transport ships that were sailing down the New England coast and attempted to settle them in several towns. Legend has it that Winslow, constantly rebuffed, left nineteen Acadians in Plymouth and abandoned the rest to the swampy coastal settlements of Louisiana. For that and other duties, Winslow was promoted to general and, upon his retirement, handsomely recompensed.

The harsh alchemy of war that rendered the Acadians homeless provided the young Warrens with a splendid new residence. Little could Mercy and James have predicted that within a decade, the teeth of the British lion would tear apart hearth and home in their own Massachusetts Colony.

Equally unsuspecting were Mercy's brother Jemmy and her father. By 1757, the elder Otis fretted over Governor Shirley's replacement by Thomas Pownall and his lieutenant governor, Thomas Hutchinson. The latter, the native-born son of a wealthy Boston merchant, was as obedient to his British superiors as his great-great-grandmother, the religious dissident Anne Hutchinson, who had resisted control from the Puritan oligarchs of Massachusetts.

Dubbed the Tall Man and Tommy-Skin-and-Bones, the gangly Harvard-educated Hutchinson was a widower who lived in a mansion in Boston's North Square with his five children. Initially, he seemed a fitting counterfoil to the many British-born governors who ruled Massachusetts, a man so dedicated to his native colony that he was writing its history.

Yet for all the lieutenant governor's sympathetic opening to his *History of the Colony and Province of Massachusetts-Bay*, Hutchinson insisted that Massachusetts "cannot subsist without the protection of our mother country."[20]

In the 1805 publication of her own *History,* Mercy described Hutchinson as "dark intriguing, insinuating, haughty and ambitious...the extreme of avarice,"[21] a man who modeled himself upon Machiavelli. Her unflattering portrait reflected a feud between Hutchinson and the Otises, initiated in 1757 when her father lost a seat to him in the Governor's Council. In compensation, the retiring Governor Pownall appointed Colonel Otis the Speaker of the House of Representatives.

Pownall's replacement was the high-handed Francis Bernard, reputed for his prodigious memory, a brood of nine children, and for being "grasping in his pursuit of fortune,"[22] as the patriot William Tudor put it. Mercy's judgment was harsher still. Bernard, she declared in her *History*, was "illy calculated to promote the interest of the people...too open and frank to disguise his intrigues."[23]

The most sticky of those intrigues was Bernard's sudden enforcement of the Molasses Act of 1733, part of the old Navigation Acts designed to discourage foreign trade. Bernard demanded a duty of six cents a gallon upon West Indian molasses, a key ingredient in the production of that prized colonial beverage rum. Still more inflammatory were the writs of assistance, or general search warrants, that Bernard ordered his customs officials to wield to force entry into the homes and shops of suspected smugglers.

Alarmed, Boston's merchants protested in newspapers and broadsides, their cries growing increasingly strident after the September 1760 death of Chief Justice Stephen Sewall. Hoping for that appointment, Colonel Otis consequently resigned his position as Speaker.

Hutchinson, or so he claimed in his *History of Massachusetts-Bay*, had no interest in the post, knowing his possession would incite "strong opposition to his administration."[24] That opposition primarily came from Jemmy Otis, who, in a private meeting, explained his father's ambitions and "vowed revenge, if he should finally fail."[25] On November 13, 1760, Hutchinson, nevertheless, became the new chief justice.

After that, the Otises, father and son, stood "at the head of every measure in opposition, not merely in those points which concerned the governor," but those affecting the "authority of Parliament," Hutchinson reported. "From so small a spark a great fire seems to have been kindled."[26]

If Colonel Otis was crushed, Jemmy was appalled. In a rousing speech to his merchant clientele, Mercy's brother reminded them that Lieutenant Governor Hutchinson was already judge of probate of Suffolk County, commander of Boston Harbor's Castle William, and now the colony's chief justice. Three of his relatives sat on the General Court. Did that not make Hutchinson the most powerful man in Massachusetts—short of becoming its monarch?

Afterward, Jemmy confronted Hutchinson, once again "swore revenge," and vowed to "set the province in flames, if he perished by the fire."[27] To fulfill that threat, Jemmy boldly protested the injustice of Bernard's writs of assistance used to enforce the Molasses Act. Stirred to action, sixty-three merchants signed a petition and begged Jemmy to plead their case in court. Mercy's brother consented immediately. To prove his dedication, he subsequently resigned his royal appointment with the Admiralty Court.

On February 24, 1761, Jemmy formally presented the grievance to the Massachusetts Superior Court, the colony's highest court. Presiding over the trial in the Council Chamber at the Town House, Boston's Old State House, sat Chief Justice Hutchinson, accompanied by five scarlet-gowned, wigged justices. Looming overhead were newly restored, life-size portraits of Charles II and James II in ermine-collared robes, symbols of the supremacy of English law.

Nearby at a long table, wigged and dressed in black gowns, were the barristers of Boston and Middlesex County, among them twenty-five-year-old John Adams.

After introductory remarks by Jemmy's colleague Oxenbridge Thatcher and his former mentor, opposing attorney Jeremiah Gridley, Mercy's brother swept authoritatively onto the floor. The writs were the "worst instrument of arbitrary power, the most destructive to English liberty, and the fundamental principles of the Constitution,"[28] he declared in a speech of steely brilliance. Similar instances of absolute power once so agitated British subjects, Jemmy reminded his audience, that they had deposed and beheaded several monarchs.

Four hours later, Jemmy was still declaiming on the fine points of English law. "Taxation without representation is tyranny,"[29] he finally announced to his riveted audience.

Fascinated, John Adams scribbled notes. "Otis was a flame of fire; with . . . classical allusions, a depth of research, a rapid summary of historical events and dates, a profusion of legal authorities, prophetic glance of his eyes into futurity, and a rapid torrent of impetuous eloquence.[30]

The case dragged on for months. In the end, the Council Chamber ruled against Jemmy, but his knowledge of British law was so comprehensive and compelling that in 1762 his constituents elected him to the Massachusetts House.

The usual method for starting a fire in colonial America was to strike flint against steel. The usual way to protest an injustice was to bring a suit to the colonial courts.

In 1761, neither Hutchinson nor the justices of the council suspected that the flinty logic of Jemmy's speech would ignite a flame that would smolder for years before exploding into an unquenchable colonial conflagration.

In Plymouth, where she tended more domestic fires, Mercy was warmed, and eventually overheated, by the consequences of Jemmy's arguments in the Council Chamber. Her 1805 *History* enshrined her brother as the patriot who "may justly claim the honor of laying the foundation of a revolution."[31]

During the early 1760s, Mercy lived quietly, birthing babies, cooking, and making candles and soap. As she later explained to her friend Hannah Fayerweather Winthrop, the second wife of the Harvard mathematics, astronomy, and natural philosophy professor John Winthrop, she was thoroughly content with the "little circle of domestic life...that Providence has wisely assigned our sex."[32]

Today, the Warren residence on the corner of Plymouth's North and Main streets remains standing but was long ago converted into a commercial building. During Mercy's lifetime, guests entered through a stately front door and were ushered into a spacious sitting room with a large fireplace whose "chimney" corner was the traditional place for the lady of the house to chat, sew, or knit. From the front door, a wainscoted staircase led to the bedrooms. A kitchen stood at the back of the house.

Outside lay the dusty grass-fringed roads of North and Main streets, where carts, carriages, and horses rumbled through Plymouth's busy thoroughfares. Nearby stood the Plymouth County Court, where Mercy's husband served as high sheriff. Just north of Mercy and James's home stood another house, a barn to its rear and a hog yard to its east. Opposite, a sloping road and brook led to Plymouth Bay and the harbor upon which bobbed vessels engaged in cod and mackerel fishing.

Mercy's first son, named after his father, James, was born on October 15, 1757, followed by Winslow, a handsome child named after her husband's maternal family, on March 24, 1759. Three years later, on April 4, 1762, Mercy birthed her third child, Charles—"the amiable youth"[33] as Mercy's friend Hannah often described him. Her fourth son, Henry, arrived on March 24, 1764, and on September 20, 1766, her fifth son, George, was delivered.

Simultaneous with the expansion of Mercy's family was the growth of the Otis mercantile business. In 1762, Mercy's second brother, Joseph, by then matured into a shrewd West Barnstable merchant, formed a partnership with the youngest Otis son, Samuel Allyne, who ran a branch of the business from Boston. For legal advice, the two partners depended upon their eldest brother, Jemmy, who, on occasional trips to the Plymouth courts, stopped to see Mercy and her family.

Another visitor to those courts was John Adams. While in 1764 he complained to his fiancée, Abigail Smith, that in Plymouth he met only "a number of bawling lawyers, drunken squires, and impertinent clients,"[34] by 1767 John had changed his mind. "In Coll. Warren and his lady I find friends,"[35] he wrote his wife, Abigail, after enjoying a Sunday dinner with Mercy and James.

It would not be until 1772 though that all four would meet. While the Adamses were considerably younger—James was eleven years older than John, and Mercy sixteen years Abigail's senior—the simpatico between them was immediate.

Subsequent to his failed writs of assistance case, Jemmy continued to harp upon the jeopardized rights of the colonists. No sooner did he join the Massachusetts House than he attacked Hutchinson for plural office holding. By 1762, Jemmy had penned *A Vindication of the Conduct of the House of Representatives of the Province of Massachusetts Bay*, in which he cited John Locke's theory that government existed "for no other end ultimately, but the good of the people."[36]

Omitted from Mercy's *History,* which extolled Jemmy as James "the Patriot" Otis and "the "first champion of American freedom,"[37] was his increasingly erratic behavior. In spite of his brilliance, Mercy's brother displayed symptoms of mental instability in speeches that skipped from one fine point of law to another without coherent explanations.

Equally unpredictable were Jemmy's collegial relationships. In 1761, af-

ter reconciling himself and his father to Governor Bernard and his lieutenant, Hutchinson, Jemmy turned on the latter. Months later, he reconciled
with Hutchinson. By 1763, he had praised him as "a clever fellow"[38] but a
few weeks later, again raged at the official.

Exasperated, Hutchinson privately dubbed him James Bluster, Esq., or
the Grand Incendiary. Jemmy's own advocates nicknamed him Furio. Even
his youngest brother, Samuel Allyne, referred to him as Esq. Bluster.

Far more admiring was a radical brewer's son named Samuel Adams. A
Harvard graduate four years Jemmy's senior, Sam was a second cousin to
John Adams. Nursed on his father's "populist" politics, Sam was "always
for softness, and delicacy, and prudence" in normal circumstances, as John
later observed. While "a man of refined policy, steadfast integrity . . . and a
universal good character," Sam, nevertheless, proved "staunch and stiff and
rigid and inflexible, in the cause."

Like his ally Jemmy, Sam was dedicated to battling political tyranny. His
flashpoint, too, had occurred at Harvard, in his case when the Land Bank—
a populist plan to issue paper money in lieu of scarce hard currency—failed
and bankrupted his father. Subsequently, Sam dedicated his life to restoring
the "dignity of free citizens."[39]

By the 1760s, Sam was a seasoned community organizer, a familiar
Boston figure in a gray wig, shabby clothes, and a stained red cloak. He
wandered the printing shops, wharves, and ropewalks of Boston daily with
his Newfoundland dog, making small talk, stirring the grievances of his
peers, and radicalizing them with lofty chatter about the fall of Rome. The
British, he insisted to his working-class audiences, were as decadent as were
the ancient Romans, but profited from their exploitation of the American
colonists.

While such conversations also took place in Boston's drawing rooms, the
stately homes of the "codfish aristocracy" of Marblehead, and the carpeted
parlors of Salem's sea captains, Sam shrewdly linked these concepts to the
everyday complaints of workers. Foremost among their concerns were
high taxes and stiff trade restrictions—largely the result of British Prime
Minister George Grenville's insistence that the American colonies shoulder
the debt of £147 million accrued during the French and Indian War.

By 1764, part of that debt was to be paid from the Revenue, or Sugar Act, which reduced taxes on molasses from six to three cents a gallon but demanded tighter surveillance of those duties, whose profits would support the ten-thousand-man army that lingered at the western borders of the British colonies.

To American colonists, however, a standing army in peacetime seemed ominous, evoking the atrocities committed against their British forbears under the military rule of Oliver Cromwell. Compounding their agitation was the March 22, 1765, passage of the Stamp Act, which required the use of special stamped paper for legal documents, newspapers, and playing cards. Substitutions were forbidden. Unless stamped with a British seal, all documents and contracts were considered void.

"The sun of liberty is set; you must light up the candles of industry and economy,"[40] Benjamin Franklin, the colonial agent to Great Britain, warned when he heard the news.

No sooner did reports about the act reach Boston in late May 1765 than "a universal murmur" arose, bringing "excesses of riot and tumult,"[41] as Mercy recalled. The first to formally protest was Virginia Colony, led by young Patrick Henry, whose words, "fearless of the cry of 'treason,'"[42] inspired a public protest.

In New York, protesters marched in the streets. Funeral bells tolled in Boston, Providence, and Philadelphia. Merchants shut their shops. Crowds stomped through the streets of Boston, carrying effigies of Grenville later burnt in bonfires.

Before long, New Englanders called for a boycott of British goods. To Jemmy, the uproar was long overdue. Since spring 1764, he had penned a series of protests, among them *The Rights of the British Colonies Asserted and Proved*, which maintained that "[e]very British subject born on the continent of America...is by the law of god and nature...entitled to all the... inherent and inseparable rights of our fellow subjects in Great Britain."[43] The Stamp Act, he announced, was one more violation of the colonists' constitutional rights.

Unfortunately, Jemmy's increasingly erratic behavior undercut his message. Less than two months after the announcement of the Stamp Act, the *Boston Evening Post* published an anonymous jeering poem called "Jemmibullero," accusing Mercy's brother of unreliability.

-<++>-

For all of the controversy surrounding that ditty, no one claimed its author-ship. To Jemmy, the satire had been penned by one of his enemies from the "little chit chat of the coffee house...magnified...into infidelity, treason, and rebellion."[44]

With typical flamboyance, Jemmy announced his intention to challenge George Grenville to a duel. More reasonably, during a meeting of the Sons of Liberty at the Warrens' Plymouth home, he called for an intercolonial congress to protest the Stamp Act. Earlier, Jemmy had accused Hutchin-son and Bernard of urging Parliament to mandate that act. Subsequent to its public announcement in May 1765, Sam Adams publicized Jemmy's accusation.

On August 15, a raging mob of Boston artisans and tradesmen, led by the Loyal Nine—the core group of the Sons of Liberty—appeared at Hutchin-son's brick mansion, demanding an explanation. Refusing to appear, the lieutenant governor fled to his hilltop country mansion in nearby Milton.

The next morning, a second mob marched through Boston carrying an effigy of Andrew Oliver, Hutchinson's brother-in-law and the new stamp collector. Chanting, the men hung the straw dummy from the Liberty Tree, burned it, broke into Oliver's house, and threatened him. At the last minute, he was saved by Hutchinson's breathless arrival with armed guards.

Gleefully, Boston's patriotic printers churned out newspapers articles, among them a broadside announcing that "the true-born Sons of liberty are desired to meet under the LIBERTY TREE at 11 o'clock. This day, to hear the public resignation, under oath, of ANDREW OLIVER, Esq. Distrib-utor of Stamps for the Province of the Massachusetts-Bay."[45]

From sheer denial or pride, Hutchinson believed the riot an aberration stirred by a few malcontents. Convinced he was still well liked, the gover-nor returned to Boston on August 26, where, while dining with his children, a neighbor warned of an approaching mob.

This time the protestors wielded axes, yelling "Liberty and Property!"[46] Still in his cambric dressing gown, Hutchinson rushed his children off to the neighbors and barely escaped himself as the crowd hacked through the front door, splintering his furniture, destroying his collection of fine wines, and scattering pages of his historical manuscript to the streets.

The next morning Hutchinson limped into Court "clothed in a manner which would have excited compassion from the hardest heart ... with tears starting from his eyes.

"I call my Maker to witness—that I never, in New England ... in Great Britain ... was ... supporting ... the Stamp Act," he claimed. "On the contrary, [I] did all in my power ... to prevent it."[47]

Within a day Mercy heard the news. She never forgot it. A few months later, that riot became the backdrop for her first political satire.

3

"Neither the pen nor the tongue of a lawyer"

"YOU HAVE NO RIGHT TO TAX AMERICA. I rejoice, that America has resisted," William Pitt, Britain's former secretary of state, declared to the House of Commons in January 1766. "On the ground of this tax...I...lift my hands and my voice against it."[1]

On March 4 the House voted to repeal the Stamp Act. By March 17, the House of Lords agreed. King George III granted his approval the next day.

In America, nine of the colonies, having met in a Stamp Act congress and supported a boycott, were meanwhile learning to survive without British goods. So it was that in March 1766, as Parliament passed Repeal of the Stamp Act, Ephraim Bowen, a Rhode Island ship owner, hosted a spinning party for eighteen Daughters of Liberty to urge the use of homespun wool for clothes.

Simultaneous with Bowen's spinning party in March 1766 was Mercy's struggle with a different kind of loss. Pregnant with her fifth son, George, the author mourned the sudden death of her twenty-eight-year-old sister, Abigail, soon followed by that of Joseph's wife, Rebecca.

In grief, Mercy wrote the poem "On the death of two lovely Sisters" recalling the "sprightly Abia...wraped beneath a shroud...who "breath'd forth her soul on a soft tender sigh" and Elizabeth, a "lovely maid...fair of form"[2] who apparently had also recently died.

Mercy's closest sibling bond was with Jemmy, who, in his letter of April 11, reminded her that "[n]o brother ever loved a sister better." Having not yet heard of the repeal, Jemmy explained his reluctance to pay his personal condolences in West Barnstable "till matters are settled in England, since every nerve is requisite to keep things from ... imprudence" in Boston. So tense was the political climate that "[t]his country must soon be at rest, or ... engaged in contests that will require neither the pen nor the tongue of a lawyer."[3]

Six weeks later, when John Hancock's brig *Harrison* arrived in Boston Harbor announcing the repeal, that rest finally seemed assured. All of Boston rejoiced. Bells pealed from church steeples. Citizens paraded through the streets. Cannons were fired from Castle William. Coffee houses and taverns offered patrons free food and drink. John Rowe, owner of Boston's busiest wharf, raised fifteen toasts to cheering fellow merchants. Fireworks burst over Boston Common.

Immediately, the colonists ended the boycott. From London, even famously thrifty Benjamin Franklin, having long pleaded for the repeal, wrote his wife, Deborah, in Philadelphia with the offer of "a new gown."[4]

By May 19, a letter from London published in the *Boston Gazette* revealed the economic damage that the boycott had wreaked upon Great Britain. "The Parliament are ... concerned [that] ... Americans should set up manufactures of their own unless they give us a free and extensive trade," the letter confessed. With the repeal, the writer had "not the least doubt the American will be on much better footing,"[5] with British merchants.

But behind those aspirations lay a trap. Simultaneous with the repeal, Parliament passed the Declaratory Act, forbidding the colonists the right to rule or tax themselves. During public exultation over the repeal, the colonists dismissed the act as a Parliamentary gesture designed to reassert authority. Only the most suspicious, among them Sam Adams, perceived it as a symbol of predatory Parliamentary intent. Few, as Mercy put it in her *History*, suspected that Parliament would actually "avail themselves of the dangerous experiment."[6]

At the time, her energies were consumed in tending to what her friend Hannah Winthrop described as the Warrens' "little flock."[7] With her new baby, George, and raising four others between the ages of three and ten, Mercy remained in Plymouth while James, elected to the General Court in 1765, served in Boston. The loneliness she expressed in a 1766 poem "to J. Warren Esq." to "leave the noisy smoky town"[8] was partly assuaged by friendships with two local women—Ellen Lothrop, a physician's wife, and James's young cousin Penny Winslow.

Exacerbating Mercy's discomfort was the December 1767 death of her mother, Mary Allyne. Few details are known other than that she died while visiting her husband in Boston where he served on the General Court. Like the deaths of Mercy's sister Abigail and sister-in-law Rebecca, Mary Allyne passed away as quickly as a flame extinguished by a candle snuffer.

Mercy never wrote a eulogistic poem about her mother. Mary Allyne's children, she once explained to Abigail Adams, were obliged to rise and call her "blessed." To do otherwise would be "unforgiven."[9] That was all.

By 1768, American colonists were expressing similar ambivalence about the mother country. In London, the new chancellor of the Exchequer, Charles "Champagne" Townshend—named for an entertaining, tipsy speech he once delivered in the House of Commons—was pondering how to pay the defense budget of £400,000, accrued during the French and Indian War.

After the retirement of America's ailing "guardian angel and savior," William Pitt, the new chancellor, consequently levied the Townshend Acts upon the American colonies. This new set of laws, which placed a tax on imported glass, lead, paint, paper, and tea, he assured Parliament, was an "internal" tax and would thus raise fewer objections than the "external" Stamp Act tax. The resultant revenues would not only pay the costs for maintenance of the British army in North America but fund the salaries of colonial officials. Most alarming as Mercy later observed, those officials became "wholly independent"[10] of the Massachusetts Assembly.

Equally unjust was the Townshend Act's authorization of writs of assistance—the same general search warrants that Jemmy had so vehemently protested in 1761.

Essentially nothing had changed in the Crown's attitude toward the Americans, except the language of its laws.

Among those horrified by the Townshend Acts was Jemmy's ally from the 1765 Stamp Act Congress, John Dickinson of Pennsylvania, whose pen produced a widely distributed series titled "Letters from a Pennsylvania Farmer." "The liberties of our common country appear . . . to be at this moment exposed to the most imminent danger," he wrote Jemmy on December 5. "If these colonies do not instantly . . . unanimously unite themselves" as they "did against the Stamp Act, the most destructive consequences must follow."[11]

By January 1768, while the Massachusetts Assembly, or General Court, formally complained to Parliament and George III, Jemmy and Sam Adams composed a "circular letter," warning other colonies that the Townshend Acts infringed upon their natural and constitutional rights.

Outraged by the colony's "seditious"[12] complaint, King George demanded that Governor Bernard force the legislature to revoke it. "Let Britain rescind her measures, or the colonies are lost forever,"[13] Jemmy, the patriot's leading spokesman, brazenly retorted.

Appalled, Bernard pressed for retraction, but the House rejected his request in a 92–13 vote. In disgust, the governor dissolved the delegates.

Within a matter of days, Boston's merchants reacted with a new non-importation agreement "to promote industry, frugality, and economy." Soon afterward, a popular ditty appeared addressed to the "Daughters of Liberty in America," warning colonial women—the prime consumers of household goods—to shun "taxables."[14]

Domestic cloth and its production became important. Spinning meetings, like the one held in 1766 in Rhode Island, were revived. In Boston, the Daughters of Liberty, spun two hundred skeins of yarn while singing liberty songs in the spring of 1769, one of sixty such events reported over the next two years. Spinning contests, too, became the vogue. Hemp and flax were cultivated for their fibers, which, when mixed with wool, produced the coarse, sturdy textile "homespun." "Wear none but your own country linen" and be proud to "show clothes of your own make and spinning,"[15] urged the *Boston News Letter*.

The "industry and frugality of American ladies must exalt their character in the eyes of the world, and...show how greatly they are contributing to...the political salvation of a whole continent,"[16] crowed the *Boston Evening Post*.

During that era, Mercy, who was already experimenting with political poetry, may have authored the "Massachusetts Liberty Song." Published in the *Boston Gazette* in autumn 1768, the ditty was a saucy retort to a Tory parody of Dickinson's "Liberty Poem." Several stanzas echoed the era's rising militancy:

Come swallow your bumpers, ye Tories, and roar,
That the sons of fair freedom are hamper'd once more; but
Know that no cut-throats our spirits can tame,
Nor host of oppressors shall smother the flame.

In freedom we're born and like sons of the brave,
We'll never surrender,
But swear to defend her,
And scorn to survive, if unable to save.[17]

Even if, as some scholars maintain, Benjamin Church authored it, Mercy's exasperation with the British and American Tories was already spilling over into her correspondence. While women were told to "leave the field of politics to men,"[18] Mercy fumed when she saw her peers sipping British tea and sporting "the rich embroidered gown... the Mechlin laces, fringes and jewels, fans of the Mother Country,"[19] as she finally protested in a 1774 poem published in the *Royal American Magazine*.

Its composition, inspired by a discussion with John Winthrop listing "those articles which female vanity has comprised under the head of necessaries," finally assailed woman's "pride of dress" as an obstacle to independence and framed it as the crux of America's conflict with the mother country.

In time, Mercy ominously predicted, a woman's "sweet temptation" for fine clothes might eventually lead to spilling of "her father's blood."[20]

Already blood was in the air. By April 1768, John Dickinson assured Jemmy that "all America is rousing in assertion of her liberty." In November, the *Massachusetts Gazette* boasted that "the whole continent from New England to Georgia seems firmly fixed: like a... well-constructed arch, the more weight... the firmer it stands."[21]

Another incentive for unification of the colonies was the arrival of British soldiers in Boston on October 1, 1768—a presence that shattered the patriots' lingering hopes for reconciliation. "The American war may be dated from the hostile parade of this day,"[22] Mercy recalled.

The catalyst for the arrival of the "lobsterbacks," as the colonists dubbed the British, was a well-publicized trade violation. Traditionally, ship owners posted bond while leaving or arriving in Boston Harbor, but under the tightened requirements of the Townshend Acts, customs agents, having discovered on June 10 that Hancock's sloop, *Liberty,* had unloaded Madeira wine without paying duty, used that violation to warn others.

Admittedly, as Mercy wrote, Hancock had been "reprehensible in permitting a part of the cargo to be unladen in a clandestine manner."[23] At dusk, customs officials had consequently slashed the *Liberty*'s ropes and towed it under the hull of a nearby British warship. The timing was deliberate, occurring just as dock workers, artisans, and tradesmen were leaving work. Appalled, the men pelted the commissioners with bricks and stones, hoisted one of their boats out of the water, dragged it to the Common, and set it ablaze.

In the wake of that uproar, Boston settled into a sullen calm, probably at the stern insistence of Sam Adams, who reprimanded the street gangs, printers, and "wharf rats" who often identified themselves as Sons of Liberty, for the rampage.

Above all, Sam and Jemmy wanted to prevent a riot like the one that had destroyed Hutchinson's mansion in August 1765, if only to stop the British from thinking of the patriots as mere "rabble" who pressed for colonial rights.

Once assured the city was calm, Mercy rode to Boston to visit James and then stopped in Cambridge to see Hannah Winthrop. A day or so later, the latter had begged her to return, but Mercy insisted she had to go home.

"I was very sorry you did not favor me with another visit before your return to Plymouth," Hannah explained on September 6, 1768. "Methinks frequent absences from that little amiable circle and the advantages you might reap from riding and change of air would conduce much to your health, give pleasure to your friends and endear you to your little ones."[24]

As subsequent events soon proved, Mercy's departure from Boston was timely, probably prompted by a warning from Jemmy. By October 1, twelve British ships of war, or by some accounts a squadron of seven vessels, arrived from Halifax. At noon, two scarlet-coated regiments appeared, followed by a third, which collectively marched to the sounds of fife and drum up King Street. At the Common, the regiments performed a sharp military drill, punctuated by sixteen musket shots before the stunned Bostonians.

Some soldiers were to be quartered in Castle William in Boston Harbor, others lodged in the Town House, the seat of Boston's court and government. Every morning, John Adams awakened in Boston's Brattle Square to the grim sounds of fife and drum. His cousin Sam grumbled about harassment from soldiers who demanded identification "a badge of slavery which none but a slave will wear."[25] In protest, he and John Adams placed anonymous essays in the newspapers.

Mercy's brother Jemmy, meanwhile, fretted over the soldiers' arrival and the implications for his own reputation. The Tories, he believed, had maliciously distorted his deeds into a demand for colonial independence— a treasonous act punishable by death. Independence had never been his intent, he insisted, but simply Parliamentary respect for the "natural" rights of American colonists.

To justify that, Jemmy invited the British commander General Thomas Gage to dine at his home but was promptly rebuffed. Few who knew Mercy's brother were surprised. Who, it was whispered in the House, could predict how Otis would respond to any legislative issue? Furio, or Esq. Bluster, rarely seemed to sustain any political course, becoming like the erratic pendulum of a too tightly wound clock.

So explosive was Jemmy over discussions about British injustices that he often embarrassed his wife, Ruth. By 1768, they quarreled so often that John Adams pitied him. "He mentioned his wife—said she was a good wife, too good for him—but she was a Tory," John wrote in his diary on January 16, 1768. "She gave him curtain lectures."[26]

Behind closed doors, Colonel Otis also complained about his son's brashness, claiming it jeopardized his own reputation in the General Court. To Jemmy, the arrival of British soldiers seemed one more indictment, which hastened "events which every good and honest man would wish delayed forever,"[27] he lamented.

Yet once having vowed to Hutchinson, who became acting governor that August, "to set the province in flames,"[28] there was little Jemmy could do to stop the colonial conflagration.

Among those fanning the smoldering coals was Sam Adams. In August 1769, he obtained the copy of a letter from a customs commissioner accusing Jemmy of obstructing the "rights of the crown and [being] disaffected to his Majesty."[29] Before long that letter reappeared in the *Boston Gazette*.

Determined to defend himself, Jemmy, accompanied by Sam, met with two commissioners on Friday, September 1, at the British Coffee House. The next morning at six, Jemmy appeared there again to no avail.

By Sunday, Jemmy had become overwrought. "Otis talks all," John Adams noted in his diary. "No other gentleman in company can find a space to put in a word . . . he grows narrative like an old man."[30]

The next day Jemmy published a letter in the *Boston Gazette* within which he labeled the commissioners "superlative blockheads." Jemmy warned that should he continue to be "misrepresented" by customs commissioner John Robinson, he had "a natural right . . . to break his head."[31] Yet none of Jemmy's patriotic friends, including John, took his threat seriously, considering it another instance of his typical bluster.

The next evening Mercy's brother again appeared at the British Coffee House. Edging menacingly toward Robinson, Jemmy demanded a "gentleman's satisfaction."

A man named John Gridley, having just entered the British Coffee House, observed the pair "engaged in . . . great wrath." After Robinson agreed to give Jemmy a "gentleman's satisfaction," the latter replied, "Then come along with me."[32]

Before Jemmy could leave the room, Robinson grabbed him by the nose. Mercy's brother struck him with a cane. In return, the British officer hit Jemmy on the head with a walking stick. A fistfight ensued while spectators, most of them British, attempted to separate the quarreling pair by "pushing and pulling" at Jemmy.

Horrified by "such foul play" and shouting that it was "dirty usage to treat a man in that manner,"[33] Gridley rushed between the men but had his wrist broken in the fray. Around him, the crowd howled for Jemmy's death.

A second eyewitness, the British office captain Mungo Mackey, reported that after entering the coffee house, he saw a hatless and wigless Jemmy "at least three [sticks] over his head, and the blood running."

Nearby stood two British officers. "You have come too late to see your friend Otis have a good drubbing," one of the officers explained. "I am very glad of it,"[34] the second one replied.

Months later, the scars were still so deep in Jemmy's forehead, recalled John Adams, that "you could lay a finger in it."[35] The wound, swore the doctors who stitched up Jemmy, was produced by an "edged weapon" or sword—a charge that Robinson later denied.

From Plymouth, where Mercy heard about Jemmy's assault, she dashed off a letter: "You know not what I suffered for you within the last twenty four hours...is it possible that we have men among us under the guise of the officers of the Crown, who have become open assassins?

"Thousands...are...daily praying for the preservation of your life. To theirs let me add my most earnest solicitations that when you recover, you will neither give or receive a challenge from any man...This I urge for the sake of your lovely babes, for the sake of your worthy and venerable father, for the sake of your many tender friends, and for...this people who stand in need of your assistance."

She was writing, Mercy explained, as "one who has your welfare more at heart, after a very few exceptions, than that of any other person in the world."[36]

Neither Mercy nor other relatives immediately grasped the effect of the assault upon Jemmy. For decades, family legend blamed the attack for the patriot's subsequent mental collapse. More likely it was a contributing factor to his already unraveling psyche.

Initially, friends and family gathered sympathetically around the stricken lawyer. Within a matter of days though, Jemmy's despair deepened, transcending the original incident and provoking remorse. "I have done more mischief to my country than can be repaired. I meant well, but am convinced that I was mistaken,"[37] he brooded.

Chagrined, Jemmy subsequently defected from the patriotic cause in support of the Tories and the newly appointed Governor Hutchinson. Then he began wandering the streets of Boston. By January 1770, John Adams privately compared him to a "ship without an helm...I fear that he is not in his perfect mind." Frequently, his comments deteriorated into "trash...obscenities...profanesss...distraction."[38] And he was drinking heavily.

On February 26, John Adams recorded that Jemmy had become "raving mad" and railed against "father, wife, brother, sister, friend."[39] Within another month—just a few days, perhaps not coincidentally, after the March 5, 1770, Boston Massacre—Mercy's brother exhibited what his friends termed "mad freak[s]."[40] One day he shattered the windows of the Massachusetts Town House. On the Sabbath, he fired guns.

To his patriotic supporters, Jemmy's deterioration was a tragedy. "I fear, I tremble, I mourn for the man, and for his country,"[41] wrote John Adams.

Predictably, Jemmy would not be reelected to the Massachusetts House that spring.

Mercy, like other worried relatives, finally realized that Jemmy's behavior suggested an encroaching insanity. Only her voice, it was said, "had power to calm him, when all else was without effect."[42]

Whether Mercy linked Jemmy's instability to her mother's dark moods or her own high-strung disposition is unclear. At the time, she praised the Creator for her own mental stability in a private poem titled "A thought on the inestimable Blessing of Reason, occasioned by its privation to a friend of very superior talents and virtues, 1770."

"What is it moves within my soul," Mercy asked in the first line. "'Tis reason, Lord, which though has given/ A ray divine, let down from Heaven," she later explained, which "Thou has bestow'd lest man should grope/In endless darkness, void of hope."[43] To save Jemmy from additional embarrassment, he was driven to the country. Miraculously, by mid-1771, he seemed recovered and was reelected to the Massachusetts House.

In the interim, the Townshend Acts had been rescinded, save for a tax on tea, prompting the colonists of Massachusetts to settle into a wary coexistence. On one side were citizens who welcomed the renewed trade with Great Britain and considered the tea tax trivial. Opposing them was a disheartened caucus of patriotic Whigs, or rebels, who, for all their resentment of British rule, seemed powerless to overthrow it.

After the five deaths of the Boston Massacre, many colonists once supportive of the patriotic cause fell away, rationalizing it was easier to pay a few British taxes than incite more military violence. Even Sam Adams's speeches seemed suspect. "How easily the people change, and give up their friends and their interest,"[44] his cousin John Adams lamented.

Fresh from a second "rest" in the country, Jemmy returned to Boston as a convert to British loyalties. One day he even appeared at Hutchinson's Milton mansion, assuring the governor that he considered him "as the representative of the King, and the Kings, as the representative of God."[45]

By then, Hutchinson, determined to remove the General Court from the political hotbed of Boston, announced its relocation to Cambridge, six miles away.

Predictably, the patriots protested. Not only was the location inconvenient and removed from Boston's newspapers and political center, but it was a radical departure from its customary location suggested by the 1691 charter of the colony. That mattered little, retorted Hutchinson, who was promptly seconded by Jemmy.

Sam Adams was appalled. So, too, was his cousin John, by then so discouraged by the Whigs' faltering resolve that he vowed to quit politics altogether. Privately, even Mercy's husband, James, confided his doubts to Sam Adams.

"Your letter expresses a noble spirit of resentment which I cannot but admire; but when you once spoke the language of despair...it gave me offense," Sam replied on March 25. There was still enough colonial resistance to British rule to advance the cause. "It is no dishonor to be in a minority in the cause of liberty and virtue." Our sons, Sam predicted, will "enjoy the happy fruits of their fathers' struggles."[46]

But not the once-inspired son of Colonel Otis. Now, for even trivial reasons, Jemmy lashed out at others—at his clients, colleagues, even at a servant who failed to place four candles at a tavern table. "He trembles. His nerves are irritable. He cannot bear fatigue,"[47] John Adams noted.

On a sweltering July day in 1771, when Jemmy's case against his British attackers was finally settled, he stunned the court by rejecting the award. The sum—£2,000—was so paltry, Jemmy sneered, that his "honor" was offended. By November, his behavior was so wild that the Otis family had him legally declared non compos mentis.

On December 3, Hutchinson gloated in his diary that Otis had been bound in a straightjacket and carried away, having, as he once vowed, enflamed the Province and destroyed himself in the process.

That same day Hannah Winthrop, who attended the hearing with her husband, wrote Mercy, "With grief did I behold the afflicted countenance of his [James Otis's] venerable father, obliged to engage in the arduous business and to restrain the over-flowings of parental affection."[48]

Mercy and her family continued to hope for Jemmy's recovery nevertheless. By spring 1772, her brother returned to Boston under the guidance of his youngest brother, Samuel Allyne. However, the following August, when the Robinson case was appealed, Jemmy suffered another relapse. This time, what Mercy delicately termed Jemmy's "beclouded reason,"[49] led him to forgive "the murderous band" that had assaulted him. Days later, the once-brilliant attorney began to rave, turning cruelly upon his anguished relatives.

No longer able to live in Boston or Barnstable, Jemmy was finally sent off to live with Captain Daniel Souther of Hull. There, for a time, he became stable enough to teach school.

It was during that anguished period that Mercy rose to champion the patriotic cause in Jemmy's place. In contrast to her erudite brother, she had no legal background. Nor as a woman was she likely to be heard. Still, as she confided to Hannah, nothing less was "at stake than that liberty for which our fathers bled & for which our sons must fall a sacrifice."[50]

So it was that by 1772, Mercy had stoked those patriotic coals into sputtering flames from her home on Plymouth's North Street.

4

The Patriots' Secret Pen

"THE GENERAL COURT IS INDEED carried to Boston but done with so ill a grace as entirely destroys all the merit of it,"[1] Hannah Winthrop complained to Mercy in June 1772. While the patriots welcomed the assembly's return to that city, they seethed over Governor Hutchinson's reason for doing so—because Cambridge was inconvenient, but not because the relocation had violated the Massachusetts charter of 1691.

In spite of his high-handed approach, James Warren thought the governor a desperate man. Hutchinson, he confided to Sam Adams, reminded him of a "poor sachem" like one of the colony's displaced American Indians, who "spent all his wampum and must appear in state equal to the noble blood running in his veins."[2]

With equal scorn Mercy later described him in her *History* as a treacherous man who professed "moderation and tenderness to his country" while simultaneously advancing the nefarious "measures of [his] administration."[3]

By October 1772 those "measures" were publicly revealed when the colonists learned that the new customs revenues not only paid Hutchinson's salary but would fund the colony's justices. Outraged, the patriotic *Boston Gazette* noted on October 17 that the "odious excise laws" made Massachusetts "officers unlimited in their power." Would not "those things hasten the day of independence"?[4]

On the chilly Monday morning of November 2, a caucus of patriots identified as the Boston Committee confronted the silk-clad Hutchinson over that question during a meeting at Faneuil Hall, forcing him to confront what he described as "black-hearted fellows whom one would not choose to meet in the dark."[5]

During that gathering, Sam Adams condemned the new mandates. Paying the Superior Court justices out of colonial customs revenues made them servants of the Crown, he declared, yet another example of "the iron hand of tyranny...ravish[ing] our laws."[6]

Amid the ensuing clamor, members of the audience demanded that Hutchinson explain the rationale for the law. In reply, the governor haughtily declared that it was not "proper," to share Parliamentary communications. A roar of protest filled the hall, demanding that he immediately reconvene the Massachusetts Assembly. Once again, Hutchinson hedged, believing the raucous crowd was only a disgruntled minority.

Sam Adams thought differently. To him, the governor's refusal was a tactical error. By November 4, he reported to James that the patriots' vowed to establish a "a committee to open communication with every town." Accordingly, he urged James to rally the patriots of Plymouth and "second Boston by appointing a committee of communication and correspondence."[7]

After receiving that town's approval, Sam replied that the Friends of Liberty were so "highly pleased with the spirit of Plymouth letter"[8] that he had published it in three newspapers. "*Nil desperandum.* That is a motto for you and me," he wrote James again on December 9, assuring him that "where there is a spark of patriotic fire, we will enkindle it."[9]

By January 1773, the smoke from that "patriotic fire" nearly choked the governor when he discovered that eighty Massachusetts towns had created their own committees and that other colonies had followed. "Unless... checked, it would mark a total separation of the colonies from Great Britain"[10] Hutchinson fretted.

To placate his restive constituents, the governor reconvened the assembly on January 6 and invited them to debate the old Massachusetts charter. His plan, Hutchinson believed, would reveal "what their constitution was, and...to join with me in supporting it or to show...where I was erroneous."[11]

Neither the Warrens nor their fellow patriots doubted that Hutchinson suffered from "erroneous" thinking. "I stand amazed at the Governor for forcing on this controversy," John Adams scrawled in his own diary that January. "He has reduced himself to a most ridiculous state."[12]

Having hosted other Sons of Liberty meetings at "One Liberty Square" in Plymouth that winter, Mercy, meanwhile, began fashioning her own version of political protest. The effort was a radical departure from her earlier work. Self-doubts arose about her abilities as a commentator, about her grasp of political events—and especially about how her work would be regarded if it was known that a woman was its author.

She was not, however, the first English-speaking woman to write on politics. Since 1763, Catharine Sawbridge Macaulay, a British radical writer five years Mercy's junior, had been publishing the controversial *The History of England from the Accession of James I to that of the Brunswick Line* in London. One of her American admirers was John Adams, through whom Mrs. Macaulay learned about Jemmy's protests over British rule of the colonies.

"Your patriotic conduct and great abilities in defense of the rights of your fellow citizens claim the respect and admiration of every lover of their country and mankind," she first wrote Jemmy in spring 1769. "The principles on which I have written the history of the Steward [Stuart] monarchs are, I flatter myself, in some measure correspondent to those of the great guardian of American liberty."[13]

By June 1773, reconciled to the fact that the "great guardian of American liberty" was insane, Mercy began writing the British author in Jemmy's place. "He has not lately been able to make these acknowledgments that are justly your due,"[14] she gingerly apologized.

She, too, Mercy explained, was "impressed with a strong sense of the natural rights of mankind which your masterly pen has so finely delineated." Realizing a "long correspondence" was unlikely, Mercy, nevertheless, wondered. "What fatal infatuation has seized the parent state, that she is...making illegal encroachments on her loyal subjects, and by every despotic measure urging these...colonies to a vigorous union in defense of their invaded rights?"

Her question was admittedly bold. Like John Adams, who had praised the British writer for her unerring ability to "strip off the gilding and false luster from worthless princes and nobles,"[15] Mercy was awed by Mrs.

Macaulay's work. Her own literary aspirations were more modest—at best, perhaps to record current events in Massachusetts under the thumb of a tyrannical governor.

Should her project fail, should she receive public "frowns" as Mercy called them in her diarylike poem "Primitive Simplicity," she intended to "quit the pen, and keep within the bounds, the narrow bounds, prescribed to female life" as "the gentle mistress, and the prudent wife."

Mercy was, nevertheless, an Otis. Once inspired, she was determined to fulfill "each fervent wish," as her poem expressed, "and thus subscribe, as the patriot's faithful friend."[16]

The result was Mercy's first political play, *The Adulateur,* a satire in blank verse portraying a Hutchinson-like character as an arch villain. The setting was the fictionalized land of Upper Servia, whose ruler, a "Bashaw" named Rapatio, vowed to avenge himself upon his foes for destruction of his personal property.

In the play, Mercy drew Hutchinson's Tory allies with equal caprice. Among them were Rapatio's brothers-in-law, "Limipit," and "Chief Justice Hazelrod"—modeled upon Superior Court justices Peter and Andrew Oliver—and their toadies, Meagre, Bagshot, and Captain Gripeall. Opposing them was the noble Brutus, representing Jemmy, and his constituents Junius, Cassius, Hortensius, and Portius.

In the first scene, a scowling Rapatio enters the stage and warns the patriots to "think of the past and tremble" about that night when they "broke my retirement ... rushed into my chamber ... [and] rifled all my secrets"— Mercy's gleeful reference to the 1765 destruction of Hutchinson's mansion. "Hell! What a night was this—and do they think I'll ever forget such treatment?" Rapatio bellows.

Supporting Rapatio's avowed destruction of Servia's rebels are his fawning Tory courtiers with "adulating tongue" who help assuage his guilt over his destruction of "the heaving struggles of expiring freedom!" Only fragments of Mercy's original script remain today. In the final scene, however, Brutus prophesizes Rapatio's ultimate defeat, after "murders, blood and carnage ... crimson the streets" of "this poor country."[17]

As Mercy wished, *The Adulateur*'s authorship was known only to her closest friends, among them Hannah Winthrop, who praised her "poetic genius,"[18] and her husband, James, who considered it one more example of her "brilliant & busy imagination."[19]

Ironically, for all her literary sophistication, Mercy had never attended a play, for Boston's Puritan tradition still forbade live theater. Citizens consequently read, rather than attended, plays. By March and April 1772, excerpts of *The Adulateur* appeared in the patriotic Isaiah Thomas's widely read *Massachusetts Spy*. So enthusiastic was its reception that a year later *The Adulateur* was republished in an expanded form to five acts, with a section on the Boston Massacre, in a pamphlet Mercy later insisted was a "plagiary."[20]

Additional testimony to its popularity was the way Massachusetts patriots used the characters' names to substitute for real ones. "Rapatio is now gone to Middleboro to consult with his Brother Hazelrod,"[21] Sam Adams reported to a friend.

Few women were better patriots than Mercy, insisted Abigail, whose play "developed the dark designs of a Rapatio."[22]

With the publication of *The Adulateur*, Mercy made her debut as the patriots' secret pen, whose barbed lampoons provoked laughter and longing for liberation from British rule.

In 1773, a scandal broke over Massachusetts that provided Mercy with fresh material. From the moment of his August 1771 appointment as governor, the Boston-born Hutchinson had promoted himself as the colony's loyal advocate, claiming that his political troubles stemmed from rebel malevolence. Not so, contended Sam Adams, who, like James, thought Hutchinson a duplicitous and contemptible[23] man. Accordingly, after Hutchinson announced his intention to reconvene the General Court in Boston in January 1773, Sam predicted he would attempt to appease its disgruntled delegates.

"I know of no line that can be drawn between the supreme authority of Parliament and the total independence of the colonies," Hutchinson said in his opening remarks on January 6. "If we might be ... altogether independent of Great Britain, could we have any claim to the protection of that government ... should we not become a prey to one or the other powers of Europe?"[24]

The governor's proposal to deny that charter's mandate for self-rule was nevertheless dismissed. "Independent we are, and independent we will be," retorted Sam Adams.[25] Then, to underscore that message, he reminded readers of the *Boston Gazette,* telling them that it was "indisputable duty to stand forth in the glorious cause of freedom,... and with a truly Roman spirit of liberty, either prevent the fastening of the infernal chains now forging you and your posterity, or nobly perish in the attempt."[26]

Among those reawakened to the cause was John Adams, who, eighteen months earlier, had quit politics and moved his family back to Braintree. However, by March 1773, John felt "under peculiar obligations to undeceive the people," revoke his "resolution," and rejoin the conflict. [27]

Simultaneously, a stunning revelation arrived from Benjamin Franklin in England in a packet addressed to Thomas Cushing, Speaker of the House.

Enclosed were letters from 1768–79 that Hutchinson, while lieutenant governor, had sent to Thomas Whately, former secretary to the British Treasury, urging punitive treatment upon Massachusetts Colony. The packet also contained hostile letters from Hutchinson's brother-in-law, Andrew Oliver.

Ironically, Franklin sent the packet to Cushing to resolve, rather than augment, political tensions—to prove that Parliament's acts against Massachusetts were a reaction to misinformation from that colony's royal appointees and not from their own malicious intent.

The letters could be shared with key patriots, Franklin wrote, but warned that they "shall not be printed."[28] Most electrifying was the discovery of Hutchinson's letter after the Stamp Act riots asking Parliament for "an abridgment of English liberties in colonial administration."[29] Another gloated, "The union of the colonies is pretty well broke: I hope I shall never see it renewed." A third demanded "standing troops... to support the authority of the government at Boston."[30]

The letters confirmed the patriots' long-held suspicions about Hutchinson, whom Mercy characterized in her *History* as "the grand incendiary, who had sown the seeds of discord, and cherished the dispute between Great Britain and the colonies."[31]

In Braintree, the Whately letters goaded John Adams into rejoining the struggle. "Bone of our bone, born and educated among us!" he lamented to his diary after reading them. "The subtlety of this serpent, is equal to that of the old one."[32]

By June 2, a gleeful Sam Adams read the Whately letters aloud to a secret session of the Massachusetts Assembly. Soon afterward, they were leaked to the public. By mid-June, Boston's patriotic printers—"hot, indiscreet men,"[33] according to John Adams—published them in the newspapers.

Even before their revelation, Mercy had been heartened by rising anti-British sentiment, even though the implications of that conflict were grim. Either, as she wrote her friend Hannah, "we must tamely acquiesce in the bonds of slavery, or repurchase our freedom at the costly expense of the best blood of the land."[34]

Tame acquiescence was never Mercy's style. By the spring of 1773, she was writing a second satirical play, *The Defeat*. Again set in Upper Servia, Mercy drew Rapatio in even darker colors, this time as a diabolical governor who bribed followers to remain loyal while hatching plans to destroy his enemies. Several characters from *The Adulateur* reappeared, among them Brutus, Cassius, Hortensius, and Limpit.

As in her earlier play, familiar political figures are pitted against one another in a power struggle, this time culminating in Rapatio's dismissal as a leader and his off-stage murder. But even that did not sate Mercy's thirst for vengeance. In the play's final scene, Rapatio returns center stage to repent his deeds in a soliloquy. Yet, as Limpit ominously warns his audience, Rapatio's hypocritical spirit still looms over the land, remaining the "dangerous foe/Of Liberty of truth, and of mankind/Who undermines their happiness below."[35]

One week after the *Boston Gazette*'s May 24 publication of *The Defeat*, Sam Adams disclosed the Whately letters to the Massachusetts Assembly. Mercy promptly added another act, which alluded to Rapatio's "cover'd sting... [and] half disguis'd plan," which stabbed "the vitals [Massachusetts] that first gave him birth."[36]

Like *The Adulateur*, only fragments of the play and its July 19 addition in the *Boston Gazette* have been preserved. Its satirical representation of the era's politicians and its affirmation of the patriotic ideals of virtue, honesty, and integrity nevertheless made *The Defeat* one of the Revolutionary era's most scorching indictments of the British abuse of colonial liberties.

Would those high-minded American virtues ultimately prevail? Privately, if not publicly, that question remained unsettled in Mercy's personal life. To observers like Hannah Winthrop, Mercy seemed blessed with every advantage—a devoted husband, two fine homes, and five healthy young sons.

"It gives me great satisfaction to contemplate the happy circumstances in which Providence has placed you," Hannah wrote to Mercy in November 1771 after a visit. "How sublime your pleasure, informing the infant mind... rearing the tender thought, and teaching the young."[37]

Abigail Adams, who met Mercy for the first time in the spring of 1773, similarly admired her "well ordered family."[38] In spite of their age difference—Abigail was then the twenty-nine-year-old mother of three, and Mercy, a forty-five-year-old mother of five—the two women became friends.

"I must beg the favor of you to communicate... the happy art of 'reading the tender thought,' teaching the young idea... and pouring such instruction over the mind," Abigail wrote on July 16, 1773, so that "the tender twigs allotted to my care, may be so cultivated."[39] Accompanying her letter was a copy of Juliana Seymour's *On the Management and Education of Children.*

In reply, Mercy explained that she did not agree with all of Mrs. Seymour's comments. Though of one childrearing principle Mercy felt certain: that love and respect for truth molded a child into a productive, ethical adult more effectively than the harsh, Calvinistic treatment of her girlhood. "I have ever thought a careful attention to... veracity in the bosom of youth the surest guard to virtue," Mercy explained. Winning "that child's confidence"[40] was the best tactic.

Nor did she, like other increasingly permissive mothers of that era, claim to have all the answers. A year later, Mercy admitted to Abigail that she was "yet looking abroad for every foreign aid" to help her "discharge a duty of the highest consequence to society."[41]

Her confession may have been related to her worries about her eldest son, James, Jr., whom she and her husband had raised strictly to set an example for his brothers. Even after the fifteen-year-old entered Harvard in late 1772, Mercy persisted in reminding him to behave with exemplary "character and conduct" because "the honor of the whole depends...on the behavior and example of the eldest branch of a family."[42]

In contrast was Mercy's more indulgent attitude toward her second and favorite son, the frivolous, charming Winslow. Even as a child, the handsome boy was attracted to "the pretty things,"[43] as his father once observed.

With the birth of each successive son, Mercy grew increasingly relaxed. When, in 1773, her brother Samuel Allyne Otis sent her three youngest sons gifts, Mercy reported their reactions with amusement. Eleven-year-old Charles had "long tired" of the gift of a "perspective"—a stereoscopic looking glass. Nine-year-old Henry plucked so vigorously upon his new violin that the strings burst; George, age seven, broke off the wheels of his new wagon. To teach the latter the value of material things, Mercy even agreed to "buy" it for fifty cents.

The boys' behavior, she wrote her brother, reminded her of "the restless pursuits of man, who like children eagerly grasp the bubbles of fancy and ...are often more miserable in the possession of their wishes than they could be in the disappointment thereof."[44]

By December 16, 1773, the Boston Tea Party had become an infamous example of those "restless pursuits." For decades, tea, steeped and poured in fine English china teapots to prosperous colonists or sipped from rude mugs by humbler ones, was one of America's most popular drinks. Though "love and scandal" were said to be "the best sweeteners of tea,"[45] as English novelist Henry Fielding had observed earlier in the century, the British duty on tea soured many Americans on the beverage.

Not, however, the Tories, who were still willing to pay the three pence tax on tea. As the patriotic poem "The Ladies Lamentation over an empty Cannister," reminded colonists:

> Come just resentment guide my pen
> And mark our mad committee men,
> Pray, what is freedom, right or laws,
> To such a vast important cause?

> Why all their malice shewn to tea
> So near, so dear—beloved by me,
> Reviving draught, when I am dry—
> Tea I just have, or I shall die.[46]

Dwindling tea sales from the East India Company, underwritten by hefty loans from the British government, had prompted the tax. To encourage the colonists to purchase that tea, Parliament consequently passed the Regulating Act, or Tea Act, in May 1773, granting the East India Company an American monopoly.

Profit, rather than respect for colonial rights, was the motive, bellowed Pennsylvania's John Dickinson; the act was one more British scheme exciting "rebellions" and sacrificing the rights of "millions for the sake of gain."[47]

Before long, several colonies joined the outcry, claiming that the Tea Act was a British bribe using inexpensive tea to buy the colonists into compliance. Again Jemmy's famous words "taxation without representation," were recalled and used to promote a new boycott.

Patriotic newspapers and handbills were thus soon denouncing tea as a "blasted herb,"[48] a "pestilential weed,"[49] which produced spasms, fevers, and spells. One song even frightened citizens into believing that tea sent to North America was "tinctured with a filth/of carcasses embalmed."[50]

Parliament, meanwhile, determined to ride out the tidal wave of colonial protest, insisted upon enforcement. By October 1773, the East India Company consequently dispatched ships to Boston, New York, and Philadelphia laden with 1,253 chests of tea. As news of the approaching fleet reached Boston, patriots rode away to warn other cities.

Philadelphia was the first to react, demanding resignation of its tea commissioners and insisting upon a citywide boycott. New York followed. On Friday, November 5, John Hancock moderated a town meeting, which resolved to prevent those ships from landing.

The East India Company's determination "to send out their tea to America,"[51] was "a violent attack upon the liberties of America," fumed the *Boston Evening Post*. Nevertheless, on November 28, the *Dartmouth*, the first of the tea ships, landed.

"The tea, that bainful weed, is arrived. Great and . . . effectual opposition has been made to the landing of it," Abigail wrote Mercy from Boston several days later. "Our citizens have been united, spirited, and firm. The flame is kindled and like lightning it catches from soul to soul."[52]

Predictably, Hutchinson supported the Crown. To ensure that the *Dartmouth* remained in port, he ordered the guns at Castle William primed in Boston Harbor. Two warships lurked nearby. Only one obstacle stood in the way—a maritime law allowing customs officials to auction unloaded cargo if it remained aboard ship after twenty days in port.

By December 16, that deadline was less than twenty-four hours away. Even after the *Dartmouth*'s owner, Francis Rotch, made a last-minute ride to Hutchinson at his country mansion in Milton, the governor refused to allow the boat to return to England without discharging its cargo.

That evening during an emotionally charged meeting at Boston's Old South Meeting House, Sam Adams threw up his hands in disgust. "This meeting can do nothing more to save the country,"[53] he declared. With that, one hundred and fifty men, their faces blackened with soot and disguised as Mohawk Indians, symbolizing America's disenfranchisement, marched to Griffin's Wharf where they dumped 342 chests of tea into the harbor.

That act of defiance, as John Adams noted the next morning, was "the most magnificent . . . of all. This destruction of the tea is so bold, so daring . . . intrepid . . . it must have so important consequences, and so lasting that I cannot but consider it an epoch in history."[54]

To memorialize that event, he asked Mercy, the most gifted American writer he knew, to write a satirical poem.

The result, Mercy meekly explained to Abigail Adams, was a poetic fantasy about a "squabble among the celestials of the sea arising from a scarcity of nectar and ambrosia." To publicize her worrisome message—the pursuit of luxury at the expense of civic good—Mercy had adopted a whimsical tone, believing that the "follies of . . . human nature exposed to ridicule . . . often have a greater tendency to reform," than "graver lessons of morality."

Written in the mock-epic style of Alexander Pope's *Rape of the Lock*, Mercy's subsequently titled "The Squabble of the Sea Nymphs; or the Sacrifice of the Tuscararoes," described how Neptune, having run out of nectar, summoned the gods, and especially its female representatives who had "influence o'er kings" to a conference. Subsequently, one of the sea nymphs, or Tuscararoes, Neptune's wife, Amphritrite, representing those faithful to the Crown, quarreled with Salacia, a rebel, over the disposition of tea. Ultimately, Salacia and her peers sacrificed the tea to thirsty aquatic deities, turning the ocean into "hyson...choice souchong...the imperial leaf." When those deities savored the "profusion of delicious teas," nearly seducing the "virtuous daughters of the mead" into drinking the "sweet inebriating dream," the latter resisted that "baneful poison" at the last moment.

In the poem's triumphant conclusion, the "daughters" rejoiced over the "confusion round Neponset Hills,"[55] symbolizing Hutchinson's country mansion in Milton.

Afterward, Mercy brooded about the merits of her poem, even though John Adams had assured her that his pen compared to hers, "conscious of its inferiority falls out of my hand."[56] Should he disapprove of the poem, Mercy insisted to Abigail that February, she would harbor no ill feelings, but simply "lay aside the pen of the poet."[57]

Ultimately there was no reason for such fears. Within a month Adams had not only arranged for the poem's publication in the *Boston Gazette,* but wrote James that Mercy's work was "one of the incontestable evidences of real genius."[58]

By 1774, John thus became Mercy's literary mentor, his praise one more spur that kept her pen primed to the quickening pace of patriotic politics.

5

"No one has at stake a larger share of domestic felicity"

ON JANUARY 19, 1774, just after Mercy sent Abigail her poem about the Boston Tea Party, she learned that her friend had been ill. "I sincerely congratulate my much esteemed friend on the restoration of . . . health," Mercy wrote, wondering if Abigail's ailment had been "as much affected by the shock of political" events as by other factors.

If so, if that "shock" was the dreaded arrival of the tea ships, perhaps the destruction of that tea might be considered one of the "cathartics" physicians often prescribed, after which British-American relations might be repaired.

Of course, as members of the "weak and timid sex" she knew that she and Abigail had no voice in that dispute. Searching for still another poetic image, Mercy compared them to a "pliant piece of clock work," with "springs of our souls [that] move slow or more rapidly"[1] depending upon the behavior of their men.

By January 1773, public sentiment raged so vehemently against the British that some Bostonians refused to eat fish "because they had drunk of the East India tea."[2] Hutchinson, it was rumored, would soon be recalled to England. Intimidated, too, were the governor's tea consignees, most of them hiding in Boston Harbor's Castle William, although at least one had been tarred, feathered, and paraded around the city.

Still another, if less violent demonstration had just occurred in Plymouth. On Monday, January 17, the day before Mercy sent Abigail "The Squabble of the Sea Nymphs," twenty-year-old Polly Watson Hutchinson arrived to visit her parents. Within minutes, Plymouth's church bells tolled, summoning the patriots to the Watson home, where they demanded that her husband, Elisha Hutchinson, the governor's son and a tea consignee, leave town. Arguing that it was twilight, Hutchinson was allowed to stay until dawn and the following morning, in spite of a blizzard, was forced to depart.

Subsequently, the *Boston Gazette* gleefully announced that once Elisha reached the home of his uncle, Lieutenant Governor Andrew Oliver, he related his "melancholy adventure to the very sympathetic Chief Justice Hazelrod."[3]

Mercy neither wrote about the incident nor its coverage in the *Boston Gazette*. Yet the newspaper's casual mention of Hazelrod revealed the enduring popularity her plays, *The Adulateur* and *The Defeat*.

Inevitably, relations between the patriots and the Tories worsened. One of Mercy's closest friends and James's Plymouth cousins was Penny Winslow, whose family were Tories. Earlier, when James had traveled to Boston as a delegate to the Massachusetts House, Penny stayed overnight with Mercy.

"I have had the agreeable company of Miss P. Winslow last night who proposes to continue this kindness through the week," Mercy wrote James in 1772. Nor, she had jested at the time, could she imagine a "singular instance of a Whig and a Tory lodging in the same bed"[4] that would have been more compatible.

After the Boston Tea Party though, such friendships became more difficult to sustain. In Plymouth as in Boston, the patriots spied on incoming ships, confiscated contraband tea, and published the names of smugglers. That behavior and other displays of "party spirit,"[5] as Abigail glumly wrote from Boston, ruins a "good neighborhood . . . good nature and humanity." Massachusetts, Mercy concurred, was in the "miserable situation of a people broken into factions."[6]

In a subsequent letter that February, Mercy shared an even more alarming thought. As wives of leading patriots, she and Abigail might be accused of treason. Should that occur, she expected that she and her Braintree friend must conduct themselves nobly, like Portia and Arria, heroines of the ancient world who sacrificed themselves for their husband's ideals instead of insisting that they "deviate from their noble principles."[7]

Soon afterward, Mercy became so ill with a respiratory infection that James rushed home from a legislative session in Boston. In spite of Mercy's ideals, her lofty discussions with Abigail and her bold satires, her nerves and her frequent illnesses, betrayed an inner fragility. "Don't let the fluttering of your heart interrupt your health or disturb your repose"[8] thus became James's frequently anxious refrain.

By late March, Mercy had recovered "tolerably well" to take up her pen again and vent her anxieties. "Even females," she confided to Hannah, could no longer remain "wholly inattentive" to the unsettled political climate. Nor should they forget that seventeenth-century quest for "liberty for which our fathers bled" that inspired their flight to North America.

Another, perhaps even greater confrontation was imminent, Mercy sensed, this time one in which "our sons must fall a sacrifice"—unless some "happy expedient"[9] intervened.

By early spring 1774, that happy expedient seemed unlikely. In mid-February the *Boston Evening Post* reported that "six ships of war and 7 regiments are ordered for America."[10] Several days later, that newspaper published a letter from Great Britain warning that its leaders intended to force "tea upon the Americans with a fleet, and troops."[11] Other rumors predicted that Parliament planned to close Boston's port.

The British were enraged, an alarmed Benjamin Franklin wrote Thomas Cushing. "We never had...so few friends in Britain." The colonists must apologize and reimburse the stockholders of the East India Company to "remove much of the prejudice now entertained against us."[12]

But to that the patriots of Massachusetts had refused, instead hoping that the Boston Tea Party would serve as a warning to the British Crown. Moreover, Parliament, as James suggested to John Adams, could easily heal the conflict "by laying the blame of the whole on their own, and East Indian company's officers, who...drove the people to this desperate step."[13]

None of the patriots doubted that such a step was essential for by then, as John noted in his diary, there was "so much of a republican spirit," that the colonists "would never submit to tyrants or oppressive projects."[14]

The rebels consequently girded themselves for punishment. Few Bostonians forgot the warning Admiral John Montagu, commander in chief of

North America, bellowed out of a window after the dumping of the tea: "Well boys, you've had a fine, pleasant evening for your Indian caper, haven't you? But mind, you have got to pay the fiddler yet."[15]

By Thursday, March 31, Sam Adams received reports from Philadelphia about the nature of that pay—that Bostonians should "expect regiments to be quartered among us." Even so, he reminded James that it was their duty "to preserve the public liberty."[16]

That same day in London, Parliament voted into law the first of the four punitive measures Americans called the Coercive, or Intolerable Acts. The first, the Boston Port Bill, ordered that the city's harbor, the busiest in America, be closed because of its "dangerous commotions and insurrections." Imported goods, including food and fuel, could no longer be landed in Boston until "full satisfaction hath been made by the inhabitants . . . to the united company of merchants of England trading to the East Indies."[17]

Thus began the Boston blockade; its sea trade, the economic lifeline of that port city, was severed with one stroke of the British sword.

On May 24, a second mandate, the Massachusetts Government Act, sheared off çolonists' remaining civil liberties by forbidding them to elect their own representatives. Formerly elected colonial officials, as Mercy recorded in her *History,* were replaced by a government-appointed "council of thirty six members appointed by *mandamus*—all judges, justices, sheriffs."[18]

The third law, the Administration of Justice Act, protected the deeds of officers who restored peace during civil riots, who, if unable to receive a fair hearing in Massachusetts, would be moved to another British jurisdiction.

The fourth, the Quartering Act of June 2, 1774, allowed British soldiers to live outside barracks in "uninhabited houses,"[19] barns, and other buildings—and even the private homes of the colonists.

News of the Boston Port Act, announced by the tolling of church bells, reached that city on May 12. Merchants shut their doors. Churches held special services for residents. Citizens, including Tories, stunned by removal of their own civil rights, donned funeral bands. Days of fasting and prayer were proclaimed throughout the colony. Patriotic messengers, among them silversmith Paul Revere, galloped to other colonies to report Great Britain's reduction of Massachusetts to a police state.

"The Act of Parliament for blockading the Town of Boston cannot be paralleled in all English history," sputtered the *Boston Gazette* on May 16. "It exhibits to every town in this province, to every colony . . . and to the whole world, what is to be expected from a government that claims an unbounded authority over us . . . to reduce us to the last distress."[20]

Within days, handbills, broadsides, and newspaper articles appeared throughout the colonies, protesting denial of the "natural rights of English citizens." Among them was Thomas Jefferson's "A Summary View of the Rights of British America," warning that such despotic acts "may yet cause further discontents and jealousies among us."[21]

In Hanover County, Virginia, it was announced that "Parliament by their proceedings have made us all and all North American parties in the present dispute."[22]

Southern plantation owners were also appalled. If the British had "a right or power to put a duty on my tea," flamed the *Georgia Gazette,* they "have an equal right to put a duty on my bread, and why not on my breath, why not only daylight and smoke, why not on everything?"[23]

Why not indeed? "This Town has received the copy of an Act of the British Parliament, wherein it appears that we have been tried and condemned," Sam Adams wrote James on May 14. "If the Parliament had a right to pass such an edict," could it not "proceed to the destruction of a community, without even the accusation of any crime?"[24]

By May 17, Mercy wrote John and Abigail, "Shall not pretend to delincate the painful ideas that arise . . . of the evils brought on this much injured country . . . shall be glad to know . . . your sentiments on the late hostile movements of state plunderers and jockeys."[25]

That same day, one of those jockeys, the unsympathetic General Thomas Gage, arrived in Boston to replace Hutchinson as governor. Determined to break the patriots' spirit, Gage placed the city under martial law.

By the terms of the Coercive Acts, as Mercy predicted, any man liable "on the slightest suspicion of treason" could be seized and transported to "any part of the king of England's dominions for trial." Legally, Gage thus had the right to "arrest the leading characters . . . and transport them beyond sea."[26]

While the general's arrival unnerved Mercy and her friends, it relieved

Hutchinson. "The present state of the Province is such, that I see no prospect of being serviceable here,"[27] the sixty-two-year-old former governor disconsolately scrawled in his diary. Yet, by a grim twist of fate, he had been compelled to remain after the March 3 death of his brother in-law, Andrew Oliver, victimized, he and his followers believed, by the constant "abuse" of the rebels.

Hutchinson, too, was demoralized. As he confessed that March to former Massachusetts Governor Bernard, the winter of 1774 had "given me as much trouble as any three months since you left."[28]

At noon on Wednesday, June 1—the same day that Hutchinson sailed to Great Britain—the blockade of Boston commenced. In place of the once-lively harbor filled with sails, clanging bells, and busy dock workers swayed a forest of bare masts and bobbing hulls; on shore stood dry-docked boats, shuttered warehouses, and deserted shipyards.

Thousands of workers lacking jobs had fled, some hauling families and household goods in wagons, others on foot, an exodus of six thousand of Boston's sixteen thousand residents.

"We have not men fit for the times. We are deficient in genius, in education, in travel, in fortune,—in every thing. I feel unutterable anxiety,"[29] brooded John Adams on June 26, as he strolled the peninsula jutting into the harbor known as Boston Neck.

In contrast to Boston, nearby towns and counties bustled with activity. Ironically, the same dusty roads that carried men and their families out of the port city were soon clogged with carts and wagons rumbling their way into Boston. From Marblehead came quintals of codfish; from Chelmsford, Wrentham, and other nearby towns, bushels of rye and herds of livestock.

Other colonies pitched in. Pennsylvania sent money and stores of flour. Connecticut dispatched flocks of sheep. From distant Carolina came shipments of rice. Still others donated money, found jobs for Boston's displaced men, and published notices of support for the blockaded city.

Hutchinson anticipated that "all our trade would be ruined," the *Boston Gazette* gloated, "that the inhabitants would then divide... and cut one another's throats... other towns thro' the province would desert the cause, and grow exasperated with the capital—that the other colonies... would leave Boston and Massachusetts to the mercy of the ministry and bluster no more about the American Rights."[30]

The opposite had already occurred.

Heartened by that intercolonial support, Bostonians stiffened their resolve. First, they refused to sell food to the British, then, to prevent construction of barracks, wood. Mysteriously, when the "lobsterbacks" collected straw for mattresses, it burst into flames. By September, Gage was nearly as frustrated as Hutchinson. "This province is supported and abetted by others beyond the concept of most people and foreseen by none,"[31] he finally complained to Lord Dartmouth in London.

Among the patriots, a "kind of predatory struggle almost universally took place," as Mercy recalled. Men and youth were drilled as "minute men," so that when "hostilities commenced,"[32] every district could provide soldiers to fight the British. Outside occupied Boston, the rebels stockpiled weapons and gunpowder, virtually under the noses of Gage's spies.

While sorely tempted to punish them, the general held back, realizing its impracticality and reasoning, "Without having recourse to *force*, we must first become masters of the country."[33]

A tense waiting game thus ensued. Restraint was critical, for any untoward act of violence could incite a battle neither side was prepared to fight.

By late May, Sam Adams urged James to "implore every friend in Boston . . . to avoid blood and tumult."[34] They would "have time enough to die. Nothing can ruin us but our violence." Above all, the American colonies must present a united front.

To do so, as John Adams noted on June 17, "a meeting of committees from several colonies on this continent"[35] was called. He and Sam were to represent Massachusetts on September 1 in Philadelphia at an assembly known as the Continental Congress.

Before his departure, John Adams asked the Warrens for their suggestions. "Though you, sire, have condescended to ask . . . to advise at this important crisis," Mercy replied, ". . . I shall not be so presumptuous as to offer anything but my fervent wishes, that the enemies of America may . . . forever tremble at the wisdom . . . of the delegates." If, however, he wished to elicit her opinion, she would happily invite him to "the northwest corner of *Liberty Square*, Plymouth, on any day you shall name previous to the twelfth of August."[36]

But Adams, then riding circuit in Maine, had no time for such a visit. His legal business, as he had groused months earlier to Mercy, was "totally annihilated these twelve months and more by the inauspicious course of public affairs."[37]

In mid-summer 1775, Mercy traveled to West Barnstable to visit her "venerable father," James Otis, Sr. After returning to Plymouth on August 8, she learned about the Quartering Act and wrote to Abigail that it was "designed to perpetuate the thralldom of America."

The only positive aspect was its timing, occurring just before the convention in Philadelphia. "Tell Mr. Adams that my best wishes . . . attend him through his journey . . . as a friend and as patriot," Mercy wrote Abigail. "May he return with satisfaction," along with, "the applauses of his constituents."

To Abigail, who dreaded her separation from John, Mercy confided her own anxieties. "No one has at stake a larger share of domestic felicity than myself," she claimed. Besides worrying about her beloved husband, James "I see no less than five sons who must buckle on the harness. And perhaps fall a sacrifice to the manes of liberty."[38]

Mercy's anxieties knew no bounds, spilling over into her letters to Hannah. Continually, she admitted, her "busy imagination" produced visions of her husband "bowing beneath the mighty conflict, and his weeping sons, buckling on the helmet and grasping the naked steel . . . [perhaps] to sacrifice at the shrine of liberty a life rendered of little value by . . . tyranny."[39]

The most immediate cause of Mercy's anxiety was James's own departure from Plymouth. Having served as chairman of the Plymouth County Convention, her husband was elected to the Massachusetts' Provincial Congress, a defiant body drawing representatives from towns outside Boston, whose decisions were to be relayed to the new Continental Congress. Vowing to "save this country or perish in the attempt,"[40] James thus journeyed to Salem for the Provincial Congress's opening sessions.

Later, when that congress temporarily moved to Cambridge, James planned to visit Boston to rendezvous with Mercy. To do so was admittedly risky for a "treasonous" character like James, but he was worried about his high-strung wife's composure. "May neither drums or any fearful apprehensions disturb your slumber or repose," he tenderly wished Mercy prior to their meeting. [41]

After the couple's reunion, Mercy visited Hannah in Cambridge, but upon her return to Plymouth confessed her anxieties about James, who had become a "marked victim by the enemies of this country, for his unimpeachable integrity and zeal in its cause."[42]

Still she tried to remain optimistic. After a visit from James that autumn in Plymouth, Mercy promised him to "behave with cheerfulness, dignity and patience ... knowing you are gone to attend your duty in the service of your country."

If only, Mercy wistfully added, they could "retire to some remote and quiet corner of the earth, where we could sit down in peace and leave the busy world with all its bustle, confusion, animosity and tumult."[43]

In nearby Braintree, Mercy's friend Abigail Adams felt even more bereft. "Five weeks have passed and not one line have I received. I had rather give a dollar for a letter by the post, though the consequence should be that I eat but one meal a day for these 3 weeks to come,"[44] she chided John in mid-September.

A week earlier, in a letter still undelivered from Philadelphia, John had written, "It is a great affliction to me that I cannot write to you oftener than I do. But there are so many hindrances, that I cannot."[45] His days in Philadelphia, John explained in another letter, were crammed from dawn to dusk with "visits, ceremonies, company business, newspapers."[46]

While September 17 was "one of the happiest days of my life," because Congress finally agreed to "support the Massachusetts or perish with her,"[47] John had tired of the deliberations. Each of his fifty colleagues, he wrote on October 10, had so much "wit, sense, learning"[48] and was accustomed to leading his own province that precious amounts of time were wasted.

After Paul Revere arrived in Philadelphia and announced that Governor Gage had dissolved the Massachusetts Assembly and was building British fortifications in Boston, the Continental Congress sprang into action. On

October 20, having denounced the Coercive Acts, the delegates approved a Declaration of Rights and Grievances and enforced it with the announcement of an intercolonial boycott to take effect on December 1.

When Mercy heard the news, she wrote Hannah an upbeat letter about the "spirit, firmness, and...happy union" that swept over the extensive colonies. "Every step" that the "infatuated Britons have been taking," she gushed, "is but a means of hastening the grandeur and glory of America."

No longer content to "leave the field of politics" to men, Mercy revealed her own ideas about government. "The grandeur, magnificence and wealth of states seldom promoted either the virtue or happiness of individuals," she maintained. "Where there is most simplicity of life and manners, there is most felicity."

Government should intervene as little as possible in the lives of citizens, Mercy maintained. Above all, a just government must never be "established in the thralldom of nations, but on a more equitable...base"[49] that respected the voice of the people.

Several factors had prompted Mercy's sudden disclosure of her ideas. Among them were the years of discourse she had once enjoyed with Jemmy, the fireside discussions she hosted for patriots at One Liberty Square, and, recently, the arrival of a letter from British radical Catharine Macaulay.

After more than a year of silence, the author had replied, blaming her delay on recuperation from a "long course of uninterrupted illness." Flattered to hear from "a woman of your sentiments and who is so nearly connected to the great patriots of the age," Catharine fretted about "the public weal of America."

In response to Mercy's question as to "whether the genius of Liberty has entirely forsaken our devoted isle," Catharine tersely replied that Parliament's recent decisions were "a complete answer." Yet they must not lose hope. Great Britain still had liberal Whigs like herself and her brother John Sawbridge, a member of Parliament "who strenuously and zealously defended the injured rights of your countrymen."[50]

The letter must have thrilled Mercy. By late December, she had thanked her new British correspondent for her "generous concern for the public embarrassments of my country." The political climate was admittedly tense. Still, the patriots hesitated to strike the first blow even while Great Britain was behaving as "an unnatural parent...ready to plunge her dagger into the bosom of her affectionate offspring."[51]

During the last months of 1774, Mercy had poured her angst over the appointment of mandamus councilors to the Massachusetts Assembly into a new satire. Anxious as usual about the quality of her work, she sent James drafts of her "new burlesque," *The Group*.

"I do not think it has sufficient merit for the public eye," Mercy admitted. Perhaps it might even be "best to suppress it."[52] Even before completing the last act, Mercy knew the *The Group* was an explosive work because of her depiction of the new mandamus councilors as money-hungry "sycophants, hungry harpies and unprincipled danglers."[53]

Still more audacious was *The Group*'s secondary theme, a pro-female message that lamented the personal hardships of war forced upon women married to greedy husbands.

Several of Mercy's earlier Tory characters—Hazelrod, Dupe, and Meagre—appeared in *The Group*. Joining them were Crusty Crowbar and Simple, caricatures of two well-known Plymouth Tories, who, in Mercy's play, wavered about pledging their loyalties to the governor as new mandamus councilors.

Initially, Crusty Crowbar admits that he is "almost sick of the parade" of honors "purchased at the price of peace."[54] His companion, Simple, meanwhile, worries over the dedication of the patriots, that "brave" and "injur'd multitude...resolv'd to die, or see their country free."[55] Ultimately, both men succumb to the royal bribes as had other, real-life characters whom Mercy pitilessly lampooned. Among the most recognizable were Brigadier Hateall, representing a notorious Plymouth lawyer named Timothy Ruggles, and a character named Beau Trumps, modeled upon Daniel Leonard, the king's attorney from Bristol County.

In a later scene, which was perhaps Mercy's strongest indictment of the colonial disregard for women and families, Hateall instructed Simple and Crusty Crowbar to ignore the likely consequences of the coming war— a "weeping maid thrown helpless on the world/ Her sire cut off...the sorrowing mother . . . her starving babes / her murder'd lord torn guiltless from her side."

A "woman's tears," after all, Hateall sneered, were only the tiresome "whinings of that trifling sex." In fact, he had married Kate years ago, only "to secure her dower" and "broke her spirits when I'd won her purse."[56]

No less shameless were Beau Trump's arguments for loyalty to the Crown. Years ago, he, too, had been a Whig who "trim'd and pimp'd," and remained only "half resolv'd" about which side to support until that "Arch Traitor," Rapatio, convinced him to defect. Justice, as Mercy predicted in the voice of an unidentified woman in the final scene, would ultimately prevail.

Suddenly it was spring, but, as the sibyl-like figure predicted, a bitter battle and a "stain'd field salute our weeping eyes." While "the tall oak, and quiv-ring willow bends" covered America's dead, the result was that the "British troops shall to Columbia yield" so that "freedom's sons are masters of the field."[57]

The battles of Lexington and Concord were still three months away, but *The Group* predicted a monumental conflict between the patriots and the British on a country green in April.

No less startling was Mercy's implication that women's oppressed marital status paralleled Parliament's suppression of the Americans' "natural rights."

"Perhaps the whole land be involved in blood"

BY LATE 1774, MERCY WAS consumed with anxiety over her new satire. While *The Group* pleaded for rights for married women, she still sought comfort and reassurance from men. "This you will dispose of as you judge proper," Mercy wrote James in Salem, enclosing two more scenes of the play. "But whatever you do with either of them...be careful that the author is not exposed."[1]

Undoubtedly, the British would consider the work treasonous. Moreover, should her identity be revealed, Mercy would be deemed a brash, meddlesome woman outspoken beyond the "narrow limits" of her gender by her fellow colonists.

Such fears, Mercy's feisty friend Abigail assured her, should immediately be dismissed, for Mercy used satire for the common good, to promote "the love of virtue" and "abhorrence of vice" among her peers. To suppress her gift "would be hiding a talent."[2]

For months, Mercy's husband, James, had reiterated that same message. By January 15, he was so enthusiastic about *The Group* that he sent John Adams the first two acts. Explaining that they were written "at my particular desire," James suggested that John provide "corrections and amendments as your good judgment shall suggest."[3] Immediately, John had the first half of the play published in Philadelphia.

On January 23, the first scenes of acts 1 and 2 appeared in the *Boston Gazette,* and on January 26 in the *Massachusetts Spy.* While an incomplete pamphlet edition was circulated in New York, by April 3 Boston's patriotic printers Edes and Gil were advertising the sale of a complete pamphlet edition.

In spite of *The Group*'s warm reception, Mercy was convinced that John's approval of the play was merely related to his enthusiasm for the patriotic cause. Privately, he must have been offended by her critical tone. "While a little personal acrimony might be justifiable in your sex, must not the female character suffer...if she indulges her pen to paint...those whom vice and venality have rendered contemptible?" she anxiously asked him on January 30.

Perhaps she had been overly encouraged by a "certain beloved friend [her husband, James]...to indulge a satirical propensity that ought to be reined in." While *The Group* was intended to be "beneficial to society," she longed to know John's "criticism...approbation, or censure." His reaction, Mercy meekly explained, might "regulate my future conduct."[4]

It would not be until March 15, six weeks after Mercy's letter, that John replied to James. Excusing his delay on an eye infirmity, he praised Mercy as "an incomparable satirist," and asked James to send "most friendly regards to a certain lady—tell her, that god Almighty (I use a bold style) has instructed her with powers for the good of the world, which...he bestows upon few of the human race. That instead of being a fault to use them, it would be criminal to neglect them."[5]

John's subsequent letter to Mercy was even more laudatory. She had no reason to apologize for *The Group* for the "faithful historian delineates characters truly, let the censure fall where it will."

Mercy had executed that task brilliantly. In fact, "of all the genius's which have yet arisen in America, there has been none, superior to one, which now shines, in this happy, this exquisite faculty...I know of none, ancient or modern, which has reached the tender, the pathetic, the keen and severe, and at the same time, the soft, the sweet, the amiable and the pure in great perfection. I am, madam, with great respect, your friend."[6]

Henceforth, John became Mercy's cherished mentor, an inspiring guide and valued judge of her subsequent work.

By the last half of 1774, the colonists were feverishly preparing for a confrontation with the British. On September 2, when Gage's troops seized hidden military supplies near Boston, the rebels vowed retribution, but at the last moment, were restrained by Sam Adams. "Blows may be spared, if possible, and all ruptures with the troops avoided,"[7] echoed John Adams from Philadelphia to his brother-in-law Richard Cranch in Braintree.

In London, the British government had also dismissed hopes of reconciliation. "The dye is now cast," George III ominously declared to Lord North on September 11. "The Colonies must either submit or triumph."[8]

In North America, relations between the Loyalists and patriots grew increasingly tense. "Affairs here are worse than even at the time of the Stamp Act," General Gage wrote London. "I don't mean in Boston but throughout the country . . . If you think ten thousand men enough send twenty; if a million [pounds] is thought enough, give two."[9]

By January 1775, the masts of British warships loomed just beyond Boston's blockaded harbor. Taunted as an "old lady" for his reluctance to crush the rebels, Gage dispatched spies to survey the Massachusetts countryside to locate the rebels' stockpiled munitions.

From Philadelphia, John Adams wrote James about new signs of intercolonial unity, epitomized by Samuel Chase, a leader of Maryland's Provincial Congress. "The Colonies will probably never be so cordially united and their spirits in a high tone than at present,"[10] John opined.

In January, new regiments of British soldiers arrived in Boston. Among them was the Queen's Guards, who settled in Marshfield near Plymouth. "People here are much at a loss . . . [about] the design of this ridiculous movement," Mercy informed Abigail, perceiving it as another British tactic to provoke the colonists into a show of force, or simply "divide and distress this country to a higher degree."[11] Just how much "higher" the country could be divided was debatable. Plymouth County itself was filled with Tories, among them her husband's Marshfield relative Nathaniel Ray Winslow, who brazenly hosted the Queen's Guards in his mansion. Equally shameless was James's cousin Ned Winslow, who entertained those same officers in his Plymouth home.

Before long, the quartering of other British troops along the Massachusetts coast created turmoil near the Adamses' cottage in Braintree. One January night after a local policeman, or member of the "town watch," offered to escort a drunken British officer to his barracks, the officer's alarmed servant summoned soldiers from a nearby tavern.

There, as a disconsolate Abigail explained to Mercy, the man "raised nine officers who were pretty well warmed with liquor and...without inquiring into the...cause, fell upon the watch." While General Gage arrested the offending officer for a court martial, Abigail predicted "we are to be in continual hazard and jeopardy of our lives from a set of dissolute... officers...who...believe that their errand here is to quell a lawless set of rebels."[12]

"We need not yet be discouraged though embarrassed and perplexed," Mercy replied. Doubtless, "the righteous cause in which the undaunted patriots of American have struggled for many years will finally succeed." While some colonists may "tremble at a speech from the throne, and others ...appalled by...a venal Parliament,"[13] a meeting of delegates to the Second Continental Congress the following May might still resolve the conflict. From her knowledge of the classics, Mercy pictured those delegates as "modern Amphictyons," similar to ancient Greek statesman who served on the republic's governing council.

The reality of the new democratic spirit though, as James unhappily reminded Mercy that March while attending the Second Provincial Congress, was far less noble. All too often that assembly was mired in pointless debates and petty quarrels.

Her spirits had been "tolerably well," Mercy replied, until she read James's account about the delegates wasting time by fomenting "divisions," which made them "easy prey to the common enemy."

Coincidentally, that same morning she awoke "trembling under the agitations of frightful dream" about an outbreak of violence. Her loved ones, Mercy believed, would be "among the first who sink beneath the torment."

While she did not doubt the "success of so righteous cause," she sensed that "some of the worthiest...in the present generation will fall in the conflict and perhaps the whole land be involved in blood."

If only, Mercy added, she could be in the "presence of my invaluable friend whose company always makes everything wear a cheerful hue."[14]

Suddenly, when on March 30 the Provincial Congress relocated to Concord and planned an adjournment for the following weekend, Mercy's longing for a reunion with James nearly came true. From Concord, he had written that he had "engaged a chamber here for my beloved." However, when a British ship arrived in Marblehead declaring Massachusetts in a state of rebellion, the adjournment—and the Warrens' reunion—was canceled.

Concord, James reported, "is full of cannon, ammunition, stores [that] ... the [British] army long for ... and want nothing but strength" to attack. The local patriots are "ready and determine to defend this country inch by inch."

How, James tenderly inquired, was Mercy and "how my little boys? I long to see you. I long to sit with you under our vines ... and have none to make us afraid ... I intend to fly home ... as soon as prudence, duty, and honor will permit."

A day later, however, James urged Mercy to pack the family trunks. "We perhaps may be forced to move,"[15] he warned. Plymouth, already menaced by the Queen's Guard in nearby Marshfield and located on a bay open to British invasion, was at risk. Even so, James reminded Mercy, "God has given you great abilities; you have improved them in great acquirements. For all these I ... love you in a degree that I can't express. They are all now to be called into action for the good of mankind" as well as for her friends' "virtue and patriotism."

Above all, he later advised, "Don't let the fluttering of your heart interrupt your health or disturb your repose."[16]

Inevitably, that repose would be disturbed. By mid-April, General Gage, determined to seize the stockpiled munitions at Concord, prepared for battle. At midnight on April 15, Paul Revere and other patriots, gazing over Boston harbor, spotted a fleet of small boats hovering under the stern of British warships. By the evening of April 18, after learning that the British intended to capture the "treasonous" Sam Adams and John Hancock, then in Lexington on their way to the Second Continental Congress, Revere galloped from Boston to warn them, stopping along the way to warn residents of Gage's imminent attack.

The Provincial Congress in Concord had just adjourned, its delegates rushing home to alert militias and nearby colonies. James, too, dashed off to Plymouth, where Mercy joined him on his ride to warn Rhode Island's Sons of Liberty.

Along the way, the couple found a house in Taunton where Mercy and her sons could hide in case of an attack upon Plymouth; by Wednesday, April 19, they had arrived in Providence.

Within hours, breathless messengers appeared, describing the first blood spilled at Lexington Green. Eight patriots and ten British soldiers had died before Gage's troops had marched to Concord. In spite of their rustic, homespun clothes, clumsy muskets, and ragged discipline, the patriots killed two hundred seventy-three British compared to their ninety-five casualties.

After the long, tense months of hesitation, news of the first shots signaling American independence shocked the Western world.

"A scene like this had never before been exhibited on her peaceful plains; and the manner in which it was executed, will leave an indelible stain on a nation, long famed for their courage, humanity and honor," Mercy triumphantly recalled in her *History*. "[S]everal regiments of the best troops in the royal army, were seen... flying before the raw, inexperienced peasantry, who... ran hastily together in defense of their lives and liberties."

While many British soldiers retreated to Boston, others, Mercy noted, "both from wound and fatigue," lagged behind. Some of the colonists "touched with humanity... opened their doors, received the distressed Britons, dressed their wounds, and contributed every relief."[17]

Other eyewitnesses confirmed that many of the redcoats refused to concede. "Fallen subjects... in a bloody battle against each other... a most terrible sight it was," Boston merchant Samuel Salisbury wrote his brother Stephen in Worcester the day after the battle. Curiously, the British seemed "very backward in owning how many men they lost."[18]

During their humiliating retreat, some of the redcoats avenged themselves upon local residents. "I saw yesterday a gentleman who conversed with the brother of a woman cut in pieces in her bed with her new born infant by her side," Mercy wrote Sarah Bowen, wife of a Rhode Island patriot. "Are these the deeds of rationals? Have we... so far debased the powers of the human soul as to blot out the sense of moral obligation?"[19]

Eight days after the battle, twenty-year-old Breck Parkman, who patrolled Charlestown with two American captains, noted in his diary "the havoc the regulars [the British]" made in the colonists' homes, most of which were abandoned when their terrified owners fled to the countryside.[20]

Other eyewitnesses such as Mercy's friend Hannah Winthrop reported that as the British tramped the Great Road from Cambridge to Lexington (today's Massachusetts Avenue), she and her sixty-one-year-old professor husband, John, fled me to a "safe" house in the nearby village of Fresh Pond. That building was "filled with women whose husbands were gone forth to meet the assailants, 70 or 80 of these with numbers of infant children, crying and agonizing for the fate of their husbands."

For a time, Hannah explained, they were "in sight of the battle, the glistening instruments of death proclaiming by an incessant fire, that much blood must be shed, that many widowed & orphaned ones be left." The next morning, Hannah and John were hustled into a cart with three others and driven fifteen miles north to the inland town of Andover.

The roads, Hannah recalled, were "filled with frightened women and children, some in carts with their tallest furniture, others on foot fleeing into the woods." Especially horrifying was "passing through the bloody field at Menotomy [now Arlington],which was strewed with...mangled...bodies," and an "affectionate father with a cart looking for his murdered son and picking up his neighbors...fallen in battle."

While she and John were safe in rural Andover, Hannah admitted it would "give me great pleasure to pay you a visit in your hospitable abode of peace & elegance, but the length of the journey & the uncertainty of the times forbid it."[21]

What Hannah idealized as Mercy's "abode of peace & elegance" was no longer safe. After escorting Rhode Island's General Nathaniel Greene and his soldiers to Massachusetts, the Warrens rushed back to Plymouth. Then James galloped off to Watertown, the new headquarters for the Massachusetts Committee of Safety and the Provincial Congress.

"I am still in a state of suspense," Mercy wrote Sarah Bowen. "[S]till uncertain whether I shall continue in my own pleasant habitation or whether in a few days I shall not be obliged to seek a retreat in the wilderness."[22]

No sooner did James arrive in Watertown than he was elected president of the Provincial Congress. Recalling the fractiousness of recent sessions, he declined, suggesting instead the younger, outspoken patriot Dr. Joseph Warren, who, in spite of his similar name, was not kin.

Having received James's note of May 3 about his safe arrival in Watertown, Mercy expressed pride that he was "instrumental . . . to promote the peace, the glory and the happiness of your country."

Should James have to travel to Connecticut on behalf of Congressional duties, she had not "the least objection for few men are better qualified for such an important embassy." If so, Mercy would ride to Providence herself to accompany him.

"Do you not think as Congress has been weakened by calling . . . several of its active members to other departments?" she suggested. Perhaps it might be time to elect "a speedy appointment of fresh hands."

As she wrote, Mercy realized she sounded opinionated and unfeminine. She had not intended to "obtrude my opinion or advice . . . [being] sensible my judgment is too weak."[23]

During that harrowing spring, Abigail Adams, whose husband, John, was riding to Philadelphia, increasingly looked to Mercy for solace and companionship. "I long most earnestly for the society of my much valued Mrs. Warren . . . I must entreat you to write to me every opportunity," she penned on May 2.

While the barges from nearby British warships frightened local residents, John's plucky young wife remained "determined to stay as long as it will be safe for any person to tarry upon the sea coast."[24]

Meanwhile, a few miles north of Braintree on a hilltop in Milton, a committee of patriots had seized Hutchinson's country home. In contrast to the riot ten years earlier at the former governor's Boston mansion, those men carefully supervised removal of Hutchinson's fine furniture, among them, horse-hair settees, red Moroccan leather chairs, and bronze busts of Shakespeare and Milton, and stored them for a future auction.

Only one item was left—a trunk containing Hutchinson's correspondence from 1771. That collection, the *Essex Gazette* announced, would "astonish everyone, who has not before been thoroughly sensible of the evil designs of that man against the liberties of this country."[25] Among them was a letter revealing that in spite of Hutchinson's insistence that he had convened the General Court in Cambridge by order of George III, his instructions had been much less specific.

Months later, from London, Hutchinson denied the allegation: He never said royal orders demanded relocation of the assembly outside Boston—only that he had received "such instruction as made it necessary."[26]

By then, such fine distinctions seemed irrelevant, for the banished Hutchinson was three thousand miles away. Far more distressing was the virtual imprisonment of Bostonians in their city.

For months, Bostonians had barely managed to survive the blockade. While food supplies continued to trickle in from sympathetic towns, the citizens subsisted largely on salt meat, cod, and beans. "Famine," as Mercy reported in her *History,* essentially "stared them in the face."

Finally, by late spring, the enraged residents complained to General Gage, who, struck a shrewd deal: In exchange for surrender of their arms, he would allow them to leave. Grudgingly, the citizens conceded, but as Mercy bitterly recounted, the "insulted people of Boston were not permitted to depart, until after several months."[27]

The situation, as Abigail lamented to Mercy that May, made her "distressed for our poor Boston friends. What course they can take, I know not. I believe they are kept in for security to the troops... O Britain... how is thy glory vanished."[28]

More encouraging was the news John reported about intercolonial reaction to Lexington and Concord. "This colony [Connecticut] is raising 6000 men. Rhode Island 1500. N. York has shut up their port, seized the custom house, arms, ammunition... called a Provincial Congress, and entered into an association to stand by whatever shall be ordered by the Continental and their Provincial Congress," he wrote Abigail.[29]

In May, Mercy became ill, ironically victimized, at least in part, by the same emotional anxieties to which she once attributed Abigail's illness after the Boston Tea Party. She was constitutionally prone to migraine headaches, and they predictably resurface during the most stressful moments of her life.

By mid-1775, with James away in Watertown, she, like other Revolutionary-era women, increasingly depended upon her female friends for solace. "Though I am very unwell scarce able to set up long enough to write, yet I must let my dear friend Mrs. Adams know it gave me great pleasure to have but a line or two from her after her very long silence," Mercy wrote from her sickbed in Plymouth on May 15. If Abigail and her sister could arrange to "run to Plymouth...but for one day,"[30] Mercy's son Winslow would serve as their escort.

After May 25, when the three "bow wows"—the British generals William Howe, John Burgoyne, and Henry Clinton—arrived in Boston with reinforcements, the patriots girded themselves for a second conflict. By mid-June, Mercy, newly recovered from her illness and edgy about James in Watertown, decided to visit her family in West Barnstable.

Among those who greeted her at the Otis homestead was Mercy's unmarried sister, Hannah, her father, her youngest brother, Samuel Allyne, and his family, recent refugees from Boston. Though her brother Joseph was in Watertown serving with James at the Provincial Congress, several of his children appeared.

On Wednesday, June 14, Mercy and her sons returned to Plymouth. A day later, she wrote her "Dearest Friend" James about the trip. Accompanying her and the boys were her sister Hannah and Joseph's twenty-one-year-old daughter, Rebecca Otis. Stopping at the Warrens' summer home in Clifford, they enjoyed Mercy's prize strawberries, "the finest I have seen," then stayed overnight before returning home to West Barnstable.

Neither their cheerful company, "the bounties of providence, nor the social intercourse of friends," Mercy admitted to James, could dispel her sense of foreboding.

Nothing, in fact, seemed to lighten her mood, "so long as my country is threatened with desolation and bloodshed, and my beloved husband not only...absent...but stationed...in a place where I am greatly apprehensive of [his] personal danger."

Rumors circulating in West Barnstable and Plymouth merely exacerbated those fears. "We hear the army is reinforced and is exceedingly formidable," Mercy wrote. "[T]he light horse are to scour the country within a week and...we are on the eve of the most bloody battle ever fought in America."[31]

That same day, warned by the patriotic Massachusetts Committee of Safety that Gage was preparing to seize both peninsulas flanking Boston— Dorchester Heights and Charlestown—General Artemus Ward decided upon a preemptive strike. By Friday night, June 16, a thousand men from Massachusetts and Connecticut, commanded by William Prescott, climbed Charlestown's Breed's Hill, and built tall fortifications.

Afterward, "Old Put," General Israel Putnam, ordered soldiers to construct similar bulwarks at the base of Bunker Hill encircled with a fence. In between the two hills nestled the peninsula of Charleston, a little jewel box of a community flanked by the Mystic and Charles rivers, admired for its townhouses and gardens.

At dawn on June 17, General Gage gazed with astonishment upon the rebel fortifications at Breed's Hill. Stunned, he ordered ships to fire and then commanded General Howe to prepare grenadiers and infantrymen to attack Charlestown.

Thus began the historic struggle known as the Battle of Bunker Hill.

Though well-informed and committed to the patriotic cause, Mercy would not yet realize that her anxious letter to James of June 16 on the "eve of the most bloody battle ever fought in America," would lead to her role as the first female reporter of the American Revolution.

PART II

Conscience of the Revolution

Reporter of Revolutionary Events

CONTRARY TO HIS USUAL COMPOSURE, James Warren was shaken by the Battle of Bunker Hill. "The extraordinary nature of the events...in the last 48 hours has interrupted that steady...intercourse which...public affairs allows me,"[1] he wrote Mercy from Watertown on June 18, after the fighting stopped.

Thirty hours earlier, General Gage's deputy William Howe led nearly two thousand men up Breed's Hill. Strangely enough, the rebels had held their fire, but, on a signal from General William Prescott, they discharged their muskets, felling the front line of redcoats like that of sheep lying "as thick in the fold."[2]

Stunned, the British retreated, reorganized, and stormed up the hill again. By then, the rebels' ammunition was nearly spent, allegedly inspiring the command "Don't shoot until you see the whites of their eyes." However, once the British advanced within thirty feet, Prescott recalled that "we gave them such a hot fire that they were obliged to retire nearly one hundred and fifty yards."[3]

The American fire was "incessant...a continued sheet of fire for near thirty minutes" killing line after line of the advancing soldiers and forcing a humiliating retreat the likes of which, as General Howe later admitted, he "never felt before."[4] After discarding their food and heavy winter gear, the British again charged up Breed's Hill, this time cutting through the patriots' lines and slaying thirty with their bayonets.

What ensued was one of the bloodiest conflicts of the Revolution, forcing the ammunition-poor Americans to hurl rocks and club the British with their muskets until, finally, Prescott ordered a retreat.

Portrait of James Warren by John Singleton Copley.
Photograph © 2008 Museum of Fine Arts, Boston.

The Americans, nevertheless, had demonstrated a "stout resistance,"[5] James explained to Mercy. But tragically, the British had torched Charlestown.

Even experienced British officers liked General John Burgoyne, who watched the battle from Boston, were overcome. It was, he later wrote, "one of the greatest scenes of war that can be conceived... to the left the enemy pouring in fresh troops by thousands. Over the land... in the arm of the sea our ships and floating batteries, cannonading them... a large and noble town in one great blaze—the church-steeples... great pyramids of fire above the rest... whole streets falling together."

It was "a complication of horror and importance beyond any"[6] Burgoyne recalled, signaling the imminent loss of Britain's American empire.

Early reports to headquarters in Watertown confirmed that the Americans had killed at least a hundred British—a count that later swelled tenfold. Among the surviving patriotic warriors were the Winthrops' son James, and Mercy's brother Jemmy. Most tragic was the fate of the Provincial Congress's beloved president, Dr. Joseph Warren, who, while tending the injured and urging the soldiers to stand their ground in the thick of battle, was fatally wounded.

Soon after fighting commenced on June 17, messengers galloped to Philadelphia asking the Continental Congress for reinforcements, munitions, and gunpowder. They "have done and are doing every thing we can wish," as James wrote Mercy. Locked in an emergency executive committee of the Provincial Congress at the Edmund Fowle House in Watertown where the delegates had met since April 22, James could "only steal" a few minutes to write. The town was in chaos, "women and children flying into the country, armed men going to the field, and wounded men returning from there."

Even in the midst of that turmoil, Mercy remained foremost in his thoughts. Above all, he hoped his "[d]ear wife" would cease fretting, "least her apprehensions... hurt her health... and if you are safe and the boys I shall be happy, fall what will... I need not say that I long to see you, perhaps never more in my life... I hope your strawberries are well taken care of and that you have fine feasting on them."[7]

Years later, Mercy's *History* included an account of the Battle of Bunker Hill and her subsequent tour of "some four hundred dwelling-houses in the center of Charlestown . . . reduced to ashes." What rankled her was that just a month earlier, its residents, moved by "humanity . . . [had opened] their doors for the relief . . . of the routed corps [of British] on the nineteenth of April."

Omitted from Mercy's *History* was her personal acquaintance with Charlestown's new homeless—among them, Hannah Winthrop's sister and brother in-law, who had provided shelter, medicine, and food to the retreating British.

Technically, the Americans lost the Battle of Bunker Hill. The British, nevertheless, as Mercy recalled in her *History,* had been "weakened by the severe engagement near Bunker Hill, sickly in the camp, and disheartened by unexpected bravery" of the patriots. Horrified, General Gage consequently ordered his men "shut up in Boston [for] the remainder of summer."[8]

Inevitably, the British barrier ringing Boston created new hardships for residents. While initially forbidden to leave the city, new food shortages and sweltering summer temperatures convinced Gage to grant some citizens passes. Meanwhile, so many soldiers deserted that the general imposed severe restrictions upon citizen behavior. Among them, Abigail wryly reported to her husband, John, was a law prohibiting Bostonians from wiping their faces with white handkerchiefs, for that was considered a "signal of mutiny."[9]

Even after the arrival of fishing boats, civilians could not buy the catch until the British were supplied. Outbreaks of disease became common, reflected by the words "very sickly" in the letters of Boston's trapped residents. Funerals, accompanied by the traditional ringing of church bells, became so commonplace that an unnerved Gage finally ordered the bells silenced. "I was a [pall]bearer for our Uncle Coffin. No bells tolled. It seemed strange," one resident recalled. [10]

Exacerbating those hardships was the forced quartering of soldiers in private homes. Epitomizing their disdain was General Burgoyne's treatment of the home of Abigail Adams's relative Samuel Quincy, whose cook had "raw meat cut and hacked upon [their] . . . mahogany tables . . . superb damask curtain and cushions exposed to the rain."[11] The British also desecrated other buildings sacred to the patriots—among them the Old South Meeting House, where they removed pews, transformed one of them into a pigsty, and converted the building into a military riding ring.

In Philadelphia, after the first reports about the Battle of Bunker Hill, communications between Massachusetts patriots and the Second Continental Congress faltered.

"I am extremely obliged to you for your favor of the 20th of June. The last fall I had a great many friends who kept me continually well informed ...but this time I have [none] except Colonel Warren of Plymouth... Colonel Palmer of Braintree, and my wife,"[12] John Adams wrote James on June 27.

That same day, James, who became president, or speaker, of the Provincial Congress after Dr. Warren's death, advised John that the army lacked "but one article [gunpowder] to enable us to act offensively." Since Bunker Hill, the patriots had "taken every precaution... for their defense." At Roxbury, he added, "they had fortified themselves in a manner almost as impregnable as Gage has done in Boston."

An eerie silence still surrounded the city. "We have no intercourse with Boston, get no intelligence... but by those who steal out... [with] accounts of the amazing slaughter made in the last action. Their men die of the slightest wounds."[13]

By early July, nearly ten weeks had passed since Mercy had seen James, and then only briefly during their frantic ride to Rhode Island. Longing to visit, Mercy consequently rode to Watertown, escorted by her sixteen-year son, Winslow.

Mercy may have shared James's second-floor bedroom in the Edmund Fowle House, across the hall from the chamber where the Executive Committee met, or she may have rented a room at Dorothy Coolidge's nearby inn, but wherever she stayed she immediately realized that her husband was transformed.

No longer was James the cool, self-assured gentleman-farmer of earlier years; he had evolved into a harried leader, constantly monitoring British movements, searching out arms and supplies for the army, and urging nearby towns to send more recruits. Longing to relieve him, Mercy served as his private secretary.

-<+>-

"In compliance with Mr. Warren's request...his application to public affairs leaves him little time to attend to the demands of private friendship ...could you look into a certain assembly you would not wonder that his time is wholly engrossed," she thus informed John Adams on July 7. There was no time, she added, to depict the "ten fold difficulties that surround us." Among them were "the plagues of famine, pestilence and tyranny" and "the artillery of war continually thundering in our ears."

Even the surrounding coastline was "degraded" by the British. Their sailors, having already plundered Boston Harbor to feed "the swarms of veteran slaves [soldiers] shut up in the town," prohibited even a "poor fisherman to cast his hook in the ocean"[14] to feed his family without a bribe.

By July 23, Adams had received Mercy's first report and was so gratified with its details that he begged James for "a continuance of her favors"[15] as a reporter.

Just before Mercy left Watertown, General George Washington arrived at the army camp in Cambridge. There James presented a "congratulatory address, expressive of their [the army's] esteem" Proudly, as Mercy reminded readers in her *History*, the general brought "letters of importance" from the Massachusetts delegates of Congress recommending her husband as a "judicious, confidential friend."[16]

From his first meeting with the tall, auburn-haired, aristocratic-looking Virginian, James was impressed. "I am much pleased with General Washington. He fully answers the character given of him,"[17] he wrote to John Adams.

Mercy probably met Washington upon that occasion as well, as suggested by Hannah Winthrop's comment about her friend's "charming"[18] portrait of the Virginian. Washington was a man of "family and fortune... a polite, but not a learned education," Mercy subsequently reminisced in her *History*, a man with "a coolness of temper, and a degree of moderation and judgment, that qualified him for the elevated station."[19]

The following December, when "Patsy"—Washington's pet name for his elegant, soft-spoken wife, Martha—rolled into Cambridge in a handsome coach, accompanied by relatives and liveried servants, Mercy offered to host her in Plymouth. Declining, Martha wrote that "[t]he General begs ...his best regards...presented to Mrs. Warren, accompanied with his sincere thanks for her . . . wishes for his honor and success; and joins in wishing Mrs. Warren, the Speaker [James], and their family, every happiness . . . derived from a speedy and honorable peace."[20]

By then, Mercy, too, had evolved from the decorous wife of an affluent patriot into a reporter for those removed from the theater of war. "It is the general opinion among us," as she wrote her friend Ellen Lothrop, "that unless [the British] administration send a much larger reinforcement . . . General Gage will not have it in his power to spread devastation."

While British reinforcements were expected, the next battles would be "only the natural struggles . . . when the genius of liberty arises to assert her rights in opposition to the ghosts of tyranny."[21]

By July 27, that "genius of liberty," represented in Philadelphia by the Constitutional Convention, had elected Mercy's husband, James, the paymaster general of the Continental Army. For weeks beforehand, John and Samuel Adams had urged James to that post—an office of "vast importance," John explained, best held by a "gentleman, whose family, fortune, education, abilities and integrity, are equal to its dignity." Three days after the election, John wrote, "the choice was unanimous! But whether we did you a kindness or a disservice I know not. And whether you can attend it . . . I know not."[22]

Having accepted the position, which included recruiting men, arranging for their salaries, and providing arms, James explained that titles meant far less to him than the success of the Revolution. "I am content to move in a small sphere," he insisted to John. "I expect no distinction but that of an honest man who has exerted every nerve." Pointedly, perhaps already sensing Adams's fondness for titles and prominence, James added, "You and I must be content without a slice from the great pudding now on the table."[23]

Soon afterward, Mercy informed the Winthrops about James's new appointment. After conveying her congratulations, Hannah added, "I catch a spark of that heavenly flame which invigorates your breast, knowing that your . . . acquaintance with those in the cabinet must enable you to form a better judgment than those who have not those advantages."[24]

Mercy, as her friend intimated, was privy to information about the early Revolution that few men and no women, including Abigail Adams, knew.

That patriotic spark, combined with her loneliness for James, prompted Mercy's repeated visits to Watertown. During her stays, she wrote John about the harrowing conditions in Boston. By August, nearly two-thirds of the city's inhabitants had fled. Smallpox and other diseases had become rampant.

On August 7, Mercy returned to Plymouth. Two days later, James apologized for failing to write after her departure. "I can assure you it has not proceeded from any abatement of affection...that is as great as ever any man had for a beloved wife and...one of the most predominant passions in my soul."

The Provincial Congress, meanwhile, had voted for a summer recess. While James was obliged to wait in Watertown for the "return of the General's express from Philadelphia," he planned to return to Plymouth as quickly as possible.

The next day James attached a postscript, thanking Mercy for her letter but chiding her for failing to write about her health. "No mention whether you are well, which is the first thing with me,"[25] he tenderly added.

During that tumultuous summer and fall of 1775, Mercy was torn between domestic and political obligations. In Plymouth, four of her sons still living at home—sixteen-year-old Winslow, thirteen-year-old Charles, eleven-year-old Henry, and nine-year-old George—resented her trips to Watertown. No less compelling were James's longings for Mercy's company. As a compromise, she often rode the rough thirty-eight-mile roads between Plymouth and Watertown alone. Her mode was probably horseback or chaise coach, a tiny coach with room for one trunk.

On August 16, Mercy headed back to Watertown, stopping, as usual, in Braintree to visit Abigail. This time the long, dusty journey in steaming summer temperatures took its toll. By the time Mercy reached the Adamses' cottage, she was ill but determined to complete the trip to Watertown. The nature of her ailment is unknown: Possibly, it was one of her "nervous headaches," or one of the more serious illnesses then sweeping the region. Whatever the cause, Mercy was laid up for several weeks, too ill to return to Plymouth.

On August 26, she wrote to Abigail that she was "in better health than

when she left" and hoped to "look homewards some time next week."
James would perhaps accompany her to Plymouth although that, as usual,
was uncertain. "Providence," after all, had "its fixed decrees to which mor-
tals must submit."

The most recent examples of such a decree were secret plans for a new
attack upon the British. In fact, Mercy hinted, if Abigail's husband, John,
then on an adjournment from the Continental Congress, could remain a few
days longer he would "hear the music of war . . . [and] have some important
intelligence to carry to Philadelphia."[26]

A day later, as Mercy had predicted, the patriots seized Ploughed Hill on
the Mystic River and moved their fortifications closer to Charlestown Neck
and Bunker Hill.

As the wife of the president of the Provincial Congress and paymaster
general of the Continental Army, Mercy felt obliged to share her perspective with her transatlantic correspondent, Catharine Macaulay.

"You have doubtless been apprized of the consequences of the hostile
movements of the 19 of April, and the spirit of freedom breathed from the
inhabitants of the surrounding villages," Mercy wrote the British author.

Congress, reluctant to "draw forth the sword against their unnatural parent," had thus petitioned George III for a reconciliation. Should, however,
the colonies be denied their "birthright of nature and the fair possession of
freedom" they vowed to create a new, purer nation than the "tottering and
corrupt"[27] one of Great Britain.

With similar spirit Mercy wrote John Adams on September 4 about the
arrival of British ships from Halifax carrying a "few potatoes and a little
wood" for Boston's starving soldiers. With them came rumors that the
Canadians feared a patriot attack. "What must be their apprehensions from
the . . . heroes who are rising up from every corner of the United Colonies
to oppose the wicked system of politics," Mercy mused.

Then, fearing she had deviated from straight reportage, Mercy added,
"I ask pardon for touching on war, politicks, or anything relative thereto, as
I think you gave me a hint in yours not to approach . . . anything so far be-
yond the line of my sex."[28]

In contrast to her deference to John was Mercy's letter to James that
same month. Hearing rumors that her husband was planning to march with

the Continental Army south of Massachusetts, Mercy inquired, "What do you mean by the part you must bear in the late military call? . . . I hope nothing is like to carry you further from me."

Illness, after all, was already rampant in the army—smallpox, "camp fever" or typhus, and the "bloodly flux," dysentery—all of them potentially fatal. In Braintree, Abigail and her children were then suffering from dysentery. That James might fall ill as well, especially while marching with the army, was a horrifying thought.

Above all, Mercy never forgot the tragedy of her brother Jemmy's life— "lost," she believed, because of his obsession with the patriotic cause. Must she also sacrifice a husband to the Revolution? His life, Mercy lectured the nearly forty-nine-year-old James, "is of great value, both to the public and to the family, as well as to one who would be miserable without you." She would rather see James join the Continental Congress, a role he had already declined, than engage in active military duty.

After voicing her fears, Mercy conceded "I know not what is best. I desire, therefore, to leave you to the care of Providence, and to trust in the divine protection to guard and guide your steps whether so ever you go."[29]

At that very moment, in fact, as James later explained to John Adams (but may never have admitted to Mercy), he was "much indisposed" with an illness but had little time to rest. The army was mired in difficulties: not only from the unruly and mutinous behavior of the "riflemen" from Pennsylvania, Maryland, and Virginia, but from a shortage of funds and gunpowder.

"Does not powder arrive?" James anxiously inquired. "I wish we may be able to give them [the British] at last one blast more . . . Money, if possible, grows scarcer than powder."[30]

In late September, Mercy's sons celebrated her overdue homecoming. The morning of her arrival, young Charles and Henry had lingered impatiently on the Warrens' front steps. "When I turned the corner . . . one of them had just finished an exclamation to the other. 'Oh, what would I give if Mamah was now in sight' . . . One leaped into the street to meet me, the other ran into the house in an ecstasy of joy," Mercy recalled.

No sooner had she opened the front door than she was greeted by "all the lovely flock." Only sixteen-year-old Winslow held back, "half affronted that I had delayed coming home so long," but finally turned "his smiling cheek to receive a kiss."

In contrast, nine-year-old George "was openly delighted," his usually serious features "not only danced in smiles, but broke into a real laugh." Then, in a burst of excitement, the boys poured "all the choice gleamings of the garden . . . into their Mamma's lap."

That day they all behaved. "Not a complaint was uttered—not a tale," Mercy recalled. By the next morning, each son "had his little grievances to repeat, as important to them as the laying of an unconstitutional tax to the patriot—or to the piratical seizure of a ship and cargo."

Having learned that her father, Colonel Otis, was "very unwell," Mercy prepared to visit him in West Barnstable, but not before tending to "every article of business" for James. "You must be a little more explicit," she added, for during their two-decade-old marriage, James had supervised the "magnific or the minutia of life."[31]

Tending to her ailing father and needy sons, worried about her overworked husband, and obliged to send reports to John Adams in Philadelphia, Mercy scurried between her family and the Revolution, an eighteenth-century version of today's "sandwich generation" of working women.

Her first concern, nevertheless, was James. Distressed by "the advantages gained by our enemies," she clung to her husband, reminding him that her "heart is more affected with what gives pain or endangers you than with everything else."[32]

After a brief sojourn with his family in Plymouth, James returned to Watertown, where on October 21, Mercy joined him once again.

In addition to the master bedroom reserved for the Speaker, the Edmund Fowle House had bedrooms available to officials, their wives, and visitors. The first floor held an office, a front parlor, and a dining room, attended by such dignitaries as George Washington, Charles Lee, and Benjamin Franklin. By August 1775, the building was so crowded that Mercy complained to Abigail, "I long for my own retirement and . . . the opportunity to seeing and entertaining my friend [James] at my own habitation."[33]

In spite of such inconveniences, Mercy realized she was better off than many of her friends. Hannah and John Winthrop were still living in rural Andover. Hannah's homeless sister and husband were "poorly accommodated"[34] in Stoneham. Sam Adams's wife, Betsy, and their children had fled from Boston to a rural cottage near Newton.

From Braintree came a distressed letter from the newly recovered Abigail about her mother's death from dysentery. "I cannot work. I cannot read. I cannot talk. O! let me write to my friend and beg her sympathetic breast to pour forth by her pen some healing balm to ease...the wounded breast," Abigail penned.

Convinced that her mother caught the disease from nursing her, Abigail wondered, "[H]ow shall I sustain the stroke?" Exacerbating her sorrow was John's absence, "that friend...whose tenderness and sympathy would alleviate my affliction."[35]

Another example of the bond between the two families was John's letter to James questioning the odd message he had received from "the excellent Marcia," Mercy's favorite nickname. Somehow, she had "misinterpreted some passage in my letter, since I never thought either politics or war, or any other science beyond the line of her sex."

Generally speaking John believed that women should be spared the "arduous cares of war and state." Yet, "I should certainly think that Marcia and Portia [Abigail], ought to be exceptions, because I have ever ascribed to those ladies, a share and no small one neither, in the conduct of our American affairs."[36]

By the last months of 1775, those "affairs" had boiled over into new instances of British treachery. Among them was the discovery that Dr. Benjamin Church, surgeon general of the Continental Army, was a spy. Nearly simultaneously came a British attack upon Bristol, Rhode Island, and the burning of Falmouth, Maine.

A few days after Mercy's return to Watertown—a trip, as Mercy wrote John Adams, that her husband requested because he "thought proper to bring back your correspondent,"[37]—she wrote about local news. Among these was a report on Abigail's improved health, her mother's death, and Dr. Church.

Even after presiding over a dinner for generals Washington, Gates, and

Lee and meeting Benjamin Franklin, the thrill of living at the political epi-center had exhausted Mercy. Echoing her earlier complaint to Abigail, she wrote John that the Edmund Fowle House was a "crowded, inconvenient place where the muses cannot dwell, or the graces of elegance reside." In spite of the surrounding din, Mercy promised to continue serving as John's reporter out of her "feelings of real friendship."[38]

Privately though, by the waning months of 1775, Mercy longed to write something original—a play, or perhaps even a history that would record the turbulent events around her.

A Still Calm Within, Violent Concussions Without

"TRUTH IS MOST LIKELY TO BE EXHIBITED by the general sense of contemporaries,"[1] Mercy maintained in her *History.* By the last half of 1775, truth to Mercy's contemporaries meant loss, loneliness, and hardship.

One of those unfortunates was her friend Hannah Winthrop, who sent an anguished account of the grave condition of her husband, John, that summer from one of the "reigning sicknesses"—typhoid, tetanus, or dysentery—sweeping through Massachusetts. "I have passed through a most painful scene in the distress of my dear partner," Hannah later explained. Finally, thanks to assistance from Mercy's husband, James, the Winthrops left Andover for Watertown, where John received "the best human help, both physicians and medicines."

Even after his recovery, Hannah remained pessimistic about the future of the colonies. If only she had Mercy's spirit. "I often wish for that equanimity of soul—of my friend, Mrs. Warren who can survey present and future in a brighter mirror... supported by... hope."[2]

From Braintree, too, arrived an achingly lonely letter from Abigail, who struggled to maintain the family farm and her children in John's absence. "I wish... you would be kind enough to write me often whilst you tarry at Watertown, and let your letters be of the journal kind; by that... I could participate in your amusements... pleasures... and sentiments."[3]

Boston, meanwhile, remained shrouded in silence. Nor had the Continental Congress in Philadelphia determined a decisive course of action. By autumn, the static situation so worried Mercy and James that they complained to John Adams.

"I think your Congress can be no longer in any doubts...about taking...
effectual strokes. We shall certainly expect it," James wrote on November 14 from Watertown. Mercy was sitting nearby, he explained, and wanted
him to relay a "paragraph of her own."

John "should no longer piddle at the threshold," Mercy suggested. "It is
time to leap into the theatre to unlock the bars, and open every gate that im-
pedes the rise and growth of the American republic."[4]

In Braintree, John's wife, Abigail, meanwhile, waiting for more news
from Mercy in Watertown, heard nothing. Only admiration for her author
friend's "historic page," as she described Mercy's newly proposed account
of the Revolution, has "kept me from complaining of my friend's laconic
epistles."[5]

To research that "historic page," Mercy, in turn, soon asked Abigail for
newspaper articles, handbills, and any other accounts she had leading up to
the outbreak of hostilities with Great Britain. By early December, she was
even begging Abigail for "part of certain private journals" that might reveal "more about certain public characters and . . . transactions."[6]

Nor was Abigail her only trusted source. From James, Mercy asked for
the "best intelligence from the army—from Philadelphia and from every
other quarter where anything of consequence can be collected. Recollect
and tell me all you know."[7]

The challenge of that project, nevertheless, did little to calm her nerves.
Soon after returning to Plymouth, Mercy suffered a series of "nervous
headaches" prompted by several tragic events. Among them was the death
of her friend Mrs. Huntington, as well as that of the "lovely" young daughter of another friend, Harriet Temple, and other friends who suffered "in-
expressible mortifications." Outwardly at least, Mercy remained cheerful,
realizing, as she wrote James, that he, the "dear companion of my life is too
distant to hear and too much engaged in matters of such magnitude and importance" to soothe her.

Her one consolation was that "necessity separates us and not voluntary
choice."[8]

Winslow, the Warrens' second son, was eligible for Harvard by late 1775,
but in his father's absence decided to remain home to help run the family
farm and business. As Mercy assured her husband, she and Winslow were

trying to keep the "wheels a going...till the happy period when you shall return."[9]

The younger Warren boys, however, missed their father so desperately that Mercy finally allowed them to visit him in Watertown. Another attempt at maintaining normalcy was Mercy's plan to host family and friends at North Street; the event was to coincide with James's return there after the Provincial Congress's winter recess. The date, as Mercy confirmed with her husband, was Sunday, December 22 .

"Particularly make my regards to the two Mrs. Adamses [Abigail and Betsy]. Tell them I shall be much disappointed if I have not the pleasure of seeing them soon,"[10] she reminded James in late November.

On a snowy December 24, Mercy's letter, however, smoldering as white-hot as the coals of a hearth at dawn, revealed that James had missed the festivities.

"If a man devotes his whole attention to the service of the public, until his fortune, his health, and his abilities are spent, he is soon forgotten and sinks into contempt," she angrily scrawled. "Or if he...serves his country with vigor and reputation, until some lucrative office is assigned him...the malice of his enemies, the envy of his neighbors, and the indiscretions of his friends often...raise a popular clamor and...defeat his usefulness."

That, Mercy bitterly observed, "is my opinion of mankind...I should not be surprised if I...live to see the most distinguished defenders of the rights of the people...become the objects of popular disgust."

Weary of the strain the patriotic duties had placed upon the Warrens' marriage, Mercy suddenly lashed out at James. "I, therefore, cannot but secretly wish to see the man...laying aside the corroding cares of state and returning into those private...walks where" free of "party prejudices [he] might taste the...enjoyments of social life—assured of a few friends."

While eager for "peace and a happy union in the land," Mercy admitted she was "less engaged about political matters" than in the past. If, she added in a moralistic tone, she could "see a little more virtue and religion among individuals, I should have more hopes of the state."

Determined that the Warrens "at least shall be an exception to [that]... hideous picture," Mercy conceded that her sour mood was exacerbated by the absence of the "cheering conversation of her kind and affectionate husband."[11]

In late December or early January, just as Mercy feared, her overworked husband became ill. Alarmed by the news, Mercy spent an uneasy day in North Street, her worries intensified by the "hollow wind that whistled around through the stormy night," seemingly a reminder of that grim moment when those "who are dear as our souls, will be agitated and broken by separation."

Soon afterward though, Mercy received a letter from "the first friend of my heart," reporting his recuperation. Happily, she responded by describing the coziness of life at North Street. Winslow, "your young historian," had just sent James an entertaining letter. "Every laudable principle I discover in my Winslow makes me happy," she gushed. "He is a promising youth indeed."

Their eldest, James, Jr., newly returned home from the classes at Harvard then held at Concord, was "reading geography at the other table." The youngest boys were in bed.

Relieved by James's recovery, she regretted the harsh tone of her December 24 letter. Mercy wrote, "I must entreat you not to be anxious on my account or solicitous for your family, until it is in your power to revisit... and then I am sure you will... add wings to your speed."

After all, "You have an heavy burden on your shoulders exclusive of domestic cares... Sickness... rages in almost every house, but heaven has hitherto given us exemption from the general calamity. May we be enabled to make the most grateful returns for such an obligation."[12]

Privately, Mercy hoped that her "grateful returns" would become an authoritative account of the Revolution. And already, thanks to a letter of January 8, 1776, from John Adams, that project seemed possible. Her mentor exclaimed that he was "charmed with three characters drawn by a most masterly pen," which he considered as good as those of "Copley's pencil." Consequently, John proposed a "bargain": He would "draw the character of every new personage I have an opportunity of knowing, on condition you will do the same."[13]

Mercy agreed. Neither she nor John were, however, sole observers of the extraordinary events of 1775. That autumn, as General Burgoyne, or Gentleman Johnny, as the flamboyant British officer, gambler, and amateur playwright was known, lived at the Samuel Quincy house, he, too, bent over his writing desk. After critiquing General Gage's rule over Boston, Burgoyne sailed for England, leaving behind a satirical play called *The Blockade of Boston*.

Though the city's old Puritan laws still forbade live theater, the British cavalierly converted Faneuil Hall into a theater. On January 8, 1776, the same day that John Adams proposed his "bargain," Burgoyne's play was presented to British officers and their wives.

The cast consisted of soldiers, some costumed as civilians, others as women, still others in blackface as Boston's African Americans. While only partially preserved today, one of *The Blockade*'s scenes introduced a caricatured General Washington in an oversize wig and wielding a rusty sword.

Another satirical figure was a rustically dressed Yankee sergeant, who announced that the rebels were "at it tooth and nail over in Charlestown."[14] At those words, cannon fire resonated through Faneuil Hall. The audience, assuming it was stage effects, guffawed and applauded. Within seconds, the cannonade grew louder, followed by the sudden appearance of General Howe, who bellowed to his officers, "Turn out! Turn out!"[15]

The cannon fire had emanated from a patriotic regiment from Connecticut, who, probably alerted by spies, had just launched a new attack upon Charlestown.

General Washington, meanwhile, urged by the Continental Congress to move the site of war beyond Boston, was already plotting a new campaign. Hours before the debut of Burgoyne's *The Blockade*, the Virginian had ordered General Charles Lee to prepare for a battle in New York City, which he felt sure was the next British target. Ten days later, Colonel Henry Knox arrived in Cambridge with bittersweet news: His soldiers had retrieved cannons from Fort Ticonderoga, yet the American siege of Quebec had failed, resulting in the death of General Richard Montgomery.

By January 20, Mercy learned the tragic news. While not personally acquainted with the "intrepid" Montgomery who had conquered Montreal that November, she sent his wife her condolences. "Whilst all America weeps the loss of the brave Montgomery, his amiable lady will permit a stranger of her own sex to mingle the sympathetic sigh and . . . pour the tear of condolences into her wounded bosom."[16]

Her husband, she assured Mrs. Montgomery, had not died in vain, for the struggle was not merely "confined to the narrow limits of a province," but supported by the "happy union of the...colonies," whose "righteous cause...engrosses not only the...American continent but...the European world."[17]

On midnight of March 2, 1776, Boston was jolted awake by the crackle of artillery fired from the guns of Ticonderoga, which the patriots had shrewdly placed in Roxbury, Cobble Hill, and Lechmere Point. The British responded with their own cannon fire, creating such a racket that ten miles away in Braintree, Abigail rose from her bed. "The house shakes...with the roar of the cannon. No sleep for me tonight,"[18] she wrote John in Philadelphia.

The next night, reverberations from booming guns and flashes of mortar shells continued. The following night, a Monday, the cannonade reached such ear-splitting levels that frightened citizens took to the streets. The weather had turned mild, and a capricious breath of spring had produced a mist shrouding the peninsula of Dorchester's hilly shoreline on the south side of Boston Harbor.

That mist, combined with the patriots' disguised barrier of hay bales, camouflaged a train of twelve hundred men inching across the Dorchester causeway. Behind them, oxen pulled carts and wagons containing chandeliers (prebuilt timber frames filled with hay) as well as fascines (bundles of brushwood), dirt-filled barrels, and some of the guns from Ticonderoga. Around ten p.m., an alarmed British officer reported that he thought the "rebels were at work on the Dorchester Heights,"[19] but his observation was ignored.

Daybreak changed everything. "My God, these fellows have done more work in one night than I could make my army do in three months,"[20] gasped General Howe, who had replaced General Gage the previous fall. Overnight, Washington's men had mounted twenty cannons on Dorchester Heights, buttressed by chandeliers, fascines, and three thousand men. Below them, lining the shore, stood the Continental Army's riflemen, poised to shoot.

Twice—first at Charlestown's Breed Hill and now at Dorchester—the patriots had surprised the British. Panicked, Howe immediately ordered his men into ships to prepare for a night attack, but once again, the weather intervened. That afternoon, as the first British transports sailed for Castle Island, a storm pelted the region with hail and sleet. That night the headwinds blew nearly at hurricane velocity. By dawn, March 5, the sixth anniversary of the Boston Massacre, a torrential rain made visibility impossible.

It was time, Howe decided, for the British army to evacuate Boston.

The patriots were stunned. A day later, from Plymouth, where he had been recuperating from a second illness, James Warren wrote Elbridge Gerry in Philadelphia of the "very imperfect" accounts he received that the army had "taken possession of Do[r]chester Hill without any opposition."[21] What puzzled him was the absence of "much firing."

An equally mystified Mercy immediately sent congratulations to her friend, Mary Lincoln, wife of Brigadier General Benjamin Lincoln. Like James, she, too, wondered about the British lack of resistance, but gleefully predicted that the Battle of Dorchester "will mark the era of George the 3 with everlasting—if you can't find a word you think more suitable, you may say glory, if your conscience will let you."

Already considering the sweep of the Revolution from a literary perspective, Mercy opined that when future generations studied the "three of the most celebrated generals in the British service" sent to subdue the American rebels in 1775, they would be amused. The first, Gage, had "shut himself up in Boston without daring once to look out the gate." Clinton, having marched south, had been "made prisoner by the Yankee Admiral." The third, Burgoyne, merely "wrote a farce and went home again."[22]

Soon after Mercy's letter, an anonymous patriot delivered a final blow to the British with a new satire. Entitled *The Blockheads of Boston*, the play jeered at the British and their Tory sympathizers as salacious, incompetent men. The clever wordplay on "blockade" was not only a sneering retort to Burgoyne's *The Blockade of Boston* but a reminder of Jemmy's famous "blockhead" comment of 1769.

While Mercy never claimed authorship, several characters from her previous political satires reappeared. Among them was Simple, now a sophisticated Tory; Meagre, a brother of Rapatio; and Officer Dupe, the secretary of state.

The authorship of *The Blockheads of Boston* remains a controversy among scholars today. In spite of thematic similarities to Mercy's earlier satires with its contrasting views of pure American values and Tory or British decadence, some experts believe its language was too bold for her hand. Within it, several characters curse, others make degrading comments about women, and still others crack vulgar jokes.

Two women, Tabaitha and Dorsa, engage in suggestive repartee about their "friendships" with British officers. Tabaitha, enthralled with a certain Lord Dapper who will "carry me to England, after the present campaign" is shocked when her snickering companion, Dorsa, retorts that her British beau has a well-known "disgrace... [and] inability." Horrified, Tabaitha explains that she hopes Lord Dapper not "wanting in *any thing* to render the marriage state agreeable." If so, she will "throw him out of window" and find a better mate—after he provides her with "dress and fashion."

Equally coarse was the Loyalist Simple's instructions to his wife about the delicate diet they must eat as faithful subjects of the Crown. Should they continue to dine upon traditional Yankee fare, the peers would surely be repulsed, for "what *goes in must come out.*"

With similar crudity, a nameless British soldier comments upon the shameful condition of his peers. "I wish *Lord North* was here, to see his brave troops... running away with their breeches down—who can help laughing at what a tom fool's errand we have sent up." Ordered to ransack the country and "hang up a parcel of leading fellows for the crows to pick ... we were drove through the country, like a pack of jack asses, nor stopped running 'til we had got within Boston where we had been fortified for six months... reduced to skeletons, our bones standing sentry through our skins."[23]

That Mercy might have indulged in such images and language is not unthinkable. As a child in West Barnstable and during her travels to and from Watertown, she undoubtedly heard similar talk. Nor did Mercy shrink from using such language herself, as illustrated in her 1775 lecture that John Adams and his fellow delegates must no longer "piddle at the threshold" over independence.

-<+>-

Since January, Mercy had been musing over another challenge John had posed—her opinion of the "form of government which ought to be preferred by a people about to shake off the fetters of monarchic and aristocratic tyranny." Warily, Mercy replied on March 10 with her own question: Was John's solicitation of her opinion sincere, or merely a jest "designed to ridicule the sex for paying any attention to political matters?"

Without waiting for a response, Mercy expressed her thoughts. Never would she welcome "a monarchy established in America, however fashionable in Europe." For years, Mercy had admired a "republican government," even before its "advantages [were] delineated in so clear and concise a manner by your pen—that if established in the genuine principles of equal liberty."

Having read Thomas Paine's pamphlet *Common Sense*, she and James were convinced that a break with Great Britain was necessary. A month earlier, in fact, James had urged Sam Adams to encourage Congress to declare America's independence, and to do so before the House of Lords responded with new challenges to their American petitions.

Again, though, Congress stalled. While Mercy knew that John advocated independence, she wondered why other delegates hesitated. "If the union of the Colonies, and a steady opposition to the disgraceful idea of foreign shackles still subsist," she hoped that "America has more than one *politician* who has abilities *to make the character of the people to extinguish vices, and follies . . . and to create the virtues he sees wanting.*"

That being expressed, Mercy referred again to her agreement to trade character portraits with John. Coyly, in a flirtatious tone, Mercy insisted he must keep his promise. After all, "you cannot recede when a lady has accepted your proposals." In return for her reportage, her "imperfect characters and observations," as Mercy described them, "I expect to be made acquainted with the genius . . . tastes . . . manners not only of the most distinguished characters in America, but of the nobility of Britain: and perhaps . . . with some of the dignified personages who have held . . . crowns . . . [and] the dancing puppets of other European courts."

America, Mercy added, must "take her rank and send her Ambassadors abroad." Then, suddenly embarrassed by her boldness, she apologized:

"The sphere of female life is too narrow to afford much entertainment to the wise and learned." She had written "beyond the limit I designed."[24]

Implicit in her outspoken letter was Mercy's emerging feminist voice. Fragile and easily quashed by even a hint of disapproval from John Adams, Mercy's ideas, nevertheless, pleaded for a hearing.

On March 8, after the patriotic triumph at Dorchester, General Howe sent three men waving a white flag across Boston Neck with a letter assuring the colonists that he had "no intention of destroying the town."[25]

Washington, noting that the letter was neither signed nor directly addressed to him, ignored it and ordered new fortifications on Dorchester's Nook's Hill. Subsequent to that unofficial truce though, both sides maintained the peace.

Initially, the Loyalists were "thunderstruck" with Howe's announcement to leave Boston and then panicked by the consequences. In preparation, soldiers marched through the streets lugging stores of munitions, hauling cannons, barrels of gunpowder, and other supplies onto their ships.

As Mercy's play *The Group* and the anonymous *The Blockheads* had predicted, the patriot victory placed Boston's twelve hundred Tories in a predicament. Most of them were merchants, elderly, infirm, or refugees from neighboring towns. Forced to leave their native land and sail with the British, many left loved ones behind, sold their property at auction, or simply abandoned it.

Even Mercy empathized with their plight. "I know, madam, your compassionate heart heaves a sigh of pity for the miserable group indiscriminately hurried on ship board to escape the . . . resentment of their . . . injured country," she wrote Dorothy Quincy Hancock in Philadelphia. "Do you think there was ever a more sudden reverse of hopes and expectations than these poor creatures suffer?"[26]

Later, as the Tories departed, Mercy described the scene even more vividly to John. "So pitiable is their condition, that it must excite the compassion of their hardest heart . . . women, children, soldiers, sailors, governors, counselors, flatterers, statesmen, and pimps, huddle promiscuously, either into fishing boats or royals barks, which ever first offered the means of escape."[27]

Ironically, the British soldiers who traveled with them were less sympathetic. "Neither hell, Hull, nor Halifax can afford worse shelter than Boston," one soldier wrote home. Another groused that taking women, children, sick, and wounded passengers aboard was "like departing your country with your wives, your servants, your household furniture and all your encumbrances."[28]

Adding to the turmoil were delays in the departure of the British fleet. Initially, General Howe had a valid excuse for high winds and choppy seas had stalled sea traffic for nearly a week. Still, even when the weather improved, the British delayed, leading Washington to suspect it was a subterfuge for another confrontation. As the days passed, British soldiers destroyed or confiscated everything that could be used by the American army—sinking cannons into the harbor, seizing woolens and linens from residents, and plundering shops for valuables.

Nor was the destination of the British fleet known. Finally, by March 16, the Virginia General had decided to force the British evacuation. The next morning, a newly constructed fort appeared on Nook's Hill; by noon a formidable line of cannons was poised upon British ships in the harbor.

General Howe instantly grasped Washington's message. At daybreak on March 17, the British abandoned their fortifications, boarded boats, and sailed with the tide, just beyond the rim of Boston Harbor. Another week passed. Still the British fleet lingered in the waters close to the fortress at Castle Island.

Suddenly, on the night of March 20, Boston and the surrounding towns were rocked by an enormous explosion as British engineers blew up Castle William. Only after that fiery spectacle did Howe's men finally set sail.

A week later, Mercy and newly recuperated James left Plymouth for Watertown, stopping first in Braintree to see Abigail. On March 27, the three friends climbed a hill near the Adamses' home and gazed upon the departing ships in the distant harbor.

"The last division of the British fleet sailed on Wednesday last," James wrote John on March 30. He, Mercy, and Abigail "had a view of them without the lighthouse from Pens Hill, about sixty or seventy sail ... What their destination is we are not able to ascertain. The general opinion is that they are gone to Halifax."[29]

No less curious, as Mercy noted to Dorothy Hancock, was the "dead silence [which] reigns through the long extended lines" around Boston—fortifications that Washington had deemed "almost impregnable."

To Mercy, "[t]he total stagnation of business within and the still calm without the walls of Boston," resembled the serenity that often "succeeds the most violent concussions in the world of nature."

Those violent concussions though had occurred in the world of man—a triumph as Mercy would later write, who "made the most costly sacrifices in the cause of liberty . . . waded through the blood of friends and foes to establish their independence and . . . support the freedom of the human mind."[30]

Yet to capture those momentous events in print seemed as daunting to Mercy as was the triumph of the Revolution itself.

"Ladies are the greatest politicians"

THE WORLD HAS "turned topsy turvey to such a degree that I can scarcely realize the present appearances of things; the enemies army fled and our own marching into other colonies," James, having returned to Watertown, wrote John Adams on March 30, 1776.

General Washington had asked James to continue as paymaster general of the Continental Army on its march to New York. Newly recovered from illness, weary from double duties as Speaker of the House and the army's paymaster generalship, James had declined. "My interest and connections here," as he explained to John, "would render it very disagreeable and scarcely honorable for me to leave this colony."

With the relocation south of the "seat of war," he and Mercy anticipated having less news to report. Instead, "All kinds of intelligence I am now to expect from you," James predicted. "When shall we hear that we are independent?"

Four days later, in a hurried postscript, James emphasized the colonists' impatience for a Congressional declaration. "I can't describe the sighing after independence; it is universal."[1]

Irritated, John retorted that the Massachusetts colony was partially responsible for the delay since its representatives had dragged their heels on that very issue. "Why don't your honors of the General Court, if you are so unanimous in this, give positive instructions to your own delegates, to promote independency," he wrote. "The S[outhern] colonies say you are afraid."[2]

By early April, meanwhile, a welcome calm had settled over the Edmund

Fowle House, enabling Mercy to secure a "convenient room." The day after her arrival she rode to the army camp at Cambridge to meet Martha Washington and was taken with the gray-haired matron's "benevolence," her "affability, candor, and gentleness." During the visit, Martha invited Mercy to join her the next morning on a tour of the land surrounding newly deserted Boston. Ironically, when a carriage rolled up at the Edmund Fowle House for Mercy and Martha to see "the deserted lines of the enemy," it was the same luxurious coach that had once belonged to Governor Hutchinson.

During the ride, the two women avoided the strait known as Boston Neck that led into the smallpox-infested city. The "ruins of Charleston" were sobering enough, Mercy later explained to Abigail, its charred townhouses, shops, and park, "a melancholy sight . . . [highlighting] the barbarity of the foe."

In return for Martha's invitation, Mercy invited her and the general to dine with her and James at the Edmund Fowle House. The day before that event, however, the general was summoned to Rhode Island on an alarm, and the dinner was canceled. Disappointed, especially since the Washingtons were preparing to leave Massachusetts, Mercy lamented to Abigail that her "object of esteem" was slipping away, "perhaps forever."

In compensation, Mercy entertained other wives of army officers at a dinner. Then she spent time "amusing myself with my book,"[3] she explained to Abigail, finally putting a name to her "historic" project.

If anyone could write such a book, John's admiring wife replied, it was Mercy. Earlier, on April 19, Abigail had asked about Martha Washington. "Should be glad of your opinion. I love characters drawn by your pen."[4]

She wished, Abigail added, several days later, she could write as well as Mercy. But she lacked the "happy talent she [Mercy] possesses above the rest of her sex . . . Cannot you communicate some of those graces to your friend," Abigail whimsically added, and allow her "to pass them upon the world for her own that she may feel a little more upon an equality with you?"[5]

Abigail was also brooding about the lack of equality accorded women in colonial affairs. In her husband's absence, she and Mercy, like other "war widows" of the era, were developing new strengths; Mercy by supervising the Warren household, farm, and business in Plymouth and riding alone to Watertown to assist James; Abigail by managing the family finances, the farm, and raising her young children alone.

"Unwomanly" though such activities might have seemed in pre-Revolutionary America, that behavior became critical to their families' survival. By mid-1776, recognition of their own abilities thus prompted Abigail and Mercy to bold new thoughts.

Five weeks after Mercy's letter of March 10, in which she had outlined her ideas about government, John responded. She had no need to apologize, he assured her. Ladies, after all, "are the greatest politicians... not only because they act upon the... principles of policy, viz. that honesty is the best policy, but because they consider questions more coolly than those who are heated with party zeal and inflamed with the bitter contentions of active public life."[6]

When Mercy described John's letter, Abigail was surprised. Her husband "writes to no one" except Portia—the nickname Mercy once gave Abigail, which she often used to sign letters. Indeed, except for her and Mercy, there was no one "in whom he has an equal confidence."[7]

Paradoxically, on April 14, just two days before John's letter to Mercy extolling women as superb politicians, he had dismissed that very idea to Abigail. Several weeks earlier, having learned that the Constitutional Convention was creating a Code of Laws defining the rights of American citizens, Abigail had advanced the notion of female equality.

"Remember the ladies," she famously said, "and be more generous and favorable to them than your ancestors. Do not put such unlimited power into the hands of the husbands. Remember all men would be tyrants if they could. If particular care and attention is not paid to the ladies, we are determined to foment a rebellion, and will not hold ourselves bound by any laws in which we have no voice, or representation."[8]

John's response to Abigail's "List of Female Grievances," she complained to Mercy in late April, was "very saucy."[9]

On April 14, he had wittily replied, "As to our extraordinary code of laws, I cannot but laugh. That children and apprentices were disobedient... schools and colleges were grown turbulent... But your letter was the first intimation that another tribe... more numerous and powerful than all the rest, were grown discontented.

"Depend upon it, we know better than to repeal our masculine system. Although they are in full force, you know they are little more than theory.

We dare not exert our power in its full latitude. We are obliged to go fair, and softly, and in practice, you know we are the subjects. We have only the name of masters and rather than give up this, which would completely subject us to the despotism of the petticoat."[10]

Chagrined, Abigail confided to Mercy on April 27, "I think I will get you to join me in a petition to Congress. I thought it was very probable our wise statesmen would erect a new government and form a new code of laws. I venture to speak a word in behalf of our sex, who are rather hardly dealt with by the laws of England which gives such unlimited power to the husband to use his wife ill."[11]

To that, Mercy made no reply. Her silence has perplexed historians for decades. Some attribute it to the fears she had expressed to John about her bold, "unwomanly" voice; others to Mercy's traditional dependence upon James; and still others to her private view that women must appear, if not be, subservient to men. As Mercy advised an unidentified young woman:

"My dear, it may be necessary for you to seem inferior, but you need not be so. Let them [the men] have their little game, since it may have been so willed. It won't hurt you; it will amuse them."[12]

Even more pressing may have been a personal incident fraught with such shame that Mercy felt compelled to drop the subject of female independence altogether.

During the spring of 1776, a urgent message arrived in Watertown from Concord, where Harvard had held classes held since autumn 1775. James Warren, Jr., then in his senior year, had suffered an emotional breakdown and, as Abigail wrote John in May 1776, was brought to Plymouth "disordered in his mind."[13]

"Do you mean that our Plymouth friends are in trouble for a disordered son! If so, I am grieved to the heart. God grant them support under so severe an affliction,"[14] he replied.

The cause of young James's breakdown was never disclosed. Scholarly theories about the youth's crisis abound—that his "disorder" was no more than the heavy drinking typical of Harvard students, or, more ominously, a symptom of the same mental illness that plagued the youth's uncle Jemmy.

Oddly enough, when the Winthrops had temporarily moved to Concord near Harvard's classes and visited young James, Hannah had reported that he seemed well.

For several weeks after her son's return to Plymouth, Mercy stopped writing friends. "My dear Mrs. Adams will undoubtedly wonder that she has not heard from me since I left Braintree, but want of health, a variety of avocations, with some anxiety of another nature must be my excuse," she wrote on May 27 in an oblique reference to her son's troubles.

"I have scarcely taken up a pen since my return to Plymouth," she added. "Indeed I feel as if I was about to quit the use of it . . . A severe nervous head ache has afflicted me for two days."[15]

No longer could Mercy pride herself upon being the perfect mother, the one Hannah had praised for informing the "infant mind[s]"[16] or whom Abigail commended as the Warrens' "well ordered family."[17]

Given the emotional upheaval of her eldest son, James, it was hardly the moment for Mercy to advocate for women's rights.

Fast company, excessive drinking, possibly even gambling and wenching in the Concord boarding house where young James Warren roomed, may have caused his "disordered mind." After receiving a message about his troubled son, his father, James, bolted from Watertown, excusing his departure upon "some private affairs,"[18] and rushed the youth to Plymouth.

Within a few weeks, young James was well enough to travel to Cambridge to prepare for Harvard's reconvened classes. Soon afterward, Mercy wrote an initially gentle letter. "I doubt not the mind of my dear James has been greatly agitated . . . since the long confinement of his mother," she began, "but [my] returning health enables me [to] . . . remind you again that . . . nature has given you a thirst for knowledge . . . and . . . taught you to soar in distinction in . . . science."

Then Mercy reverted to a lecture. The "great business of life," she began, "is the regulation of the passions and the subjugation of those appetites which tend to . . . weaken the powers of the mind." The young often make mistakes. Yet there was a difference between succumbing once to an "evil influence" and repeating it. Companions might tease James for refusing temptations, but their smirks were "the grin of fools."

Once again, Mercy reiterated the close relation between the achievements of her sons and her own sense of pride. As a mother, she had "laid my account high with regard to my children and if disappointed the shock will be in proportion to the height I have soared."[19]

Young James's reaction to his mother's letter, if there was one, has not been preserved. Mercy, meanwhile, continued to brood. After visiting her that summer, Abigail confided to John that Mercy was "almost heartbroken," for she had valiantly attempted to "train them [her sons] up in the way in which they ought to go." Young James was "impaired in health...in mind...in morals...a situation truly deplorable." Even so, John must not "mention the matter—not even to them by the slightest hint. Tis a wound which cannot be touched."[20]

Other events conspired to make 1776 a still more challenging year. In Watertown, Mercy's husband continued to serve on the Board of War, supervising requisitions for soldiers, recruiting men, and ensuring the safety of the Massachusetts coast.

Then James was named to the Superior Court. Taken aback, he wrote Adams, who had nominated him, that he must have been a choice of last resort. "So barren is our poor country that they have been obliged to appoint the most unsuitable man in the world," James mused, explaining that he was "embarrassed beyond measure." While fearing John's "displeasure" and puzzled by "the solicitations of friends," James refused the post, rationalizing that his acceptance would only "injure his country and expose himself."[21]

John blamed his friend's refusal on another reason. The Superior Court appointment, he bitterly told Abigail in late May, "must be disagreeable to him and his lady, because he loves to be upon his farm and they both love to be together, but you must tell them of a couple of their friends, who are as fond of living together who are obliged to sacrifice their rural amusements and domestic happiness to the requisitions of the public."[22] A private man, James had scrupulously avoided mentioning the turmoil created by his eldest son. Almost certainly, it contributed to his refusal.

Subsequently, James would be nominated or elected to other high positions, but to John's frustration, he repeatedly declined. "Warren has both talents and virtues beyond most men in this world," John again confided to Abigail in August 1776, "yet his character ["will"] has never been in proportion."[23]

After rejecting the Superior Court nomination, James traveled to Plymouth to spend time with Mercy and their youngest four sons at his "little farm" on the Eel River. Daily, he and Mercy waited anxiously for news about the document from Philadelphia that would place America in a new relationship with Great Britain—the Declaration of Independence.

By May 20, John had maintained that "[w]e can't be very remote from the most decisive measures and the most critical events."[24] Yet it would not be until July 1 that the Continental Congress scheduled a vote and then, at the last minute, postponed it a day. On July 2, soon after Congress convened, twelve of the colonies voted for independence.

"I have the pleasure to inform you that a determined resolution of the delegates...to push the question of independency has had a most happy effect,"[25] Elbridge Gerry wrote James from Philadelphia on July 5. Enclosed in Gerry's letter was a copy of the first broadside edition of the Declaration of Independence.

Five days later, in Plymouth, James had still not received the news. "When are we to hear of our proceedings?" he impatiently wrote John. "What alliances and confederations have you agreed on?...Our borders seem to be in a state of peace and tranquility; how long they will continue so I know not."[26]

Simultaneously, another worry threatened to destroy the "peace and tranquility" of Massachusetts—a smallpox epidemic that killed one of every three victims. Colonists rushed into Boston for treatment at one of the city's newly established "smallpox hospitals." Among them was John's wife, Abigail, whose uncle Isaac Smith, offered the use of his vacant Boston home for relatives and friends. The Warrens joined them.

While Abigail's four young children went with her, Mercy and James arrived alone. Perhaps the Smith house, already crammed with the Adamses, Abigail's sisters Elizabeth Cranch and Mary Shaw, and their husbands, had no more room.

Just as likely though, Mercy, fearing she would be too ill to nurse her sons if they were inoculated all at once, decided to have them treated later.

On Saturday, July 13, Mercy and James appeared in Boston carting with them temporary straw mattresses, sheets, and other necessities. The city's post-British "alteration and gloomy appearance" was sobering, James reported to John, a place with "no business, no busy faces, but those of physicians, ruins of buildings, wharfs."

Smallpox, its prevention, and its "cure" had even drawn James "into its vortex and brought me with my *other self* [Mercy] into the crowd of patients with which this town is now filled." Boston had been transformed into a "great hospital for inoculation."[27]

Everything, it seemed, revolved around inoculations and their after-effects. Still that was understandable, for even by the primitive standards of eighteenth-century medicine the inoculation, or variolation, process was daunting. Adapted from an ancient Turkish treatment, Revolutionary-era physicians injected colonists with fluid extracted from the pustule of a sufferer. Several days later, recipients spiked fevers, and suffered headaches, abdominal pain, and nausea.

The reaction, which lasted three or four weeks, terminated with sores or pustules, some even on the inside of the eye. Even so, the cure was less severe than the original disease and guaranteed lifetime immunity.

The variolation, nevertheless, had certain risks. Some patients developed full-blown cases of smallpox and died. Others remained listless and weak for months. Still others suffered permanent damage to internal organs and joints. Many were left with devastating eye problems, including blindness. Even so, nearly everyone thought the treatment was worth the risk.

Within hours of the Warrens' arrival in Boston, Abigail Adams received a letter from Philadelphia. "Yesterday the greatest question was decided, which ever was debated in America, and greater perhaps, never was or will be decided among men," read John's triumphant message of July 5. "A resolution was passed without one dissenting colony 'that these united colonies are, and of right ought to be free and independent states.' "

In a few days, John promised his wife, "You will see a declaration setting forth the causes, which have impelled us to this mighty revolution."[28]

Finally, on Saturday, July 15, an official copy of the Declaration of Independence arrived in Boston. Its appearance "diffused a general joy," the newly inoculated James informed John. "Every one of us feels more important than ever; we now congratulate each other as freeman. It has really raised our spirits...beneficial to mitigate the malignity of the small pox...[and] seems to animate...every one to support and defend the independency."[29]

With similar enthusiasm Abigail's brother-in-law, Richard Cranch wrote, "The Declaration of Independency...was received accordingly by the loudest acclamations of the people, who shouted–God Save the United STATES of America!"[30]

Either Mercy's response was not preserved, or perhaps she was too ill to write. Years later in her *History*, she recalled the Declaration's dramatic impact upon the colonists. Thereafter, "Americans could now no more be considered as rebels, in their proposals for treaties of peace and conciliation with Britain; they were a distinct people who claimed the rights...faith and ...respect of nations, uncontrolled by any foreign power."[31]

John's subsequent response to James included an odd request. His survival of earlier variolation, John believed, had been the sole "merit, which originally, recommended me to this lofty station."[32] Now that others were immunized or had survived smallpox, he wanted to leave the Continental Congress. "I wish to be released from Philadelphia forever," he explained, for he longed to return to his family in Braintree. "My face has grown pale, my eyes weak and inflamed, my nerves tremulous, and my mind weak as water." It was time to "take a little rest."[33]

Others should "come here and see the beauties and sublimities of a Continental Congress." Perhaps James might take his place. After all, John teased, "[a] ride to Philadelphia, after the small pox, will contribute prodigiously to the restoration of your health."[34]

Like other patients, James regained his strength only gradually, so troubled by eye problems that he was unable to write for days. Finally, on August 7, he promised to find a replacement for John. Four days later James wrote again, pressing John for a Congressional appointment of a major general to head the few regiments still protecting Boston.

"Mrs. Adams will inform you by this post that she and the children are well," he added. The only exception was Charles, the Adamses' second son, who "has not yet had the small pox."

As to Mercy's condition, James simply reported that "Mrs. Warren and myself have been fortunate enough to have it very cleverly [clearly] and propose going home this week."[35] Perhaps, either from the strain of writing or a tendency to gloss over such details, James described neither the course of his own illness nor that of his wife's.

The only comment about Mercy's reaction to the variolation came from Abigail, who reported that while she and James were rapidly recovering, Mercy still suffered "faintings and langor."[36]

By summer's end James had returned to Watertown to resume his duties. Among them were supervision of Boston's nearly unprotected harbor, raising new recruits for New York, and finding a replacement for John Adams.

Mercy, meanwhile, had returned to Plymouth. From there she wrote Abigail on September 4 that she savored the "rustling of the gentle breezes in my own little garden... and the return of my little flock from school,"[37] but was still too frail to receive company. While relieved to survive the variolation, she missed James.

The preceding spring, Mercy had penned a praiseworthy poem about her husband. Titled "To Fidelio" who was "Long absent on the great public cause, which agitated all America, in 1776," Mercy described strolling sadly alone along the "gurgling rills" and the "beauties of the adjacent hills" of Clifford.

Her message, for with Mercy there was always one, indicated that while she longed to see an end to the "dread din of war" and a return to "each joy domestic life can yield," she remained proud of James's sacrifices.

Patriotic virtue, she prayed:

> May free this country from despotic chains
> Long life I ask, and blessing to descend,
> And crown the efforts of my constant friend.[38]

⋘⋙

By mid-September though, Mercy was no longer as enthusiastic about James's "patriotic zeal." Earlier that month, the Massachusetts legislature had appointed him a major general of the Rhode Island regiments—one of three officers slated to wrest that colony from British control. Afterward, he and those militias were expected to join Washington and his army in New York.

On Sunday, September 15, learning that James had "thoughts of taking the command," Mercy grew hysterical. From her desk she wrote, "How earnestly did I ever entreat my dear Mr. Warren not to accept of an appointment which...would involve me in the depth so distress? With my eyes now swimming in tears do I recollect how many honorable, how many profitable, and how many useful employments you have refused, and accepted of this one which...was...a dagger in my bosom!"

Then, more gently, "But I will not reproach you...for if you march to New York in your feeble state, I do not imagine you can have much expectation of returning." In view of his recently compromised health, "You can never endure winter's campaign."

Should James insist upon accepting the post, she would not stand in his way, but instead, Mercy impetuously announced, "I must march with you and take my lodgment in the neighborhood of the camp. I hardly know what I write...it is Providence which has destined me this affliction...I feel...as if I should sink only under the weight of my fears."

In a postscript written later that day, a calmer Mercy explained that she had received news of James's appointment just before dinner and, losing her appetite, retired to her room. After weeping and a "little reflection," she had "almost persuaded myself of the improbability of your leaving this province...Your talents and capacity in the legislative will do more service to our country," she insisted, "...than your military abilities can do in the camp."

Doubtless James would be an exemplary military leader. "Did your health permit, I have no doubts of your being distinguished...I hope for a letter tomorrow and thereby to know your determination."

In the meanwhile, Mercy dutifully promised to "endeavor to learn submission to the designations of heaven, but when contrary to my wishes, oh, how involuntary the resignation!"[39]

10

"The hand often shrunk back from the task"

A DAY OR TWO AFTER receiving Mercy's distraught letter, James refused the appointment as major general of Massachusetts. His health, he wrote John Adams, "could not . . . support the fatigue"[1] of active duty at that moment. Months later, he confided that the tensions between local militias and the Continental Army were another factor, that the former were "despised . . . [and] directed by the Continental Generals."[2] Had he assumed the major generalship, officers of the Continental Army would have been his superiors—an awkward reversal for James, their former paymaster general.

In spite of James's decision, Mercy grew increasingly anxious over his suddenly tardy letters. "I hear from every quarter that you are exceedingly engaged. Your laconic [tardy] style confirm this report," she observed. Realizing then that she sounded shrill, Mercy conceded that certain "secrets of state" might be "too deep for the female ear or too intricate for her consideration."

Exacerbating her sense of abandonment was the failing health of her father, Colonel Otis. Her beloved parent, she wrote James, "flatters himself, notwithstanding . . . that a little attention and . . . more riding will yet restore him to health."[3]

By November 25 and 26, worries about smallpox led Mercy to place her sons in a new Plymouth inoculation hospital. On Sunday, December 1, having attended to her feverish sons, she returned to North Street and, in an "hour of solitude," wrote a self-pitying letter to Abigail.

Ironically, at that very moment, her friend was enjoying a rare visit from John, then on leave from Congress. Her own husband, Mercy complained, was in Boston, her eldest son "absent, my other four at...hospital ill with the small pox, my father on a bed of pain...no sisters at hand nor even a friend to step in." How fortunate that dear "Portia" had John by her side and was "encircled by her children in full health."[4]

Three days later on December 4, a "darksome dreary day," Mercy bent over her desk again, this time writing to Hannah Lincoln, whose husband, Benjamin, had assumed the major generalship in James's place "My mind has been almost wholly engrossed since my return from Boston by preparation to put my large family into an inoculating hospital,"[5] Mercy explained.

In between her domestic duties, Mercy, nevertheless, brooded over her lack of progress on her *History*. Indeed, as she later confessed in its introduction, her "trembling heart...recoiled at the magnitude of the undertaking, and the hand often shrunk back from the task."[6] Yet, even during those difficult moments, Mercy continued to collect information about the Revolution, not merely from published reports but from American friends.

"You may remember that you gave me an extract or two from the foreword of your good brother,"[7] she thus reminded Hannah Lincoln. Having misplaced it, she asked for a second copy.

Her loneliness, if nothing else, led Mercy to later remind readers of her *History* that "every domestic enjoyment depends on the unimpaired possession of civil and religious liberty."[8] By the winter of 1776, Mercy's own life dramatically epitomized that fragile relationship.

In the final months of 1776, possession of that "civil and religious liberty" seemed as elusive as the snow chilling the retreating American army after their defeat at Fort Washington. As General Washington predicted, Howe's men had sailed from Halifax to New York. Moreover, Parliament had reinforced Howe's troops with twenty-three thousand soldiers and nearly seventeen thousand German mercenaries or Hessians (a number that later swelled to thirty thousand), raising enemy presence in New York to fifty-five thousand men. Nearly half of Great Britain's formidable armada served by twenty-eight thousand sailors also hovered along the East Coast.

"Perhaps at no period of the great struggle for independence, were the affairs of the United States at so low an ebb as at the present,"[9] Mercy wrote in early winter 1776. Though even after learning about the suspicious capture of General Charles Lee, she remained certain that a benevolent Providence would enable the Revolution's success to inspire a worldwide rebirth of "virtue, religion and morality." On December 26, she uncannily predicted to James that "this day and evening, amidst a thousand gloomy anecdotes . . . God was about to bring us deliverance, by means which we cannot foresee."[10]

As it happened, the means of deliverance that same day was the victorious Battle of Trenton. Twenty-one Hessians lay dead in the streets, ninety others were wounded, and nine hundred were taken as prisoners. News of that triumph, Mercy reported to her husband on December 31, did wonders for local morale and "raised the sad countenance of our people . . . high."[11]

It was nearly February before Abigail finally replied to Mercy's unhappy letter of December 1. "My eyes ever since the smallpox have been great sufferers. Writing puts them to great pain,"[12] she explained. While congratulating Mercy on her sons' recoveries, the Braintree matron was seething.

For nearly two years, Mercy had been able to visit James in Watertown, while Abigail lived alone with her children in Braintree during John's long absences in Philadelphia. The result, as Abigail had complained to Mercy months earlier, was that she found herself not only "doubled in wedlock but multiplied in cares to which I know myself unequal, in the education of my little flock."[13] After reading Mercy's morose letter of December 1, Abigail had little sympathy.

James's absence while his sons were being inoculated in Plymouth, Abigail sharply responded, must finally have forced Mercy to understand "what I passed through the summer past only with this difference—that your friend [James] was within a day's ride of you and mine hundreds of miles distant."

Abigail then sought sympathy. "O Marcia, how many hundred miles this moment separate us [her and John]—my heart bleeds at the recollection," she wrote. "Many circumstances conspire to make this separation more grievous . . . than any . . . The distance, the difficulty of communication and the many hazards . . . render me . . . very unhappy."

While longing to dissuade John from leaving, Abigail knew that "our public affairs . . . wore so gloomy an aspect that I thought if ever his assistance was wanted, it must be at such a time."

The result, was "much anxiety and many melancholy hours for this year to come."[14] Suggested but never explicitly stated was that Abigail had become pregnant during John's recent visit. In all probability, her husband would be absent when she delivered her fifth child.

Earnest as Abigail's letter was, it took Mercy aback. For six weeks she did not respond. Instead, she continued to spin wool into skeins and sent it along to her Braintree friend for the poor.

When on March 1, 1777, Mercy finally wrote, she blamed her delay upon a return of postvariolation symptoms, which included "weakness . . . feebleness of my limbs, and pains . . . sufficient to damp the vigor of thought, and check . . . literary employment."

In a cursory acknowledgment of Abigail's complaint, Mercy wrote, "I do not wonder at the regret you express at the distance and absence of your excellent husband." Even so, she stiffly reminded Abigail about their former admiration for classical heroines. "Why should not the same heroic virtue, the same fortitude . . . that crowns the memory of the ancient matron, adorn the . . . modern fair who adopts the signature of Portia? Surely Rome had not severer trials than America."[15]

That Mercy's own spirits had flagged, that she had begged James to remain in Massachusetts, remained unmentioned.

In addition to its military presence upon American soil, the Crown waged war on the colonies on the high seas, making the transcontinental delivery of goods and letters risky.

When on February 1 Mercy learned that a Plymouth man planned to sail to Great Britain, she dashed off a letter to Catharine Macaulay, reporting that the Crown had forced "the peasant and the statesman . . . [to] struggle even in *blood* to secure to themselves and . . . posterity the claims they derive from heaven."

Indeed, the political climate was so mutable and complex, Mercy observed, that she lacked the ability to record its nuances. Such a task would require "the pen of a Macaulay to trace the origin, to paint the prime actors, and give . . . true coloring to the . . . war."[16]

Two weeks later, learning that still another Plymouth citizen would sail to England, Mercy wrote Catharine again. After describing General Charles Lee's suspicious "capture" and the patriotic victories at Princeton and Elizabethtown, Mercy noted that the Revolution had riveted international attention and would "probably light half Europe in flames."[17]

Whatever hopes Mercy harbored for James's permanent return to Plymouth were scuttled in May 1777, when he was named one of the three directors of the new Navy Board. James had repeatedly written John Adams about the importance of establishing a national fleet in the Atlantic. By May 6, John proudly reported that such a board had been approved for several districts, among them Boston.

"I hope you will engage in this business and conduct it with spirit," John urged. The nature of the post, which included supervision of shipbuilding, the appointment of naval officers, and the establishment of arsenals, would mean that James must resign as Speaker of the House. The recompense was low, but the work critically important. "It will be an honorable endeavor," John opined, "to be so capitally concerned in laying a foundation of a great navy."[18]

James contemplated the offer while visiting Mercy in Plymouth and escorting her to visit the pregnant Abigail in Braintree. By June 5, having briefly enjoyed a taste of domesticity, he replied to John from Watertown, thanking him for that "late instance of . . . friendship," but explaining that he had lately "taken such a lurch . . . for a more private way of life" that he was inclined to refuse the Navy Board post.

Among his objections was the requirement that Navy Board directors must live in Boston. Nevertheless, James acknowledged he was "very glad there is a board established. Never such a thing was wanted more."[19]

Ultimately James did accept the post regardless of Mercy's ongoing complaints about loneliness. Increasingly, Mercy was brooding over the eventuality that her sons would be fully grown. Only two—eleven-year-old George and thirteen-year-old Henry—were still home. The Warrens' middle son, Charles, had just entered Harvard, where her eldest, James, Jr., was completing his final year. Even her favorite, Winslow, dividing his time between the Warren farm and his father's mercantile business, appeared only sporadically.

Intensifying Mercy's sense of marginality was Plymouth itself, bitterly divided between patriots and Tories—a town she now disliked, she admitted to James on June 14, "were it not the interest of the best of husbands to reside there," inhabited by a "people defective . . . in literary and polite education and soured by the bitterness of party resentment." What rankled her most about the divided town was its disregard for her beloved James, who had devoted "time and fortune in their service" for nearly a decade. Where she lived, Mercy suddenly realized, was inconsequential, "provided I have the company of that man of whose friendship I have had more than twenty years . . . and without whom life has few charms."

While reaffirming her hope that James would be "instrumental in the salvation" of America, she reminded him that he had done his best. Should the British triumph, "You can, after a ten years ineffectual struggle, quit . . . public life and retire with the consolations of a peaceful conscience."[20]

Omitted from Mercy's unhappy letter was mention of the return of a post-variolation symptom. That same day, she wrote to Abigail, she had "been deprived the use of one eye."[21] By July 7 Mercy was recovered enough to write Abigail again, this time wishing her an easy time with the birth of another "young patriot."[22]

Two days later, Abigail began shaking and, after several anguished days, delivered a stillborn baby girl. Several weeks passed before Mercy heard the news. Chagrined, she congratulated Abigail on her recovery "after pain, peril and disappointment."[23] With equanimity, that matron replied on August 14—a date, she reminded Mercy, was "memorable, the twelfth anniversary" of the destruction of Hutchinson's mansion.

"Since that time what have we endured? What have we suffered?" Abigail mused. Worried that Mercy had faltered writing her *History*, she pointedly added, "Many . . . memorable events which ought to be handed down to posterity will be buried in oblivion, merely for want of a proper hand to record them. I have always been sorry that a certain person who once put their hand to the pen, should be discouraged and give up so important a service. Many things would have been recorded by the penetrating genius . . . which will . . . escape the notice of any future historian."[24]

Resiliency, as Abigail had recently proven, was critical in the face of hardship. She expected no less from Mercy.

-<+>-

"Had ever any man so many rascally cousins as I have?"[25] James grumbled to Elbridge Gerry about his Tory relatives in Plymouth. Among the most treacherous was his cousin little Ned Winslow, the brother of Mercy's friend Penny, who, in April 1775, rode with a British regiment to Lexington and Concord. No less rascally was Ned's father, Edward Winslow, one of the five men the Massachusetts House accused of "endeavoring since the 19 of April, 1775, to counteract the struggles of this and the United States."

By 1777, disenchantment with the war, disruptions in trade, and a thirst for imported goods also discouraged other Americans from the Revolution. Some of them had already resorted to hoarding and smuggling. Others, hedging their bets between the British and the patriots—the "neutralists" and those still faithful to the Crown, now called Loyalists—furtively traded with British privateers to obtain goods, rums, and wines. Still others, observing the growing scarcity of commodities like flour, wheat, and cloth, cornered the market, resulting in runaway inflation.

"The price of every thing is extravagant, and the extortion of sellers... unbounded,"[26] James consequently complained to Elbridge Gerry that winter. By April, as the economy worsened, the nervous delegates of the Massachusetts legislature also wavered, sometimes adopting leniency toward the Loyalists, at other times putting them in prison.

Privately, Mercy continued to practice domestic economy in keeping with the concept of patriotic independence. From wool clipped, washed, and combed from sheep at Clifford Farm, she spun skeins for her household, then sent the rest on to Abigail for the poor. Their example, she wrote her Braintree friend, might set an example of "industry and economy" for others—except those "so depraved...as to prefer the modes of Paris...to the linsey-woolsey of their own country and the simplicity and Puritanism of New England."[27]

Still, home economy, no matter how rigorously practiced, could not compensate for a shortage of essential goods. In their absence, Mercy attempted to purchase cloth and household commodities through her son Winslow, who had established an importing business on the Continent.

If able to purchase "a yard of... good Irish linen,"[28] Mercy promised to send it to Abigail. But by the summer of 1777, such imports were as scarce as imported foodstuffs. "I have not yet been able to purchase any coffee. Shall remember you when I do," Mercy assured Abigail, as well as "any thing suitable for children's wear."[29]

Domestic profiteering and hoarding, combined with the flight of farm workers into the army, had also eroded supplies of domestic commodities. "If I would give a guinea for a pound of flour, I don't think I could purchase it," Abigail had groused to John earlier that year. "There is such a cry for bread in the town of Boston...the bakers deal out but a loaf a day to the largest families."[30]

With the distanced drumbeat of the Revolution, the chink of coins suddenly became more important than commitment to the cause.

During that spring of 1777, Mercy received an invitation to dine with several Loyalists—a Captain Martin, a Mrs. E., and their friends. Before she could decline, the Loyalist woman had appeared at her door "to acknowledge the obligation," and shamed Mercy into acceptance. She acceded, she later explained to James, because it seemed "prudent to lay aside party distinctions."

While she did "not love the society of those people who love us so little," Mercy also objected to the "malignancy which rages where party prejudices run high." Ever conscious of the sympathetic portraits she had drawn in *The Group* and *The Adulateur* of women helplessly tied to Loyalist husbands, Mercy thus attempted to remain open-minded. Above all, the conscience-stricken author reminded John, she had to meet "the approbation of my own mind...little affected by...any party."[31]

The "simplicity and Puritanism of New England" Mercy had mentioned in her letter to Abigail epitomized the values of the original patriots—fair treatment to others, sacrifice for the common good, equality of civil rights, and a just appeal of grievances to government authorities. In contrast were the more worldly values of money, luxury, and high living that many Americans, neutralists as well as Tories, now embraced.

John Adams disagreed. From his perspective, citizen ambivalence stemmed from another source—the new republic's inability to create a unified government. "It is our weakness and want of power to protect the people that makes Tories and deserters,"[32] he insisted to James in spring 1777. Once the new government was stronger, disloyalties would disappear.

Proof of underlying patriotic sentiment was soon confirmed by the arrival of fifteen thousand men to Saratoga, New York, from the militias of New England, New York, and Virginia. After an initial advance near the town, Burgoyne's army—a motley blend of British, Hessians, Iroquois Indians, and Loyalists—surrendered. By the terms of the treaty, fifty-seven hundred British soldiers agreed to withdraw to Boston before returning to Great Britain.

Months after the Battle of Saratoga—the turning point in the Revolution Mercy felt vindicated after learning that Burgoyne described the Loyalist regiments under his command as the same self-serving lot she had portrayed in *The Adulateur* and *The Group*.

The Loyalists, General Burgoyne reported to Parliament, were a disparate group of men with such "various interests ... [which] rendered all arrangement of them impracticable. One man's views went to the profit he was to enjoy ... another, to the protection of [his] ... district ... a third ... intent upon revenge against his personal enemies."[33] Triumphantly, Mercy later included Burgoyne's report in the index to her *History*.

Even after the victory at Saratoga, many colonists remained ambivalent about the British. From Cambridge, where Burgoyne's men were to be quartered at Harvard, Hannah Winthrop wrote in mid-November that the redcoats were "prancing and patrolling every corner of the town, ornamented with their glittering side of arms," behaving more like a triumphant army than one recently defeated.

Some of her neighbors, the "polite ones say, we ought not to look on them as prisoners ... [but as] persons of distinguished rank ... not view them in the lights of enemies," Hannah added with disgust.

Rumor had it that seven thousand soldiers were to be quartered in Cambridge, provoking her to question the rationale for insisting that "the first University in America ... [be] disbanded for their more genteel accommodation." Where, she lamented to Mercy, "is the stern virtue of an A[dams] who opposed such an infraction in former days?"[34]

Less than a month later, Congress, fearing that the "stern virtue" of the

Revolution was compromised in France, had recalled Commissioner Silas Deane and replaced him with John Adams.

Horrified, Abigail confided her sorrow to Mercy that John, who had recently returned to Braintree from Philadelphia, was again about to leave her and the children, this time on a hazardous transatlantic trip. While empathetic to what Abigail termed John's "painful absence," Mercy, nevertheless, applauded his appointment.

"Great Advantages are often attended with great inconveniences," she wrote Abigail. "If your dearest friend had not abilities to render such important services to his country, he would not be called." Abigail, in fact, was to be congratulated for being "nearly connected with a gentleman whose learning, patriotism and prudence qualify him to negotiate at foreign courts."

Assured of her friend's "public spirit and fortitude," Mercy felt sure that Abigail would never stand in John's way. "Why should you? You are yet young and may set down together many years in peace after he has finished the work to his own honor . . . the satisfaction of his constituents and . . . his conscience."

Moreover, Mercy reminded her, "you cannot, my dear, avoid anticipating the advantages that will probably redound from this honorable embassy to yourself . . . your children and your country."[35]

Without admitting it, Mercy also hoped to reap those advantages for herself. She asked Abigail to remind John of a "certain bargain" he made with her in January 1776 to exchange portraits of the era's important characters. Her own contributions, as Mercy previously explained, would be woefully "inadequate" in comparison to John's new post, which would acquaint him "with the genius . . . taste, and manners . . . of the nobility of Britain, and perhaps . . . [other] dignified personages."

Newly inspired to resume her *History*, Mercy admitted she would even be "gratified with one letter from the Court of France."[36]

In February 1778, the same month that Adams and his ten-year-old son, John Quincy, departed for France, the Massachusetts legislature ordered the Loyalists to take a vow of allegiance. Among them was James's sixty-four-year-old cousin, Edward Winslow, that "most malignant of your foes," Mercy wrote, who subsequently appeared at a Plymouth town meeting and "cast the illiberal reflections"[37] upon her husband.

That May James lost the election as Plymouth representative to the Massachusetts House. Stunned, James complained to Sam Adams that "the cunning of a party, here...have even made use of the Tories to prevent my being chose by my town."[38]

Simultaneous with that loss was the rise of the neutralist party, headed by John Hancock, Boston's wealthiest merchant and the former president of the Continental Congress. Longing to become the first governor of the State of Massachusetts, Hancock had shrewdly been increasing his visibility for years. In 1777, having returned from Philadelphia "under the escort of light dragoons...the ringing of bells...discharge of thirteen cannon,"[39] he donated vast sums to the restoration of Boston.

Hancock's gifts to the city and its citizens were nearly legendary: the revival of Boston Common, the payment of the rents of widows and orphans, the repair of tenant properties, the donation of one hundred fifty cords of wood to the public almshouse, and the forgiveness of debts in paper money rather than in scarce hard currency. By December 1777, Hancock was accordingly chosen moderator of Boston's town meetings and reelected to the Continental Congress.

The following March, the merchant received another boost in status when owners of a privateer presented him with a handsome gold-hued coach. Thereafter, the carriage became Hancock's official vehicle, accompanied by his handsomely liveried servants, caparisoned horses, and fifty horsemen from his private corps of cadets.

To Mercy's husband, James, Hancock's display was a "pompous parade." The American public "must have an idol," he complained to Sam Adams, who had bitterly tangled with Hancock during the Hutchinson administration.

Pitted against Hancock's glamorous and paradoxically aristocratic image, the self-sacrificing "virtues" of the Warrens and their patriotic circle seemed dull and stern. The result of Hancock's largesse—his bribes, as James described them to Sam—was that "[y]our dear town have...lost their compass and...lost sight of their old principles and policy."[40]

While James morosely accepted his defeat in the Massachusetts House,

Mercy fumed that Plymouth had forsaken "a man who for many years . . . at the expense of his own health, fortune, and happiness . . . aimed to promote their interest."

Nevertheless, she saw one advantage to James's forced retirement from Massachusetts politics; finally they might have more time together. Perhaps, as Mercy hoped in a letter to her husband during the summer of 1778, "your duty will not urge you in future to be much separated from your family, that we may shortly sit down in private tranquility until nature [death] makes the last demand."[41]

11

"War has ever been unfriendly to virtue"

FOR TWO YEARS, Mercy had worried about her father, James Otis, Sr., whose days were spent "on a bed of pain verging fast towards the closing scene."[1] When on November 8 or 9, 1778, a messenger arrived at North Street, announcing that Colonel Otis's condition was grave, Mercy rushed off to West Barnstable.

By the time she arrived, it was too late. "I saw my father no more, as my foreboding heart presaged. He breathed his last sigh . . . before I reached his now desolate mansion,"[2] she sadly wrote Abigail weeks later.

Today, the slate-gray tombstone of James Otis, Sr., etched with the face of a winged cherub, stands above other headstones near the stone wall bordering Old King's Highway, a memorial to the self-taught lawyer who sent his eldest daughter across the road to study with Rev. John Russell.

As the winds of the North Atlantic blew across Boston's South Shore, bringing the snow of a particularly harsh winter to Plymouth, other events set Mercy on edge. The first was the shipwreck of the twenty-gun brig *General Arnold*, which, having sailed from Boston, had anchored on Christmas Eve in Plymouth bay. During the night, heavy currents loosened the anchor, moving the vessel onto the White Flats sandbar and forcing the one-hundred-seven-man crew to scramble onto the quarter deck. By Christmas night, high winds and a raging blizzard had killed seventy of the sailors from frostbite.

Coincidental with the *General Arnold*'s departure from Boston, the Warrens' third son, Charles, sailed to Plymouth on another ship. A dutiful, attractive youth, Charles was "Goodness itself"[3] as Mercy once scribbled upon one of his letters from Harvard.

The hours had ticked away on Christmas Day without news of the youth's whereabouts, until finally Mercy learned that the sloop carrying Charles had survived the storm.

Two other Warren sons were also missing from North Street that Christmas. James, Jr., was a lieutenant in the Navy's flagship thirty-six-gun frigate the *Alliance*. Less explicable was the absence of Winslow, who, rumor had it, spent that fall in "gaming, and the fashionable amusements."[4] But of that Mercy remained silent, discreetly writing John Adams that December that her eldest sons had reached "an age that makes it proper they should leave the parental roof."[5]

Nevertheless, with only two sons "in the parlor," the recent death of her father, and James's year-round duties to the Navy Board, Mercy felt abandoned. To alleviate her loneliness, Abigail sent her namesake, pretty Abigail II, or Nabby, for an extended visit to Plymouth. In return, a grateful Mercy offered to tutor the thirteen-year-old.

That arrangement pleased everyone. "If your little good girl is unhappy she conceals it from me, for she smiles as if she enjoyed herself and says Plymouth is as pleasant as either Boston or Braintree,"[6] Mercy assured Abigail on January 18.

Gratified, Abigail replied that she had sent Nabby to Plymouth hoping "her company might . . . elude the lonely hour," and knowing the girl would "reap advantages from residing with a lady she could not fail . . . loving and respecting."[7]

In February, Nabby confided to her teenage cousin Elizabeth Cranch, "I am quite contented here."[8] The Warren sons Henry and George were pleasant companions, and she had enjoyed visiting Mercy's closest neighbor and friend, Ellen Lothrop. She also befriended young Sallie and Betsy Watson, whose Loyalists affiliations, at Mercy's insistence, she had overlooked. "I don't think myself capable of meddling with politics," Nabby explained, "and therefore can have friends upon either party."[9]

One glittering March morning after an ice storm, Mercy wrote Abigail that Nabby was a girl "who I really love, and love her more the longer she resides with me. In future I shall call her my Nabby and back my claim with the promise of her papa to whom I shall appeal if you monopolize too much."

Enclosed was Nabby's "manuscript," a collection of her studies at North Street. The youngster's stay had proven "an agreeable entertainment,"[10] Mercy reiterated, one apparently so mutual that Nabby stayed until May.

"So I must give up my little companion, my young friend," Mercy finally wrote that spring. "Your claim is prior, your title cannot be contested, but remember she is not all *your own.*"[11]

A year later, the teenager still talked about the winter she "so agreeably spent with" Mercy.[12] Two years later, Nabby begged to return, but Abigail had refused, admitting, "I am jealous of trusting her there again least she should love it better than home."[13]

Along with Mercy's delight in Nabby was despair over her historical project. "Alas Clio [the Greek muse of history] is deaf," she admitted to Abigail, "perhaps irrecoverably stunned till the noise of war shall cease." In fact, the nine muses, "sickened by the unpromising aspect of this decayed village" had probably "bid an everlasting adieu."[14]

Mercy's isolation on Boston's South Shore was only partly to blame. With the theater of war relocated to New York and the south, reports about battles drifted in slowly. John Adams's trip to France was another obstacle. He still considered Mercy "the most accomplished lady in America"[15] (besides his wife, Abigail), but his letters arrived infrequently.

No less frustrated was James at the Navy Board. While "determined never to desert the colors I helped to boost,"[16] as he had promised John, keeping those colors aloft was difficult because of a lack of funds.

By May 1778, while six American ships awaited repairs in Boston Harbor, the French fleet, under the command of Charles-Henri, Count d'Estaing, arrived with badly needed supplies for the Continental Army. Those ships, too, demanded expensive refitting.

"Remember the embarrassment of the Navy Board for want of money," James reminded Sam Adams in Philadelphia; the board, at that moment, could not "command 500 dollar."[17]

Equally embarrassing was the penurious stipend allowed James and his fellow board members for living expenses—sums lower than those paid naval carpenters and riggers—which forced him and fellow directors to subsidize their own room and board.

Another aggravation was the interference of certain members of the Continental Congress. "Why, when you have appointed captains . . . can't it be left to us to say which shall go in any ship here?"[18] James complained.

Essentially, Congress seemed indifferent to the Navy's potentially key role in the war, even after that summer's failed American-French effort to retake Newport, Rhode Island.

By late October, James sent a letter of resignation to Sam Adams to be forwarded to the president of the Continental Congress. "This business is very laborious, requiring close and constant attention," James explained, leaving him "no time to attend to my family and private affairs. The honor of holding this place will not compensate."[19]

Alarmed, Sam begged James to change his mind. "If the war should continue longer . . . it will be conducted in such a manner as will render a large army less necessary . . . [enabling] us to be at greater expense for an American navy."[20] Ultimately, James agreed.

Meanwhile, he and Mercy became increasingly dismayed by what they realized was the rise of a new materialistic class, weary with the deprivations of the Revolution.

Admittedly, "[a] state of war has ever been . . . unfriendly to virtue," Mercy wrote John that autumn. Nevertheless, she was stunned at the "total change of manners" among her countrymen. Rapacity, she added, in phrases as fiery as those from the Reverend Russell's pulpit, combined with "profusion, pride and servility and almost every vice" had become the vogue.

The only remedy would be the arrival of some undiscovered "genius" to reveal the "feet of clay" belonging to the ostentatious John Hancock, whose cunning courtship of the public mesmerized them into believing that his values were "pure gold."[21]

Nor did Mercy restrict her despair to her private letters. By October 10, 1778, she had poured her outrage into a poem, "The Genius of America weeping the absurd Follies of the Day," which was published in the *Boston Gazette*.

The concept, Mercy explained years later, was inspired by a "remarkable depravity of manners" precipitated by "a state of war; a relaxation of government; the sudden acquisition of fortune; a depreciating currency; and a new intercourse with foreign nations."[22]

Like her satirical plays, Mercy's imagery in that poem is bold—almost blatantly sexual. The seductive pleasures of black market or smuggled goods were "selfish passions" tempted by "pleasure's soft debilitating charms," which swooned in "full riot in cold avarice' arms." Even as "our country bleeds and bleeds at every pore," gold became "the deity whom all adore."[23]

Equally moralistic was the anonymous publication of *The Motley Assembly*, a satire mocking the colonists' wavering, self-serving political affiliations. The play opens with a Mrs. Taxall and Mrs. Flourish, whose ambitious daughters, mourning the departure of British frivolities, were now forced to endure the more sober amusements of the Whigs.

"O why has Heaven permitted our passive sex to be so long deceived ... by the idle and groundless opinion of the superior wisdom of the male sex!" Mrs. Flourish moans in one of *The Motley Assembly*'s opening lines.

Mr. Runt and Mr. Turncoat, in turn, admit that their sudden new "sympathies" for the Whigs are merely a contrivance, adopted to win over America's newly "patriotic" women. Underscoring the theme of political insincerity are warnings from Careless to his amoral friend, Aid, to beware of those "who professes themselves Whigs;—They are ... the most dangerous characters among you."[24]

Not only did *The Motley Assembly*'s author explain he was a man but Mercy's usual cast of characters was missing. The play's message, nevertheless, echoed the "absurd follies of the day" portrayed in Mercy's "The Genius of America," leading some scholars to attribute it to her.

In May 1779, James was reelected to the House of Representatives and appointed to the Continental Congress. By early June, he had refused the latter post, writing Mercy that her "little trembling nerves" were "among the influential reasons."[25]

Those nerves probably related to the sorrow she felt after learning about the May 24 death of Hannah Winthrop's beloved husband, John. To console her friend, Mercy wrote a poem titled "On the Death of the Hon. John Winthrop Esq., L.L.D. Hollisian Professor of Mathematics and Natural

Philosophy, at Harvard College," addressed "to his Lady," which appeared on the front page of the *Independent Chronicle* on October 21, 1778.

In a memorial to the couple's fierce patriotism, Mercy compared them to the heroic figures of ancient Greece and Rome, extolling them as the "good Cornelias and her Arrias fair," who "nobly struggle in a vicious age / To stem the torrent of despotic rage."[26]

One consequence of that rage was inflation. "You can hardly conceive what state things are in here," James wrote Elbridge Gerry in March 1779. "We suffer in common the depreciation of our currency, and...have a real scarcity of provisions. Bread, especially of which in some places there is actually a famine. Meal...23 dollars bushel, flour 40 dollars."[27]

By June, the economic situation had become even grimmer. "Bohea tea was 40 dollars a pound, Indian corn was 40 dollars per bushel and meat from 6 to 8 per pound," James reported to John Adams. Paradoxically, the colonists snapped up costly European luxury goods, exacerbating America's foundering balance of payments. "If the subject was not serious...it would be laughable," James added, describing how Bostonians lusted after "gauze" and "other geegaws" characteristic of the era's "vanity, folly and extravagance."[28]

How much longer, Mercy asked John, did he think the patriots would be "distressed by...gamblers, courtiers and stock jobbers." In Boston, "the votaries of pleasure...the men of taste and refinement, make no inconsiderable figure. Some deify...fashion...in a French, a British or American dress: while others worship...at the shrine of Plutus [god of wealth]."

Even so, she noted, "the old Republicans (a solitary few)...still persevere, their hands unstained by bribes, though poverty stares them in the face."[29]

Weeks after John's unexpected return from France, Mercy's letter arrived in Boston, where he was writing a new constitution for Massachusetts. Agreeing that the "factious demagogue...assisted by a numerous band of mercantile speculators...on both side[s] the water" had shattered the old patriotic concepts, John predicted the trend would persist. Nevertheless, he assured Mercy, those who "corrupt our simplicity will be restrained."[30]

Perhaps Adams was right: Patriotism, a return of sincerity, hard work, and respect for the rights of the people would eventually triumph, Mercy opined in her poem "Simplicity." Within it, Mercy traced man's birth in "virgin form" through the fall of Rome to "George's folly." Yet the latter would inspire revenge upon "Proud Thames," whose commercial ports would be possess'd by hated foreign courts" once "heaven confirms the independent states."

Even so, Mercy warned, America might also perish "in the vortex of European crimes"[31] if its citizens failed to return to patriotic values.

Henceforth, that theme became Mercy's signature, displayed in printer's ink as boldly as the banner of thirteen stars and stripes sewn by a widowed Philadelphia seamstress that waved above the battlefields of the Continental Army.

For all Mercy and James's resentment of fashionable frivolities, their son Winslow courted the high life. During rare visits to Plymouth, the young man appeared dutiful enough, but by late autumn 1779, more rumors spread that he was gambling. At first, the elder Warrens were not concerned, for as youngsters their sons had probably played card games like whist and loo at Mercy's embroidered card table.

But gambling for high stakes in the backrooms of coffee houses, taverns, and private drawing rooms was a different matter. Exacerbating the elder Warrens' fears were reports that Winslow socialized with a notorious man who drew youth into high-stakes games.

Mercy, accordingly, dashed off a warning to Winslow on December 1, followed three days later by another. His companion was a "character dangerous to society," known for his "external appearance of affluence and... gaudy show of wealth," beneath which were "paws extended as a beast of prey" upon the sons of rich men.

"I wish to see you soon," Mercy announced, believing that it was his duty to write her "as she descends" in life, expecting that "her children will smooth the declivity" and "oblige the... affectionate mother."[32]

Even with the approach of Christmas and the arrival of her beloved husband, James, and other relatives at North Street, Winslow had not appeared. Soon afterward, Mercy's disappointment turned to rage when he responded with a cheeky letter that expressed admiration for *Chesterfield's Letters.*

Reminiscent of *The Prince* by seventeenth-century Florentine writer Niccolò Machiavelli, Lord Chesterfield's book of manners urged young men to behave cunningly to achieve status and wealth. In London, where the *Letters* were first published in 1774 by Philip Dormer Stanhope, the fourth earl of Chesterfield, the book immediately became controversial. The volume taught "the morals of a whore, and the manners of a dancing master," observed Dr. Samuel Johnson. Even so, if the "immorality was removed," *Chesterfield's Letters* "should be put into the hands of every young gentleman."[33]

Above all, Chesterfield believed that "the manner of doing things is often more important than the things themselves." Since the purpose of his *Letters* was "to enable worldly advancement," civility had less to do with compassion than with self-interest. To treat people well was important, but only because they may "some time or other . . . have it in their power to be of use to you."[34]

Mercy was appalled. Tactfully, she conceded that she understood Winslow's admiration of the *Letters*'s fine diction and harmonious prose. Yet, when Chesterfield "sacrifices truth to convenience, probity to pleasure, virtue to the graces . . . we cannot but pity the man as much as we admire the author. I think it by no means necessary that a gentleman . . . of good breeding, should drop his humanity . . . renounce the moral feelings, or . . . his life should be a contrast to every precept of Christianity."[35]

Especially obnoxious was Chesterfield's attitude toward women, whom he described as "only children of a larger growth . . . [with] entertaining tattle, and sometimes wit . . . A man of sense only trifles with them, plays with them . . . flatters them, as he does a sprightly, forward child; but . . . neither consult them . . . nor trusts them with serious matters; though he often makes them believe that he does both."[36]

Seething, Mercy informed Winslow that she thought Chesterfield's "contempt poured upon so fair a part of the creation . . . beneath the resentment of a woman of education and reflection." Above all, "I ever considered human nature as the same in both sexes."

Hoping, nevertheless, that Winslow would visit, Mercy closed her letter with another appeal to his filial loyalty. "I expect the pleasure of seeing you here daily. . . and [not] neglect a point of politeness to a lady, as well as duty, to a most affectionate mother."[37]

In Braintree, Abigail Adams, who had just finished reading *Chesterfield's Letters,* was also outraged. "I found enough to satisfy me, that his Lordship with all his elegance and graces, was a hypocritical polished libertine," Abigail bristled to Mercy on February 28.

Most rankling was Chesterfield's approval of deception, prompting "the most immoral pernicious and libertine principals into the mind of youth." The writer may have had an "elegant pen," but was "poisoned with . . . libertinism."

Abigail then asked for a copy of Mercy's letter to Winslow. Determined to correct Chesterfield's "abuse of our sex,"[38] John Adams's feisty wife arranged for its subsequent publication in the January 1781 *Independent Chronicle.*

If nothing else, Winslow's elusiveness, combined with rumors about his gambling, forced Mercy to realize that the patriotic ideals of honesty, fairness, and equality were passé. A shift in moral values had taken place, a tidal wave that swept away New England's Puritanical values and neoclassical ideals on a frothy tide of new money, profiteering, and materialism.

"Fellows who would have cleaned my shoes five years ago, have amassed fortunes, and are riding in chariots,"[39] James had grumbled to John Adams the previous summer. Boston suddenly teemed with men who acquired "new money" through dubious means and displayed it through ostentatious "dress, furniture, equipage and living."[40]

Years later, Mercy accounted for that transformation in her *History* by a "depreciation of paper [money] . . . a sudden accumulation of property by privateering, by speculation, by accident, or fraud, [which] placed many in the lap of affluence."[41] Essentially, Mercy was describing the nouveau riche of the Revolution, who, like the profiteers of any war, shrewdly amassed their fortunes.

By late 1779, while "drudging at the Navy Board,"[42] James, after learning that Congress had failed to appoint him to its Board of Admiralty, once again threatened to resign.

From Philadelphia, Massachusetts patriot James Lovell blamed the slight upon anonymous letters accusing James of pocketing handsome commissions. Furious, James retorted that he had engaged in public service "from the purest principles," sacrificing time, his business, and his family for the common good. Such accusations were not only "groundless and ridiculous," but the obvious work of certain "displaced officers and connections" who harbored "resentment and revenge."[43]

Foremost among those connections was John Hancock, a man whom James had long resented for his ostentation and bribes, but with whom he had maintained a cordial relationship. Subsequent to the defeat at Newport, Hancock had lavished huge sums of money upon the French with banquets and entertainments at a time when, James peevishly noted, American sailors and officers of the Navy Board were "starving on their bare pay."[44] When Hancock preempted decisions about the refitting of French vessels, which, to the former merchant's credit, he subsidized out of his personal fortune, James remained silent.

One incident in September 1778 had finally broken James's patience—Hancock's *faux pas* at a dinner for French officers at his Beacon Hill banquet hall. The guests of honor were generals d'Estaing and Lafayette, accompanied by James and other Navy Board directors, officers, and legislators. The dinner began smoothly enough with a series of toasts to the French, punctuated by thirteen salutes from cannons adjacent to Hancock's mansion, but when they toasted the U.S. Congress, no cannons sounded.

Embarrassed by that breach in protocol, James later confronted Hancock, demanding to know why Congress was not "treated with the highest marks of respect." Curtly, Hancock replied that "he had his orders."[45] After that, the two men became estranged. Nor, in the ensuing months, would their differences be resolved, even though Hancock—the great man,[46] as the patriots mockingly dubbed him—worked assiduously to preserve French goodwill.

A month later, when Hancock hosted a ball in his concert hall to commemorate the departure of the French to the South, James, Sam Adams, and other patriots refused to attend because they considered it another insult to American sailors.

On September 4, 1780, Hancock won a landslide victory for governorship of Massachusetts. The Warrens were hardly surprised. Should James be reelected to the assembly, he intended to nominate Sam Adams as secretary even while knowing that those who "don't worship devoutly" at Hancock's feet were unlikely to succeed. In point of fact, Mercy's husband explained, he was "content to retire into private life where I can...say that I have in no instance deviated from the principles I professed."[47]

When, in November 1780, James was reelected and offered the lieutenant governorship of Massachusetts under Hancock, he refused it. "I am now a member of the Navy Board," he rationalized to Jeremiah Powell, president of the Massachusetts Senate, explaining that was "incompatible ...while I should be Lieutenant Governor."[48]

Privately, James was also disgusted with the public's attitude toward Sam Adams. "Neither your beloved town, the county, the state or the two houses have shown any gratitude for your...great services...the man who had the greatest hand in the great revolution in the world," he wrote his friend.[49]

While James knew his standards were passé, he and Mercy expected their sons to honor them: James, Jr., was already serving as a marine lieutenant on the *Alliance*. Winslow, however, had suddenly announced his plans to travel to the Netherlands as a commission agent. He would sail at the earliest possible date, as soon as frozen Boston Harbor thawed.

His announcement sent Mercy into a panic. Writing James on March 15 from the "gloomy northeast corner of her room" as the "rough Boreas [wind] whistles in my ear...and...no mortal voice" was heard, she whimpered that "[m]y children leave me early and I seem to grow useless to them."

In a self-flagellating assessment of her fifty-two years, the author plaintively added, "I am sometimes ready to think you could serve the public as well, and perhaps, better, unencumbered by anxieties for me."[50]

Two days later Mercy wrote James again. "No Winslow yet, and it seems by your letter he is soon to leave America." The youth "knows not, nor ever will, the affectionate fondness that agitates my frame." Even so, should he arrive, she was determined to "put on a cheerful face."[51]

Prevented from traveling to Boston because of the harsh weather, Mercy resorted to her pen, again lecturing Winslow about the "barriers of virtue" he would encounter in Europe with its "prostitution of moral sentiment." While having no reason to suspect Winslow of "criminal passions," she again warned that his "taste for elegant amusements may be carried too high."[52]

She was, or so it now seemed to Mercy, always abandoned by key male figures in her life. "I will not complain, but is it not singular that I am always so long in expectation?" she fretted to James on March 26.

"Do I raise my hopes too high? ... Is it not natural ... for the mother to look with longing eyes after her children? I begin to think Winslow does not intend [to visit]. I have been so many times disappointed that I feel ... as if I never was to see him more."

In an uncharacteristically peevish rage, Mercy then scrawled, "What a trifle it appears to me for a man to go from Boston to Plymouth! I would have rode it over twenty times since last December to have saved one of my family half the pain I have felt in a week, shut out from all communication with them ... What signifies to sit at midnight and sigh after distant friends and tell how I love and long to see my children—my husband? I will not. I give them my best wishes and will try to repose on the pillow of rest the weary lids of your affectionate ... M. Warren."[53]

PART III

The Patriot Historian

12

Views from Neponset Hill

THE HARSH STORMS THAT BATTERED New England in late March 1781 delayed Mercy's letter to James for nearly a week.

His affection, James finally replied on a blustery Sunday, April 2, was "as ardent as ever." He hoped to return to Plymouth in a few weeks' time. "Don't you think I love my boys? You can't tell how often I think of their smiling countenances... How often do you think my imagination forms a picture of their mamma? An imagination must be good indeed to draw... all the sweetness of the original."[1]

Winslow, James added, was traveling to Plymouth the next day, accompanied by several friends. In preparation, Mercy had scurried around Plymouth buying delicacies to honor the Warrens' hospitable reputation. "I hope," she confided to James that same stormy Sunday, "they will keep the appointment, as you know the difficulties of... entertain[ing] strangers in such a barren place."[2]

A day or two later Winslow arrived alone, explaining that his friends had canceled at the last moment. Infuriated by their "frivolous excuse," Mercy restrained herself, venting privately to James that "I have had more fatigue and... expense in the... last year to make preparation for good company than fifty dinners would have been in Boston." The time, she bitterly noted, might have been spent instead "to apply more to my book."[3]

Even so, Mercy savored every moment of Winslow's visit, but became morose when on April 5 he announced he was leaving for Barton the next morning. He promised to return before his ship sailed, but Mercy was dubious. Indeed, as the weeks passed and Winslow's sailing date approached, she decided to join him in Boston. There, while waiting to see Winslow, she wrote John Adams, asking him to look after her son. Winslow's interests, she explained, "are chiefly of a commercial nature," but with John's help and advice, they might be "properly improved by industry and observation."[4]

On Friday morning, May 19, the date of Winslow's scheduled departure, the sky looked strange. At dawn, the sun rose blood-red and the clouds had an odd "brassy appearance,"[5] as Dr. Cotton Tufts, Abigail Adams's uncle, noted. After a thundershower, a heavy black cloud loomed overhead, turning the sky so dark that by eleven a.m., reported the *Boston Country Journal*, even "in a room with three windows . . . large print could not be read."[6]

As the encroaching blackness covered the skies, nervous schoolmasters dismissed their students. Citizens crowded into the churches. Families ate their noon dinner by candlelight. Fowls took to their roost, woodcocks "whistled . . . frogs peeped."

"People in the streets grew melancholy, and fear seized on all except sailors,"[7]noted a diarist in Salem. To the religious and superstitious the darkness implied Judgment Day. More scientifically inclined citizens blamed it on a planetary disturbance, a comet, or the eruption of a volcano.

By late afternoon, the sky finally lightened, but the sun turned "extremely red." The air smelled like swamp fire, and, subsequently, a smoky scum settled upon tubs of rainwater. A similar film also appeared on New Hampshire's snow-capped mountains. Ultimately, scientific men like Dr. Tufts concluded the cause was heavy smoke drifting toward the coast "brought along by air currents"[8] from forest fires in upstate New York.

Mercy, who disdained superstition, probably accepted that explanation. Still, the advent of the Dark Day, as it was later called, must have worsened her anxieties about Winslow's journey.

Soon afterward, still more gloomy news arrived about the May 12 fall of Charleston, South Carolina. Its impact upon the departure of the *Pallas* is unknown, but in any case, Winslow's sail date was postponed until June 3. That same day in Plymouth, Mercy's friend Ellen Lothrop died.

"What unspeakable loss do I sustain in the death of this worthy woman?" Mercy wrote James from North Street, lamenting the other "excellent friends" she had lost in recent years. Still not knowing of Winslow's departure, she added, "Had he everything he needed, and did he go off in good spirits?" If not, "tell him . . . I expect to hear from him, and by every opportunity afterward."[9]

For all of Mercy's pleas, it was months before either she or James heard from Winslow. During the *Pallas*'s transatlantic crossing, a British squadron commanded by Admiral Richard Edwards seized the ship at Newfoundland and forced it to land at St. John's. There the *Pallas* bobbed at anchor for weeks, awaiting instructions from British authorities.

By August 18, the Warrens had heard the news. Before Mercy loomed images of Winslow as a prisoner of war, "pale and emaciated by hunger and hardship reduced to . . . distresses."

The next day, however, by an extraordinary coincidence, the *Alliance*, the thirty-six-gun frigate upon which their eldest son, James, served, arrived in Boston from Newfoundland after encountering the captured *Pallas*. From reports passed between the ships he learned that Admiral Edwards had treated Winslow well.

Heartened, Mercy wrote Winslow, "I now understand you have not fallen into the hands of an ungenerous enemy—but that humanity and politeness . . . distinguish the commander . . . at St. John's." In the meanwhile, she hoped Winslow would make the most of his anticipated release in England before traveling to the Netherlands. Possibly the sojourn would have even "greater advantages than if you had pursued your first plan."[10]

Simultaneous with Winslow's capture had been his oldest brother James's tumultuous crossing from France with the *Alliance*'s commander, Captain Pierre Landais. In spring of 1780, Landais had bitterly quarreled with squadron commander John Paul Jones and even ordered the frigate to fire upon the *Bonhomme Richard* during a sea battle. In reaction, Benjamin Franklin, then minister plenipotentiary and head of the European Marine Committee, informed Captain Landais of his imminent dismissal.

Disregarding Franklin, Landais appealed to his rival and ministerial colleague Arthur Lee, who permitted him to sail for Boston on June 1. Once at sea, the overwrought Landais ordered several officers into the brig, gave orders to reverse course, and even menaced Arthur Lee with a carving knife for helping himself first to roast pig in the wardroom.

Twice the *Alliance*'s exasperated crew mutinied until finally they coerced the raving captain into ceding control of the ship. Subsequent to the *Alliance*'s arrival in Boston, Captain Landais was carried off the ship for a court martial.

That summer, too, a scorching drought had raged over Massachusetts, parching the hay and corn and resulting in a thin harvest. By August, as drying leaves began to fall, Mercy realized that her sons, too, were inevitably drifting away. The Warrens' third son, Charles, had returned to study at Harvard, where he would be joined by his younger brother Henry. With Winslow overseas and James, Jr., in the Navy, that meant only fourteen-year-old George remained at home.

"To allay her fears about loneliness," Mercy wrote Charles of her expectation to enjoy "the society of my three young sons," in isolated Plymouth that winter. She remained there only out of "maternal duty" while "your good father must necessarily continue almost wholly at Boston."

The winter of 1781, she predicted, would be the Warren brothers' last time together for "the calls of education or business must separate you...I hope, therefore, it will be spent in a manner that will enable each one to look back with pleasure on...January and February."[11]

Even Mercy's lonely friend Abigail Adams noted, during a visit, that Plymouth seemed incompatible with Mercy's appetite. "You must quit Plymouth, you who so well love society and who always adorn it, must not be secluded," she urged Mercy on September 1. If only she could move to Braintree, which would "have greatly added to the happiness of your ever affectionate, Abigail."[12]

A new home near Boston would not only bring Mercy's family closer together, but provide more immediate access to news about the Revolution.

In Cambridge, the same day of Abigail's letter, Hannah Winthrop was also thinking about Mercy's *History*. Prompted by an announcement in the *Boston Advertiser* that the "Lady of M. General Warren intended to favor the world with the History of America," Hannah congratulated her on the news. Like Mercy's other friends, she was proud of her talents and looked forward to a book from "the fair hand of so good a penwoman."

That notice also mentioned the plans of a "History of a particular state from the other lady," but, Hannah added, that writer was no competition.

Mercy, above others, would "oblige the world, for the honor of America, with her arrangement of facts, which will certainly make as conspicuous a figure as any era in the history of the world."[13]

The *Advertiser*'s announcement that Mercy had resumed work on her *History* appeared after her meeting with Arthur Lee. Apparently, Mercy had charmed the former minister plenipotentiary, for subsequently he wrote James that it was "no flattery to say that I never met with a lady whose conversation pleased me more."[14]

Later, when James described his comments to John Adams, the latter wryly responded, "My most profound respect to Mrs. Warren. I dread her History more than that of the Abbey [the Catholic church]. I want to know in what colors she will draw Brother Lee. He little knew what eyes were upon him."[15]

By late summer 1781, Winslow had arrived in England, where he befriended three young fellow Americans—John Temple, the son-in-law of James Bowdoin; John Tyler, in London on business; and artist John Trumbull, son of the Connecticut governor. The Warrens' son, Trumbull noted, was a "somewhat amphibious character, and withal young, handsome and giddy."[16] For six weeks the foursome gadded around London, enjoying its sights, theaters, and gaming tables. All seemed well until they heard about Benedict Arnold's treasonous attempts to capture West Point.

Even before that news the British treated foreigners suspected of espionage harshly. One recent victim was Henry Laurens, former president of the Continental Congress and a passenger aboard the *Pallas* that summer, who was seized for carrying "treasonous" papers and imprisoned in London's infamous Tower. By Saturday, November 18, subsequent to the news about Benedict Arnold, John Trumbull was arrested. Then came a warrant for John Tyler, whom Winslow helped escape to the Continent. Mysteriously, the Warrens' son lingered in London.

Two days after Tyler's escape, Mercy received a letter from her son—the first since his departure. Delighted by Winslow's assurances that his days were spent "reading, writing and reflecting," Mercy assumed he must by then have sailed for France or Holland where he would meet "some of the first characters in Europe." Still, she could not resist reminding her son that while his letters of introduction would lead to a "polite reception" to important men, it was Winslow's "own honor and probity that will secure" him "esteem."[17]

In January 1781, British authorities seized those "introductory letters" and Mercy's correspondence when they placed Winslow in prison. Four days later, Lord Hillsborough, secretary of state for the colonies, having read them, ordered a meeting with the youth. After reprimanding Winslow for visiting the imprisoned John Trumbull, Hillsborough confided that he was "prepossessed" in Winslow's favor.

"He and others to whom my papers were consigned, lavished many praises on my mother's letters—said 'they would do honor to the greatest writer that ever wrote' and added 'Mr. Warren, hope you will profit by her instructions and advice,'"[18] Winslow reported to Mercy.

Subsequent to his release, Winslow sailed for France where, presumably, he would visit John Adams.

During their winter recess from Harvard, Charles and Henry Warren dutifully returned to Plymouth. By then, memories of Nabby's company the previous winter had prompted Mercy to invite a new guest to North Street—this time her niece Betsy Sever. One December day as a fierce storm whiplashed the region, blanketing Plymouth and Boston in snow, Mercy suggested that her sons and Betsy write descriptions of the weather.

Charles, Mercy proudly reported to James, wrote "blank verse at once descriptive, poetical, sentimental and moral. Henry sketched in prose his ideas . . . George attempted a letter to Papa . . . but disliking his own composition . . . postponed till Monday. Betsy . . . complained to me . . . that she was very cold, by a good fire, and wished Aunt Warren would finish her letter."[19]

Within a few weeks they were all scattered again—Betsy, back to her parents in Weymouth, Charles and Henry to Cambridge.

By January 2, during still another heavy snowstorm, Hannah Winthrop described her delight in Henry, who, like his brothers before him, boarded with her at Harvard.

"Young Henry trips down stairs from his studies . . . thinks I should not be so much alone. His young susceptible heart [was] compassionate [about] my solitude," Hannah wrote, even though he did not grasp the "subject of my contemplation"—memories of her late husband, John. "Teach me," Hannah pleaded, "to loosen these cords of affliction." Longing to see Mercy, she remained disappointed "at your not favoring me with a visit, especially, considering your attractions at Cambridge."[20]

Several factors had prevented that trip, the first, the unusually harsh winter weather of 1780–81, which created deep snowdrifts along the icy roads. A second deterrent was Mercy's eye infection, a "cold fixing there"[21] as she wrote Abigail.

Brighter news arrived on January 28 from Mercy's husband, James, who had just purchased Governor Hutchinson's former country home in Milton on Neponset Hill. Its seller, a Mr. Broome, had demanded a high price— a steep £3,000—which, as James later explained to Winslow, commanded "every resource"[22] not otherwise invested. Even so, the house seemed worth it, for it was elegant, airy, and close to Boston.

Thrilled, Mercy jested about "what sort of a mistress shall I make at the head of a family of husbandmen and dairymaids." Although the Hutchinson property was pricey, she hoped James "would not be anxious about paying for the place," for "we shall get through that by and by."[23]

The main house, a spacious pitched-roof and gabled dwelling of English white oak, stood on a hill near a bridge over the Neponset River. Years earlier Hutchinson had planted two majestic rows of elm trees that still lined its entrance. To the east stood a coach house, stables, and barns; to the west, a farmhouse and outbuildings. Overlooking Boston Harbor, the property included fields and orchards. Added to those features was the property's location only eleven miles from Boston and six from the Adamses' cottage in Braintree.

In addition to its beauty and convenience, the newly purchased estate symbolized the Warrens' revenge over Hutchinson. Nor could the couple have forgotten Mercy's triumphant lines of "The Squabble of the Sea Nymphs," published seventeen years earlier, whose nymphs, having rejected British tea, celebrated, as "the ocean rebounds and songs of triumph rings...Neponset Hills."[24]

Ironically, other troubles clouded the Warrens' delight. In January 1781 after reading an alarming newspaper story, Mercy wrote Winslow, "Not a word have we had since ours of August twenty third but we hear you took passage in the vestal frigate which . . . we learn arrival safely in England and that the honorable Mr. Laurens was immediately committed to the Tower." Did he expect that "your mamma, always so apprehensive for your safety, can be quite easy till she hears you have left that hostile island?"[25]

In contrast to Winslow's ongoing silence were the doting attentions of Mercy's two sons at Harvard. On March 4, Abigail wrote that a day earlier Charles and Henry stopped in Braintree to breakfast with her en route to Plymouth. Delighted, she felt for "these young gentlemen a particular affection, not only from their own amiable . . . dispositions," but for the sincere "affection which I bear to their most excellent mamma."

Best of all, Abigail added, she took "particular satisfaction . . . in the idea of soon having her for her neighbor." For months from Europe, John had been sending his straitened wife foreign goods that she, in turn, sold to friends and neighbors—among them tea, paper, fabrics, and handkerchiefs. Often, Mercy acted as her agent and sold them with varying degrees of success in Plymouth.

"With regard to our commercial affairs, you must have misunderstood me with regard to tea, because I never had any," Abigail thus explained in her letter. "The handkerchiefs sent the other day were a mistake, the flowered papers . . . always contained the colored handkerchiefs and I did not think to open them."[26]

Henceforth, their proximity would prevent such miscommunications.

In late May 1781 the Warrens finally heard from Winslow in Holland. His letter was a great relief, his father, James, replied on June 3—the same day he, Mercy, and George arrived "to reside at Milton upon the farm that was Gov. Hutchinson's." Winslow would be thrilled with "our new habitation . . . [which] falls within your taste."

More worrisome was Mercy's health. "Your mamma has been very ill during the winter & spring & still continues so, having an inveterate humor settled in her eyes which baffles all applications and medicine," James explained. The ailment had "deprived her of . . . reading & writing for several months . . . impaired her health in other respects." Hopefully, their move to Milton combined with fresh "air, exercise and a fine season will soon restore her."[27]

Less explicable than Mercy's vision problems was the silence surround-
ing Winslow's visit to John Adams. After an unpleasant tangle with Charles
Grazier, Count de Vergennes, in Paris and a grudging concession from
Benjamin Franklin, America's minister plenipotentiary, John traveled to the
Netherlands in July 1780 on a "fishing expedition"[28] for funds. That expedi-
tion lasted longer than anticipated, and John was still in Amsterdam in
May 1781, negotiating a treaty in place of imprisoned Henry Laurens when
Winslow arrived. But of that visit, Adams had not written.

Nor a year later would he mention a second meeting that Winslow
claimed they had in Paris. Wary, Mercy finally wrote John. Had "any part
of his [Winslow's] conduct since in Europe rendered him unworthy that
Mr. Adams has never once named him," she asked. "If he has, your tenderness will...impose silence, if not, the fluttering hopes of mother will be
strengthened [by] your next letter."[29]

By the time she wrote that second letter, other events had dampened
some of Mercy's maternal "fluttering hopes." By mid-spring 1781, she and
James worried over the disappearance of the *Alliance*, which had sailed in
March from France but never arrived in Boston.

That spring the Warrens' fourth son, Henry, became ill at Harvard with
a consumption-like cough. Hoping sunshine and the fresh sea air wafting
over the Warrens' new hilltop estate would provide a cure, the Warrens
completed the move and by Monday, June 4, were waiting for the arrival of
their furniture.

Coincidentally, in faraway Virginia, Governor Thomas Jefferson and
members of the Virginia Assembly had just escaped Lord Cornwallis and
his men in Charlottesville. Five days later, the *Alliance* finally arrived in
Boston Harbor.

Lookouts, observing the *Alliance*'s unsteady sail into the harbor, realized
something was amiss. Once the ship anchored, they learned that the vessel's
main yard, spars, and rigging were destroyed during a May 28 battle in
Newfoundland against the *Atlanta* and the *Trespassy*, British sloops of war.
Four Americans had died, and the *Alliance*'s Captain Barry was seriously
wounded.

James Warren, Jr., had survived, but his right knee was so badly shattered that sailors carried him by stretcher through the front door of the former Hutchinson mansion as a stunned Mercy and James watched.

Six days later, Mercy's husband wrote Winslow that young James "now lies very ill and it is doubtful whether he will recover with or without the loss of his leg. He has behaved . . . like a man and in the action like a hero . . . if he dies, he will be regarded as a brave man that falls in the cause of his country."

Previously, Mercy had seemed to be "recovering fast," but now, James added, her son's condition had "created such anxiety, agitation and fatigue as I fear will carry her back again."[30]

It would not be until September 28 that Mercy could finally write to Winslow. "My pen has so long lain useless that I feel a little awkward in the resumption. My decayed health and weakened eyes have prevented me writing a line to any one since . . . January last," she explained. Since his father wrote regularly about "business and the present politics of this country," Mercy confined her letter to the "domestic circle."

The family planned to spend the following winter at Milton Hill, a "pleasant spot . . . health and contentment brightens every countenance, except a little gloom at times on the brow of one who has suffered much in the public service."

Young James, Mercy added, had "sustained the action with a bravery that did him honor . . . though by the amputation of a limb, he is made a cripple in the vigor of life."

His other brothers were well, all except Charles, who, nevertheless, persisted in his studies. Henry was the "same amiable, active, obliging youth that you knew him to be at Plymouth . . . George studies geography, history, etc. but notwithstanding the pleasure he takes in his delightful apartment [on Milton Hill] he sometimes . . . [has] an inclination to ramble."

"We should," she pointedly reminded Winslow, "be all happy in your speedy return."[31]

In spite of Winslow's long silences, the Warrens continued to write regularly. Penning a letter through dimmed eyes on September 28, Mercy warned that he should avoid "the dread influence of vice clothed in the specious disguise of politeness."[32]

By mid-November her eyesight had only slightly improved. Mercy, nevertheless, wrote a second time, apologizing that her handwriting "may be less intelligible" than usual. [33]

For her, a woman with a lively and treasured correspondence, the incapacity was particularly cruel. Few if any letters were consequently exchanged between her and Abigail in that period—a time, as the latter nostalgically recalled from France several years later, during which they enjoyed "sweet communion" and passed many "pleasant hours."[34] Fortunately, Tremont, the name Mercy dubbed the new Milton home, and the Adamses' cottage in Braintree were only six miles apart, making frequent visits possible.

Other friends, however, did not necessarily understand the extent of Mercy's disability. "A letter from Mrs. Warren would afford me much pleasure," Hannah plaintively wrote from Cambridge in January 1782. "I hope your eyes are recovered. If not, pray make use of some other pen!"[35]

Mercy could make no immediate response. Her poor sight also prevented work on the *History*, creating what must have been a frustrating delay—especially after news about the October 1781 victory at Yorktown.

Had Mercy been superstitious, she may have attributed that lapse as a punishment wreaked upon her by a vengeful Hutchinson ghost, but she was rooted in the rationalism of the Enlightenment. She considered the new Milton home, she wrote Janet Montgomery months later, "my own little pleasant villa."[36]

By the time Mercy's eyes had improved so that she could write about Yorktown, it was months after the fact. That definitive contest had taken place, she lyrically extolled in her *History*, in the "Virginian fields, the germ of the New World, the first British plantation in America, a state dignified for its uniform ... and firm defense of the natural rights of mankind."[37]

Subsequently, during research on the battle, Mercy had obtained a copy of Cornwallis's surrender, which he dispatched to Sir Henry Clinton, one of the British "bow-wows" who had instigated the 1775 Boston blockade.

"I have the mortification to inform your excellency, that I have been forced to give up the posts of York and Gloucester, and to surrender the troops under my command, by capitulation, on the 19 instant, as prisoners of war, to the combined forces of America and France,"[38] read Cornwallis's letter.

Triumphantly, Mercy had included that in the index to her *History*.

13

Hope Is an Airy Queen

WINSLOW, MERCY RUEFULLY CONFIDED to her niece Sally Sever in December 1781, was "perhaps too much the object of tender anxiety to my fond heart."[1] Even that moment of self-perception did not stop Mercy from sending Winslow a string of letters, inquiring after his affairs, reminding him to avoid temptations, and begging him to return home in spring.

His father, James, Mercy had explained in November, could no longer help him with the diplomatic post, since he had "very little influence with the reigning power" in Massachusetts, whose leaders espoused principles "repugnant to every idea of a virtuous republic."[2]

By December 16, Mercy alluded to the problems surrounding Winslow's importing business in Boston. Only a day earlier, she had "flattered herself" that his father could have "furnished you (on his own credit) with bills to the amount of 5 or 500 sterling"[3] but he could buy none in Boston. Equally frustrating was James's inability to sell the goods that Winslow imported to Boston; those consequent debts might harm his credit abroad.

To those and other letters, Winslow did not reply, leading Mercy to express her anxieties in a poem called "To a Young Gentleman, residing in France." Written on January 1, 1782, Mercy prayed for her son's "Long health, long peace and long happiness" and return to "sweet Tremont" after abandoning his ambitions and the "fopperies of a foreign court." She begged Winslow to return "for nothing else we need/ To see thee happy, would be bliss indeed."[4]

Though Winslow could not provide such bliss, Mercy spent the winter of 1781–82 in a happier frame of mind than in previous seasons in Plymouth.

Portrait of Winslow Warren by John Singleton Copley.
Photograph © 2008 Museum of Fine Arts, Boston.

The convenience of Milton Hill, she wrote Sally Sever, had surrounded her with the "best of friends...a number of amiable youth enlivening the day and smiling...when their excellent father sets his foot on the threshold... at night."

In spite of her fondness for Clifford, Mercy was entranced with her new hilltop home, especially its "shady walks, the pleasant groves...delightful landscape from the parlor window"—domestic pleasures she believed better than the "whirl of dissipation, the ostentation, pomp and noise of the convivial board" and the "drawing room" of fashionable Boston.

Like Sally, who had a crush upon her "favorite" cousin, Winslow, Mercy admitted that one of her trials was waiting "almost impatiently...[for] the arrival of a vessel" carrying European mail. Not that Winslow was lax, she assured Sally. Her son wrote "by all opportunities" with sentiments "pleasing to the mother and the friend."

She would write again, Mercy promised, albeit infrequently. "Remember, the weak optics [eyes] are employed this way the present winter only for the use of a dear absent son."[5]

Subsequent to the surrender of Yorktown in October 1781, James's obligations to the Navy Board declined and by early 1782 had ended. Embroiled for nearly two decades in public duties, his reputation battered by Hancock, James became embittered. One of his biggest complaints, beyond the Congressional refusal to name him to the Admiralty Board, had been the lack of recompense for his maimed son, James, Jr. Ironically, that was an oversight that James, as the Army's first paymaster general and a director of the Navy Board, had conscientiously sought to avoid for the men under his command.

By March, James appealed for help from his friend and Congressional ally Major General Benjamin Lincoln. "It would be tedious to enter into the detail of my son's suffering," James began in a businesslike tone. "Yet the young man has received but a trifle from the many prizes"—the British ships he had helped capture. If his son could be recompensed for his service as well as "the loss of his limb...your friendship as well as humanity"[6] would be appreciated.

In spite of James's discontent and Mercy's comment that he had "little influence" in Massachusetts, he was again elected to the Massachusetts legislature in the spring of 1782, followed in autumn by his nomination to the Continental Congress. For a second time though, Mercy's husband declined the latter post. Those chosen, he tersely wrote John Adams were "Gerry, Osgood, S. Higginson, Gorham, Holton and J. W. [James Warren]. I believe the last must stay at home and cultivate his farm."[7]

The return to farming was only one reason for James's refusal. A few weeks earlier, he had complained to John about his power-hungry peers. "My friend, the divine science of politics is composed of the same materials here as in Europe. There is something...exceedingly singular in our country. None...was more distinguished by its virtue and public spirit, and no country ever" so quickly adopted "the vices of others."[8]

For months, James, accordingly, had planned to escape the political arena and devote himself to home, hearth, and horticulture—the same idyllic existence that John had so often wanted himself.

"I wish I had fortune enough to purchase me an equal farm upon Pens Hills and enter into an emulation with you, which should make his hill the brightest,"[9] John had jested with James that July.

In reply, James admitted that he welcomed John's eventual "return to our hills" to go "roving with you among the partridges, squirrels," and share the "science of husbandry,"[10] but on November 1 he acknowledged that John's role as minister plenipotentiary to France meant he had a "large field before you."[11]

For over a year, John had been cultivating that field, and by autumn 1782, had harvested it as a cash crop with a five-million-guilder loan from the Dutch. Proudly, on the eve of that agreement, John finally wrote about a "harmony so entire between France, America and Holland" that augured a "good conclusion."

He had only one request, John added, that "Mrs. Warren will give my Dutch negotiation a place in her History. It [the alliance] is one of the most extraordinary in all...diplomatic records."[12]

To that, Mercy enthusiastically agreed. "Any historian must be very negligent of fame, who is not ambitious that the diplomatic transactions of this extraordinary period should stand conspicuous in his or her work. Therefore depend upon it, sir, a blank shall be left in *Certain* annals for your Dutch negotiations"—amplified, perhaps, by his addition of a few "authentic documents."

Ruefully, she admitted that lately her *History* had "languished under the hand of time" because the "the muse [had] grown too timid amidst the noise of war."[13] Long delays in reports about the final battles of the Revolution, compounded by Mercy's eye problems, had also undermined her confidence.

Another copy of that correspondence preserved in her letterbook suggests that Mercy was still insecure about John's enthusiasm for her *History*. "I know not whether to consider a request in your last, in a serious or a satirical light," she fretted. Simultaneously flirtatious and threatening, she then added, "If the last [satirical], let me tell you, its poignancy is felt . . . by a susceptible heart—and some . . . revenge will arise."

Nor, she added "is any office so illustrious, nor any character so sacred, but he must submit, if he provokes . . . the threats of a woman."[14]

John did not receive Mercy's letter until January 27, 1783, and probably noticed its strident similarity to a letter from Abigail the previous June. "Patriotism in the female sex is the most disinterested of all virtues," his lonely wife had asserted. "Excluded from honors and offices, we cannot attach ourselves to the state or government yet all history and every age exhibit instances of patriotic virtue in the female sex . . . we are called upon to exhibit our fortitude . . . when you offer your blood to the state, it is ours . . . In giving it our sons and husbands, we give more than ourselves."[15]

From that and Mercy's letter, women's roles and rights was obviously a topic of conversation in Braintree and Milton—a debate that John again sidestepped, just as he had in 1776, while placating "the most accomplished lady in America."[16]

Insisting that he meant nothing derogatory by his comment, the statesman replied, "I assure you, Madam, what I said about certain annals was no sarcasm. I have the utmost veneration for them." Disingenuously, he added that if Mercy included the Dutch treaty in her *History*, he hoped she would not mention his "patience." "I hate most to be praised for my patience. I had rather you should immortalize my impudence. I rather think it was this quality, than the other which produced the effect in Holland."[17]

Within that same letter John also described his meetings with Winslow, but realizing its dubious flavor, finally crossed out the passage. A copy of the original, nevertheless, remained in his letterbook. "I have never had an opportunity, Madam to see your son since he has been in Europe, but once or twice at Amsterdam . . . He has been traveling from place to place; and although I have often enquired after him . . . seldom been able to hear of him," John wrote. "I have heard nothing to his disadvantage, except a shyness and secrecy . . . and a reputation which he brought with him from Boston of loving play. But I have not been able to learn that he has indulged it improperly in Europe."[18]

In its place, John substituted a paragraph reiterating his hopes for James's appearance as a delegate to the Continental Congress that spring. "It is too soon for Mr. Warren or me to retire. Stability and dignity must, be given to the law, or our labors have all been in vain . . . the old hands must do this or it will not be done."[19]

On February 4, 1783, Great Britain proclaimed an end to hostilities. Six weeks later, on April 15, Congress ratified the provisional articles of peace. In keeping with the resultant celebrations, some of the old hands reappeared. Among them was Jemmy, who, after years of retreat at an Andover farm, was driven to Boston during the summer of 1782 by his nephew Harrison Gray Otis, the son of Samuel Allyne.

Visitors, curious to meet the famous patriot, found Jemmy a changed man, no longer the firebrand who had sparked the "greatest Revolution in the world."[20] Stouter, slower, and sadder, the fifty-seven-year-old patriot had seemingly recovered his sanity, although his ravings had scarred his children. His son, James, had died in 1777 in a British prison. Against his wishes, his daughter Elizabeth had married a British officer and lived overseas. Only Jemmy's third child, Polly, remained home with his wife, Ruth, with whom he had settled into a muted domesticity.

Instead of rabid speeches and patriotic zeal, Mercy's brother favored books and quiet evenings by the fireside. Nevertheless, admirers continued to flock to his home, making it the "resort of much company calling."[21] At the insistence of old friends, Jemmy took on several legal cases and even argued one in the Court of Common Pleas.

Of his return, Mercy wrote little. Governor Hancock though insisted upon arranging a public celebration to commemorate Jemmy's return. Initially, the famous patriot had declined, fearing that a public appearance might stir painful memories. Yet by the spring of 1783, the eighth anniversary of the battles of Lexington and Concord, Jemmy was persuaded to accept the governor's invitation. During the formal dinner at Hancock's banquet hall, toasts were raised again and again, as Samuel Allyne and his son hovered nearby. After observing a "visible oscillation in his intellect,"[22] they quietly left with Jemmy.

By then, however, it was too late. The crowds, the commemorations, and the speeches had so upset Jemmy's balance that he began to rave, causing Samuel Allyne to rush him back to Andover.

Mortality again became Jemmy's obsession. The next morning, still restless and upset, he chopped away the lower branches of a nearby pine thicket. That day, or soon afterward, he gathered his papers and burned them in a bonfire, destroying dozens of precious documents detailing the early days of the Revolution. With the return of spring came occasional thunderstorms, and the dramatic play of light and sound that always fascinated Jemmy. On Friday afternoon, May 23, the famous patriot stood in the doorway of the Osgood house, leaning on his late father's silver-headed cane and enjoying a storm. Suddenly he was struck by a bolt of lightening. "James the Patriot" died instantly.

He was "as extraordinary in death as in life," wrote John Adams from France. "He has left a character that will never die while the memory of the American Revolution remains."[23]

No less stunned was Mercy, especially when she realized that her beloved brother had perished just as he always wished. "My dear sister," he once told her, "I hope when God Almighty, in his righteous providence, shall take me out of time into eternity, that it will be by a flash of lightening."[24]

For two weeks Mercy was too numb to write Winslow. His uncle's genius, she finally wrote her son on June 8, was "too big to be circumscribed or too extensive for enjoyment in this limited sphere" and likely prompted the "sovereign arbiter" to remove "the greatest yet most unhappy of men" from earth.

History, she believed, would ultimately honor Jemmy's character and contributions. "The pen of a sister," Mercy wrote her favorite son, "can scarcely touch the outlines."[25]

◄‹›►

That letter was sent to Pennsylvania instead of France, for just before Jemmy's death, Mercy and James had endured a shock of their own—an announcement that Winslow had arrived in Philadelphia.

Learning that her son had traveled there in anticipation of his father's service to the Continental Congress, Mercy euphorically wrote, "And is my son—my dear Winslow again on the same continent with myself? Words cannot express the joy—the gratitude that pervaded my bosom when the tidings reached my ear." He was, she gushed, the one for whom she "waked and watched though many weary night... It is three years this day since I bid you adieu... My God has heard, has returned you."

Tenderly, Mercy added, "I know not how to restrain my impatience to see you. Yet, if a journey this way immediately, would materially injure your interest—I will a little longer, suspend my wishes."[26]

At James's request, Elbridge Gerry wrote Congressional delegate Samuel Holton, to help Winslow obtain "an appointment to the office of consul." While others clamored for such a post, the young man had "personal qualifications and "patriotic connections"[27] above the ordinary.

While James also thanked Benjamin Lincoln for the initial "civilities and friendship shown my son at Philadelphia,"[28] he was privately discouraged about Winslow's European business ventures. Having paid many of his son's bills during his time abroad and attempted to sell his imports in a "miserable market," James now suggested that his "applications in future must be to true solid business."

Winslow might well "derive great advantages from seeing some merchants of eminence here [in Boston]... You should, therefore, contrive to spend some time here."[29]

On September 3, 1783, John Adams, Benjamin Franklin, and John Jay signed the Treaty of Paris, which formally ended the war with Great Britain. After seven years of violence and bloodshed, the mother country finally recognized the United States as a separate nation.

"The discordant sounds of war that had long grated the ears of the children of America, were now suspended... harmony soothed their wounded feelings, and they flattered themselves the dread summons to slaughter and death would not again resound on their shores," Mercy proudly wrote in her *History*. With the "independence of America...every prospect of tranquility appeared."[30]

Tranquility also reigned in the Warren household on Neponset Hill. James was happily "at work among my potatoes, instead of being in Congress,"[31] as he reported to John Adams that October. Winslow was so charmed with the new home's pastoral setting, its views of Boston Harbor, and his room overlooking the garden that he even promised to stay until receiving a diplomatic appointment.

James, Jr., while still occasionally suffering from "disagreeable spasms"[32] when tired or upset, was steadily improving. Charles's health had stabilized enough to return to Harvard with Henry. Seventeen-year-old George pored over his books in preparation for more advanced studies in Rhode Island. All told, autumn and the early winter of 1783, capped by a holiday reunion of the five sons at Neponset Hill, had been joyful.

Yet life, as Mercy once observed in a poem about fatalism, often seemed "deceptive," an "airy queen" who "holds a false mirror to the dazzled sight."[33] That autumn Mercy's observation was again tested when Governor Hancock announced his resignation.

Crippled with gout, exhausted from his public duties, plagued with complaints from protesting citizens about high taxes, and eager to spend more time with his five-year-old son, Hancock, too, longed to retire.

"I have not the vanity to think that I have been of very extensive service in our late unhappy contest," the former merchant confided to his long-time associate Captain James Scott in London. Nevertheless, he was proud that "I set out upon honest principles and strictly adhered to them...I have lost many thousand sterling, but, thank God, my country is saved...I am determined, in the course of this month to resign my command of this Commonwealth."[34]

But to do so midterm, warned Hancock's lieutenant governor, Thomas Cushing, was unwise, would make him appear a quitter, and would ruin his reputation for posterity. Impressed with Cushing's perspective, Hancock stayed on, not only to fulfill his term but to reenter the 1774 gubernatorial race.

Infuriated, Mercy's husband, James, sarcastically informed Elbridge Gerry, "For our comfort and consolation...we may still be happy in the possession of a chief magistrate, whose merits are ... extraordinary" and behavior above "ridicule or contempt."[35]

Hancock, nonetheless, faced anything but a happy political situation, for Massachusetts was hobbled by rapidly rising deficits, prompted at least in part by the Congressional insistence that it assume part of the debt for the Revolution.

To that, James and other citizens had protested, believing it unfair that their state, the "cradle of liberty," must shoulder the heftiest burden for national independence in the sum of $1. 6 million.

Having neither the authority nor the courage to raise taxes from the states—that being the issue that sparked the Revolution—Congress had churned out paper currency, "continentals," to recompense veterans for their military service. With little silver or gold specie behind them, they soon became so worthless that citizens protested and even rioted. Faced with a growing shortfall from states unable to pay their assigned debts, Congress consequently looked to the collection of imposts, or taxes upon foreign goods, to make up the difference.

"I am exceeding sorry to find Congress still pursing the plan of general taxes,"[36] James wrote Congressional delegate Benjamin Lincoln, referring to the imposts and excises on foreign goods that he felt sure would be the "ruin of commerce."

Already, thanks to the "imbecility"[37] of the Hancock administration, taxes in Massachusetts had risen as high as 25 percent on certain foreign goods .

During his stay in Milton, Winslow, who took a keen interest in his mother's literary work, convinced Mercy to write about the quest for liberty using a foreign example from history. Accordingly, as she explained in the introduction to her tragedy, *The Ladies of Castile,* she chose an "ancient story in the annals of Spain, in her last struggles for liberty."[38] Echoing earlier conversations with Abigail about women's contributions and behavior during the American Revolution, the *Ladies of Castile* depicted the contrasting reactions of two Spanish widows to the deaths of their husbands during the reign of sixteenth-century Holy Roman Emperor Charles V.

The first widow, Doña Maria, in spite of what she admitted was the "weakness of my sex," vowed to behave courageously in support of her husband Juan de Padilla's fight for liberty. Becoming his widow, but refusing to "wail...in vulgar grief" or "in slavery meet a lingering death / Beneath a tyrant's foot,"[39] Doña Maria schemed to strip the Toledo cathedral of its wealth in support of her late husband's cause.

Mercy depicted the weak-willed Doña Louisa in a different light; She was the daughter of royalist Don Velasco, high constable of Castile, who, like Rapatio in Mercy's earlier plays, planned to "chase the miscreants from the land." When Lousia's husband, the more liberal, Torylike Don Francis, died, her cowardly solution was suicide.

A plea for recognition of the sacrificing women of the Revolution and empathy for those caught between love and political allegiances, Mercy's *The Ladies of Castile* was the most feminist of her patriotic plays. As her heroine, Doña Maria, reminded her audience:

> Though weak compassion sinks the female mind
> And our frail sex dissolve in pity's tears;
> Yet justice' sword can never be resheath'd
> 'Till Charles is taught to know we will be free;
> And learns the duty that a monarch owes,
> To heaven—the people—and the rights of man.[40]

-<+>-

In ironical contrast to her message in *The Ladies of Castile*, Mercy did not always follow her own plea for womanly self-sufficiency.

"We have had what we call a tight winter and have been continually tortured with cold,"[41] James reported to Elbridge Gerry on February 25, 1784, just after Mercy had completed the play. Added to the difficulties of the bitter weather were the winds of loneliness and despair that gripped Mercy after her sons, with the exception of the crippled James, Jr., left Plymouth.

The departure of her youngest, George, for his studies in Rhode Island especially disturbed fifty-six-year-old Mercy. "The day you left me...my spirits depressed. I felt as if I had finished my work, and had nothing more to do but to...[but] record my sentiments, opinions for the...felicity of my children,"[42] she wrote on January 5.

Within a few weeks Mercy received reports that Charles had suffered a setback in his health, followed by news that Henry, too, was ill. Nor, in spite of his earlier promise, did Winslow remain in Milton but instead moved to Boston, from where he announced his intended return to Europe—this time to Lisbon, Portugal.

Again Mercy wrote of her disappointment. Following a storm that prevented Winslow's visit in March, Mercy wrote that older people tended to "prize the interview of an hour, seize the day with avidity, and consider… a week… much higher… than perhaps you can affix to that of a year."[43]

While he finally returned for a brief visit, she reported to Sally Sever that "[t]he day of his return looks distant indeed." Disconsolately, she added, "My Henry goes soon, a voyage merely in pursuit of health."[44]

That voyage—a bracing sea journey to Halifax—had a dual purpose, for the city was also a Tory sanctuary where James's relative Edward Winslow, who owed him money from before the Revolution, had fled. Prompted by reports from Edward's daughter Sarah that the Winslows dwelled there "elegantly situated in a good house upon the Parade,"[45] Henry thus expected to collect upon his father's loans.

After his arrival, Henry quickly realized the truth: Not only was the seventy-one-year-old Edward impecunious, but in failing health. Three days into Henry's visit he died. "Ned behaved like a brute and so I have lost my money," James later wrote Winslow. "And so the tide sets yet."[46]

On Sunday, June 20, two weeks before Henry's return, the tides also carried Mercy's beloved Braintree friend and daughter on the *Active* to Great Britain. "Mrs. Adams and Miss Nabby left us last Sunday… with a very fine wind which has continued here ever since and promises her a fine passage,"[47] James reported to John Adams.

Of that departure, as so often in Mercy's life when confronted with conflicting emotions, she wrote nothing. Glad as she must have been for Abigail's reunion with her husband after four years, Mercy thus lost her trusted, feisty confidante.

14

The Public Is a Monster
Seldom Guided by Reason

WHATEVER LONELINESS MERCY FELT subsequent to Abigail's departure was partially dispelled by the arrival of Catharine Macaulay that July. Officially, the British author planned to tour the United States and meet the patriots whose liberties she had long championed. Privately, the visit would provide Catharine with respite from the cloud of controversy surrounding her in Great Britain.

The reasons for that disapproval were complex. Along with supporting the American Revolution, Catharine had horrified her British readers by criticizing the reigns of William III and Charles I in the newest volumes of her *History of England*. The second blow to her reputation was her 1778 marriage to twenty-one-year-old William Graham, "a young stripling school-boy"[1] as the powerful *St. James Chronicle* sneered.

"I should not have thought it strange if Mrs. Macaulay had crossed the Atlantic to marry some arch rebel...but to unite herself with a boy, and a Scotch boy is quite out of the path of such a comet,"[2] snickered Elizabeth Montague, leader of London's literary "bluestocking" salon.

Catharine's union, opined Horace Walpole, creator of the gothic novel, was "but an uncouth match."[3] With it, her reputation had "irrevocably fallen," sneered poet-essayist Edmund Rack. "Her passions, even at 52, were too strong for her reason; and she has taken to bed a stout brawny Scotchman of 21. For shame!"[4]

As rapidly as the author's reputation had flared to national prominence, it collapsed into ridicule and satire. By July 1779, London audiences flocked to Haymarket Theater to watch *A Widow—No Widow*, featuring a famous author who extorted money from admirers before eloping with a young captain. To the public, Catharine thus became a dangerous free-thinker whose politics and personal life threatened the very roots of civilized society.

In contrast, America celebrated "Mrs. Macaulay-Graham" as a revered defender of human liberties. No sooner did she and her husband step off the gangplank of the *Rosamund* onto a Boston wharf than they were ushered into Hancock's golden coach and whisked off to his Beacon Hill mansion. During the ensuing weeks, Catharine and young James were feted at dinners and balls.

Even Mercy, for all her prim ideas about marriage, hotly defended Catharine. "Doubtless that lady's independency of spirit led her to suppose she might associate for the remainder of life with an inoffensive obliging youth with the same impunity a gentleman of three score and ten might marry a damsel of fifteen,"[5] Mercy insisted to John Adams.

In mid-August, after Mercy dined with Catharine, she invited her and her husband to Neponset Hill. One bright morning in early November, the British couple arrived at the Warrens' mansion. The contrast between the two women must have been extraordinary: Mercy, in an unadorned American-made dress, her graying hair neatly tucked under a mob cap; the slender British author in a fashionable gown, her face "painted" as usual in the French style.

No less striking must have been their conversation, especially Catharine's surprise at the public's disdain for the old Revolutionary values of simplicity, frugality, and brotherhood. Seven months later, Abigail Adams, hearing rumors of the British author's reaction, reported to Mercy that Catharine believed she had arrived in the United States "ten years too late."[6]

Catharine's presence, nevertheless, reinspired Mercy. "I mean to employ myself in writing, the ensuing winter, if my health and other circumstances will admit," Mercy wrote Winslow on November 10. Privately, she also conceded that Catharine's marriage was an embarrassment. "I blush for the imperfections of human nature, and when I consider her as my friend, I draw a veil over the foibles of the woman,"[7] Mercy delicately added.

From the bucolic village of Auteuil, France—"a kind of Pens Hill" as John Adams described the town where he, Abigail, and their children lived

—he anticipated that Americans would overlook Catharine's unorthodox union. "Her literary character, and the honor she has done to those political principles we profess should secure her a respectful reception in Boston," he wrote. While the author's marriage "was not discreet," the world had pardoned far "greater indiscretions, in infinitely less meritorious characters."

For the past decade, John grumbled in the letter, he "devoted myself wholly to the public affairs." Literary pursuits were once part of his "youthful desires," but now he was "too old, and too blind, ever to resume them with much ardor, or any prospect of success."[8]

Implied was Adamses' hope that Mercy would complete her history of the Revolution and feature him as a lead figure in that struggle.

Awed by Catharine, Mercy confided to John that the author was verbose "both in conversation and composition"—and even finally told her so. Readers, after all, Mercy added (perhaps as much to remind herself), should never suffer from "fatigue while listening to the humiliating story of human conduct."[9]

To Mercy that humiliating story was again confirmed during the winter of 1784–85 when James was elected to Congress. Once again he had declined. His "attachment to private life," as Mercy wrote Winslow, had become increasingly "incompatible with his long labors in the field of politics." By then, James thought nothing more "irksome" than leaving Milton to try again to save "a new-formed Republic from the consequences of their own folly," especially from men who were "indifferent to the principles of the revolution."

In Massachusetts, those men, Mercy claimed, were the "engines of Hancock," that flamboyant patriot who won the gubernatorial election each spring. "Depend upon it, nothing less than an American monarchy is in contemplation,"[10] she warned.

In spite of Hancock's seeming invincibility, the citizens of Massachusetts were discontent. Ironically, much of that grumbling arose from fellow merchants who protested rising currency imbalances that hobbled trade because of "an amazing scarcity of [hard] cash."

The problem, Mercy believed, could be solved by creating domestic industries, "independent of the fashions or taste of foreign nations."[11] That failure, after all, had left the residents of Massachusetts with a lack of basic commodities, which, ironically, was coupled with a flood of English luxuries into the marketplace.

"The scarcity of money ... in consequence of our excessive and extravagant importations of British frippery, has occasioned stagnation of trade, stopping discounts at the bank and other embarrassments,"[12] James similarly explained to Elbridge Gerry.

In 1780 the national debt was $11 million, a sum to which the states were expected to contribute but, faced with maintenance of local militias, often failed to honor. By the mid-1780s, rising interest costs, the depreciating value of the continental currency issued by Congress, the loss of profiteering, war-time contracts, and misguided international trade policies were sinking the new republic in a post-war depression.

Pennsylvania owed £4,646,000 by 1783. So large was Virginia's obligation that the state allocated £207,000 of its income of £256,000 to interest. South Carolina spent £83,184 of its budget of £103,526 in interest to keep the state budget afloat.

Massachusetts, which owed £1.6 million, was in equally dire straits. Its veterans, struggling to redeem the value of the falling "continentals" finally received for military service, joined the heavily mortgaged farmers of western Massachusetts to ask the legislature to produce paper money—an option bitterly opposed by coastal merchants.

By late 1784, the economic climate was so unstable that even James struggled to pay the mortgage at Neponset Hill. To raise cash, he had considered selling his "Eastern lands," but, as he wrote Winslow, interest on money was "so high that those few [with cash] will not purchase land."[13]

As the post-Revolutionary economy unraveled, bankruptcies became common. During the crisis, Mercy's brother Samuel Allyne Otis had overextended his credit with British traders. So, too, had his brother Joseph in West Barnstable, who by spring 1785, teetered on the edge of bankruptcy. "Is there no possibility of selling the farm?"[14] Samuel Allyne wrote with alarm.

Torn between the prospect of debtors' prison and loss of the family holdings, Joseph shrewdly transferred the farm and other Otis holdings to his children. "Grandfather's estate is responsible for the payment," Mercy explained to Winslow. "What a reverse in one of the oldest and most respectable families in [the] eastern states."[15]

In Boston, Samuel Allyne was less fortunate. By September 1785, the once-prosperous merchant was forced to declare bankruptcy.

Until 1784, Mercy's warnings about the danger of purchasing European luxuries was restricted to her private letters. Even her retort to Winslow about *Chesterfield's Letters,* which Abigail Adams published in a January 1781 edition of the *Independent Chronicle,* had appeared without a byline.

When, however, the newly established *Boston Magazine,* in imitation of London's recognition of female authors, invited "the fair sex to become candidates for literary fame"[16] in 1784, Mercy decided to reprint her critique under her own name. After that, "Mrs. Warren" became a symbol of Old Colony values—just as was her husband, James.

Undermining those values was the rise of Boston's new society accompanied by the establishment of fashionable new clubs. Among the most exclusive was the Sans Souci, or "free and easy," an elite bimonthly salon or "tea assembly," featuring music, dining, dancing, and gambling. To Mercy, the club seemed a "ridiculous institution" for the struggling new nation, and its cent gambling fee, she thought, was likely to prompt "consequences of a most alarming nature."[17]

Not so, scoffed Hancock's followers, who defended the Sans Souci as the epicenter of a stylish new Boston. The club, a member insisted in the *Massachusetts Centinel,* would be "very useful in polishing the manners and promoting harmony and social intercourse in the town."[18]

Another well-publicized affirmation of the Sans Souci was appearances by Catharine Macaulay. Those visits, a horrified Mercy confided to her son George, "cast a shade on her character,"[19] contradicting the author's 1783 "Treatise on the Immutability of Moral Truth," which had condemned luxury.

Simultaneous with Mercy's private critique came protests from Boston's old-line Puritans and patriots, who decried the Sans Souci for mimicking British-style elitism and decadence. On January 15 the matter attracted widespread attention with William Warden and Benjamin Russell's publication of "A new farce, SANS SOUCI, Alias Free And Easy, or, an Evening's Peep into a Polite Circle."

That pamphlet, billed as an "Entertainment in Three Acts," depicted a Mrs. W____n paired with the "Republican Heroine," Catharine Macaulay,

who, expecting to find "a cultivation of manners . . . similar to the public re-
solves," had been shocked by the American admiration for "British gew-
gaws, etiquette and parade." For years she had admired the courageous new
nation, but now understood that her views were "mere chimeras of my own
imagination."

"D__m the old musty rules of decency and decorum—national character— Spartan virtues—republican principles," retorted Little Pert, a Sans
Souci member. "Fashion and etiquette are more agreeable to my ideas of
life—this is the independence I aim at—the free and easy air which distin-
guishes the man of fashion . . . from the republican."[20]

As anticipated, the farce provoked a controversy reflected in the *Massachusetts Centinel*'s warning that "[we] are prostituting all our glory as a
people for new modes of pleasure" that were "injurious to virtue" and
"detrimental to the well being of society."

In that same issue Sam Adams fumed, "Why do you thus suffer all the in-
temperances of Great Britain to be fostered in our bosom, in all their vile
luxuriance?"[21]

In reaction, tongues wagged, tempers flared, and citizens snickered
at Adams and his constituents as old-fashioned, despotic arbitrators of
morality.

To Mercy the furor seemed trivial and did nothing to correct the human
desire for "every species of luxury"[22] as she groused to John Adams. For
that reason, she explained to Winslow, she took "no part in the enjoyment,
the castigation, or the vindication of this puerile enjoyment."[23]

Mercy's silence would not, however, protect her from persecution. By
early 1785, when newspaper articles condemned the Sans Souci farce and
Hancock's influence upon the club, rumors circulated that Mercy had written them. "I hope I shall never write anything I should be so much ashamed
to avow as that little indigested farrago," Mercy fumed to George. "Yet I
have been in one of the papers as the author of that and several satirical
pieces." Such accusations, she surmised, could be "traced to the Hancock
party."[24]

Inadvertently, Mercy's role as America's foremost female advocate of
old patriotic values had become a political target, fueled by Hancock's announcement to retire and James's subsequent nomination as his replacement.

"The private opinion of most people is...in favor of your Father," Mercy wrote Winslow. "But perhaps...his enemies may prevail." The public, she added "is a monster seldom guided by reason, nor is it possible ...to judge which way the furious beast will leap, till it is known what kind of bait will be thrown."[25]

As a critic of the high life and the wife of James Warren, Mercy had already become that bait.

Nor was the monster public the only one deceived. "From the...mention of my name in the farce and my particular acquaintance with Mrs. Macaulay, some ill natured persons suggested to her that your mama was the author,"[26] Mercy morosely wrote her son George.

The breach between the two women would be healed, but it left a scar. In July 1785, on the eve of her departure for England, Catharine's letter to Mercy alluded to the "animated severity which...has sometimes offended the delicacy of your friend's sentiment." Tactfully, Catharine then dropped the subject and thanked Mercy for her friendship, her "many endearing obligations"[27] at Milton, and her letter of introduction to the Washingtons.

From Virginia, Martha Washington had already thanked Mercy for "introducing a lady so well known in the literary world as Mrs. Macaulay Graham." Moreover, added that matron, "the friendship which subsisted between General Warren and Mr. Washington will never be forgotten by the latter; it was among the first formed, and most lasting, at Cambridge, and with equal pleasure would be renewed by him."[28]

No less enthusiastic was the support rallied for James by his followers for his candidacy for the Massachusetts governorship. But surprisingly, Sam Adams supported James Bowdoin, and in the ensuing power struggle, Mercy was ridiculed.

The *Boston Gazette* wrote that while Mercy was a lady "whose literary accomplishments are known," she "prostitutes her time and talents...to blast the character of some of the most worthy of our citizens." In fact, the "whole artillery of her scandal and abuse, is leveled at a character [John Hancock] who was one of the first that stepped forth in defense of our country."

Mrs. Warren's motives were "consistent" with her tendency to "find fault with men and manners, because the public have no better opinion on her dear G-n-r-l's [General Warren's] ability . . . His refusing to go to R-e [Rhode Island] when ordered by the G-l C-t [General Court] at a time when his country was in the greatest difficulty and danger; and the flimsy and vague reasons he assigned for not going (vs. that he would not be under the command of a C-t C-l) [Continental Guard] can never be effaced."

Like Warren, Mercy suffered a "depravity of heart." Moreover, her writings were mediocre, reflecting "no great honor on either the goodness of her heart or the brilliancy of her pen." Instead of satirizing others, the *Gazette* recommended she "follow the example of a celebrated female historian." If she did so, Mercy might even achieve a degree of "perfection which she certainly never will attain by the composition of F-rc-s [farces], or the illiberal abuse of news-paper essays."[29]

Mercy made no reply, though Sam Adams had urged her to do so. She had lived "long enough to see so much of the baseness and ingratitude of mankind," she finally explained to Sam, to think it wise that she "continue a silent spectator of . . . bold ambition."

Fuming over his support for Bowdoin, Mercy caustically added, "While my family and connections, *whom you sir very well know,* seem to be forgotten and my husband in private life, I think the quiet contemplation of the instability of human affairs . . . the most becoming line of conduct for your friend."[30]

Ultimately, James Bowdoin won the patriot party's nomination for the governorship over Hancock's candidate, Thomas Cushing.

"Our new Governor has issued his proclamation for the encouragement of piety, virtue, education and manners and for the suppression of vice," Sam Adams announced to John Adams that spring. "This with the good example of a first Magistrate and others may *perhaps* restore our virtue."[31]

Still nothing changed. Sam's hopes for a return of virtue, Mercy later observed in her *History,* remained unfulfilled. In 1785, a "cloud of chagrin" sat "on almost every brow, and a general uneasiness," as citizens complained about Congress, "whose powers were too feeble for the redress of private wrongs, or the more public and general purposes of government."[32]

No less disquieting to the Warrens during that period was Charles's failing health. In an effort to recover, the twenty-two-year-old traveled in August 1784 to Hispaniola, today's Haiti and the Dominican Republic. By October, his health had not improved, even though, as Mercy reminded her son, that trip seemed "the only chance...to escape the rigors of another Northern winter."

Winslow, she reported, had just written from Lisbon that he understood that Charles planned to return home and then sail to Europe to join him. He, too, was unhappy, and he detested Lisbon, whose citizens seemed "sunk into the vilest depths of superstition."[33]

Even so, Winslow had lived well overseas. On his way to Lisbon, he stopped in London, where the expatriate John Singleton Copley painted his portrait. From Lisbon, he sent his parents canned grapes and a large, handsome carpet. Yet such gifts did little to relieve Mercy's maternal anxieties. By late 1784, she felt her life oddly "suspended and fully balanced by my fears for both my dear absent sons." While others "adventured" for gain, Mercy pictured herself engaged in a different kind of "speculation abroad ...more valuable than gold," in the lives of her sons. "If my treasures return without alloy, I shall think myself more fortunate than him who sees every favorable breeze wafting him the rich productions of the Eastern and Western world."[34]

In the winter of 1785, Mercy received an alarming letter from Charles about a new illness that dimmed her speculation, even as he assured her of his recovery and anticipated return to Boston in April.

Nor, in Lisbon, did her second speculation, Winslow, fare much better. "The consular appointments will certainly be made in a short time and I have no doubt of your succeeding,"[35] Mercy had assured him on April 30. Yet by June, nothing was settled.

To divert herself from that winter's disquieting events, Mercy retreated into writing, once again creating "something in the dramatic line" in a foreign setting. Drawing upon events described in Gibbon's *The Decline and Fall of the Roman Empire*, the resultant *The Sack of Rome* focused upon two of Mercy's favorite themes: patriotic virtues threatened by vice and the masculine exploitation of women.

The setting, as the introduction explained, was fifth-century Rome, when "the character of man was sunk to the lowest stage of depravity" and its citizens were corrupted by "every species of luxury." Nor, Mercy pointedly added, "have more enlightened and polished ages been taught by their examples to shun the luxurious vices."[36]

As the play's title suggests, the plot centers around the fall of Rome, which was caused by internal intrigues and an accompanying degradation of several noblewomen. Among the most important is Eudocia, daughter of Emperor Valentinian, who struggles over conflicting allegiances of filial duty and love. She is betrothed to noble Gaudentius, who wants to kill the emperor to avenge his father's death; Eudocia tempers him by explaining that such an act would make him unfit to become her husband. Instead, she longs to escape with him to enjoy "the sacred walks, the silent grots, where virtue once reclin'd." Crushing those hopes is "the distant din of arms—alarms—and shouts," followed by a twisting plot in which another vengeful Roman noble, Maximus, kills the emperor Valentinian.[37]

Later in the play, Eudocia's mother, the newly widowed empress Edoxia, horrified by the prospect of a forced marriage to her late husband's murderer, Maximus, summons the Vandal king Genseric for help. Simultaneous with the Vandal plunder of Rome, Genseric's son Hunneric plans to forcibly wed Eudocia. In the final scene, Hunneric kills Eudocia's beloved, Gaudentius; this is followed by her self-inflicted death on his corpse.

The Sack of Rome was Mercy's eighteenth-century version of an English morality play, a warning that luxury, political corruption, and thoughtless revenge similarly threatened America.

"A female bard still asks your candid eye," Mercy's epilogue explains, and hopes that "the politeness of an infant nation" would not "damn the play, and hiss it out of fashion." Instead, she implored its readers to "let is pass at least a night or two," so that they "might learn their follies ere it was too late."[38]

By August 1785 Mercy had sent a draft of *The Sack of Rome* to George, who critiqued it for a lack of dramatic passion and "too many similes," poetic descriptions, and "moral observations."

In September, she dispatched a reworked version to Winslow. While it may not "afford equal entertainment with the compositions of a Corneille," she admitted, she hoped "you will find pleasure" in it.[39]

Mercy knew that *The Sack of Rome* was one of her least successful works, but it had been composed to heal the affronts she and James had silently suffered the preceding spring.

⊰⊹⊱

Winslow's reaction to the play, if there was one, has not been preserved. That summer, as usual, Mercy waited for his letters. Only a few arrived, and, when they did, as she complained to George, they were "short and . . . full of business."

By then Charles had returned from Hispaniola to plan a voyage to Cádiz, Spain; from there he intended to travel to Lisbon. The trip filled Mercy with dread, even though she vowed to "see him off with fortitude and cheerfulness and . . . leave it calmly to the choice of heaven, wither we meet again."

Clearly, there was no easy solution. If Charles sailed, she wrote George, "it is my opinion he will never return." Yet if he stayed in New England that winter, his recovery was even more unlikely. Watching Charles struggle with his health that spring and summer had been heartbreaking. "While he sometimes appears better for a few days . . . we flatter ourselves he may recover; but a shower—a breeze—a social hour—or some lesser accident frequently threatens."

The eldest Warren son, James, Jr., meanwhile, had moved to Hingham to teach school. Henry was studying business in Boston. Since George had lived in Northampton, Massachusetts, for the past year, it was the "opinion of your father and the whole family that you should make us a visit."[40]

As it happened, Mercy had more company that winter than anticipated. One chill morning in early December 1785, as Mercy sat by the fire at a "lonely hour . . . contemplating the situation of my sons at a distance of a thousand leagues," she heard a familiar voice greeting her from the first floor. Rushing downstairs, to her "astonished eyes" she discovered Winslow, who had arrived unannounced from Portugal. Apparently, he had never received Mercy's letters informing him that Charles was en route to him in Lisbon.

"My next thought," Mercy immediately wrote Charles, "was the disappointment you must suffer by the absence of a brother whose kind offices you may . . . need and whose . . . knowledge of foreign nations might have been greatly advantageous."[41]

Charles would never receive her letter. Some weeks later, Mercy and James learned that their amiable twenty-three-year-old son had died of consumption on November 30 in St. Lucar, Spain.

15

"The fair fabric of a free, strong and national republic"

WHILE SHOCKED, MERCY HAD ANTICIPATED the death of her son Charles. He "had long stood on the brink of eternity and viewed life as a bursting bubble," she somberly reminded her youngest son, George, in January 1786. His last years were "made perfect through suffering" and he "died as he lived, with . . . calm, uniform dignity and virtue."

Was it therefore wise that "we wish him to return from the society of the blessed? . . . No. He has done his work—he has entered before us," perhaps even "to bid welcome to the eternal shores those he so tenderly loved."

While Mercy mourned for herself, for James, and for her "surviving children who have lost such an invaluable companion," she felt "an inexpressive calmness"[1] for Charles.

Far less calming were the events surrounding Winslow's arrival from Portugal. Having learned he would not receive a diplomatic post in Lisbon because Congress thought Portugal vulnerable to Barbary invasions from North Africa, Winslow had booked passage to Boston. Almost certainly, he knew that the ailing Charles was on his way to meet him in Lisbon.

Pressing debts, according to scholarly opinion, probably prompted Winslow's departure. Some of them, at least according to Mercy and James, were accrued during his months of waiting in Lisbon for a diplomatic appointment. Others, though, likely emanated from his business losses and from his penchant for "loving play."[2] What is certain is that by late 1785 Winslow had failed to make payments toward a debt of £570 owed prominent Dutch banking brothers Jacob and Nicolas Van Staphorst—the same men who lent money to the United States through John Adams.

Having returned to Boston, Winslow had anticipated help from his father not only for the Van Staphorsts' debt, but those owed Boston creditors John Codman and a Mr. Lowell. To his surprise, his father had financial difficulties of his own and was then so strapped that he decided to sell the Warrens' Milton home.

Compounding the Warrens' financial difficulties were funds James had advanced to pay the salaries of sailors while a director of the Navy Board. Those payments had been generous—£1,000—a sum confirmed in 1785 by a treasury commissioner.

In October 1786, however, a second treasury official arrived in Boston and accused James of faulty record-keeping. The man was "a very singular character," James had complained to Elbridge Gerry at the time, "dark, reserved, disgusts everybody, affronts or ill treats all, is abused in return, and bears it as a dull horse does a whip."[3] Predictably, James was never recompensed, a situation he hoped to remedy in early 1786 by sending Winslow to Congress with records of his accounts.

Dutifully, the young man rode the icy roads to New York in February 1787, hoping that besides delivering James's accounts, his personal appearance before Congressional delegates might win him a diplomatic appointment. At month's end with nothing decided about either, Winslow began the long ride back to Massachusetts.

On Monday, March 6, just after Winslow's return, James received an apologetic letter from Nathaniel Gorham, a former patriot of the Massachusetts Board of War and soon the new president of Congress. Gorham explained that the "great inattention and negligence of the states . . . renders it impossible for Congress to pass upon this report." Other debts first had to be paid, especially "applications from our foreign creditors."[4]

As usual for travelers like Winslow riding between Boston and Philadelphia, he stayed overnight at certain inns along the way. No sooner had he returned to a New Haven inn than Sheriff John Chandler served him with papers filed by the Van Staphorsts of Holland demanding his appearance in court that April.

Someone, Winslow ruminated as he rode back to Plymouth, had watched his movements and anticipated his return to New Haven—a someone who could only have been his frustrated American creditor, John Codman. Prevented from collecting his own debts in Massachusetts because of James Warren's political influence, Codman had filed a suit in Connecticut on behalf of the Van Staphorsts.

Vowed to take revenge, Winslow thus appeared on March 12 at one p.m. at Boston's Stock Exchange, the hour when merchants traditionally convened. That day the Warrens' friend Revolutionary war hero General Henry Knox was also present and stunned to observe an argument on the floor of the Exchange that culminated into a "caning match between Mr. John Codman and Mr. Winslow Warren." The latter, he recalled, "attacked Mr. Codman with a very heavy cane without giving him at the least precious notice," rendering him "much bruised."[5]

To Mercy, the incident was all too reminiscent of her brother Jemmy's fracas with British officer John Robinson eighteen years earlier.

In contrast to the ugly rumors surrounding Winslow came a flood of condolences about Charles. If only she had the words "to pour... the healing balm" upon Mercy about the death of that "amiable youth,"[6] wrote Hannah Winthrop in recollection of the years he had boarded with her at Harvard.

From London, Abigail Adams similarly mourned the loss of that "dear and amiable youth who, while "young in years... mature in virtue... lived beloved and died lamented."

She also consoled Mercy about the accusations leveled against her husband, James, during the 1785 gubernatorial election. She must ignore the "popular torrent which... sets against your worthy partner." Time, Abigail insisted, "will convince the world who are their approved and unshaken friends."

Within that same letter, Abigail expressed the disappointment she shared with her husband, John, over James's refusals to serve in Congress. The public's spiteful reaction, Abigail implied, was understandable, one even she had predicted "when I so earnestly pressed the General to accept his last appointment and attend Congress."[7]

By late spring 1786, the economy of the State of Massachusetts, straining under a federal obligation of $300,000 per year, was faltering. To boost the state coffers, the legislature under Governor Bowdoin raised property taxes upon the state's struggling farmers, toppling their tenuous hold upon mortgaged farms financed by federal "continentals" and plunging them into bankruptcies.

The courts sold the repossessed properties to speculators at a fraction of their worth. Not only were their taxes exorbitant, howled the farmers, but Massachusetts had demanded payment in specie, or hard currency, which was hard to come by in rural counties. Equally unjust was the double advantage held by the region's justices, many of whom served as delegates to the Massachusetts Assembly, which set the state's fiscal policies. Since, moreover, the "continentals" churned out by Congress to pay the farmer-veterans of the Revolution were becoming worthless, they clamored for Massachusetts to produce its own paper currency.

A bitter battle between the farmers of western Massachusetts—and its merchants, lawyers, and legislative delegates—erupted. "Commerce is ruined and, what is worse, the husbandry and manufactures of the country cannot be supported," James had predicted a year earlier in a letter to John Adams.

While the state legislature had debated various solutions, they ultimately did "little" to ameliorate the situation. Exacerbating the financial crisis was the public's "total change in principles and manners" toward self-interest and wealth, a situation, James claimed, that "seems verging to confusion and anarchy."[8]

During that period, John had complained in a letter to Mercy, "I wish my friend Warren in public life, because I know he would have been useful there...his numerous refusals, I am informed, are made use of against him."[9]

The "picture you draw of the ruin of the country is horrible," John finally replied to James on July 4. Yet, "bad as it may be, paper money or a suspension of law processes...would make it much worse. I cannot be of your opinion that there is 'total change in principles and manners' nor that 'interest is the only pursuit' nor that 'riches only are respected.'"

If James recalled the years between 1760 and 1774, he would realize that self-interest and the pursuit of wealth always prevailed. "Our countrymen, are not, and never were, 'Spartans' when it came to wealth." Moreover, John added, "I am never apprehensive of anarchy, because I know there is wisdom...enough to prevent it."[10]

On that last point though, John was overly optimistic. By the summer of

1786, a number of Massachusetts towns refused to pay taxes. Even so, the state legislature had adjourned without offering remedies against foreclosures, prompting James to fume that the delegates had irresponsibly "dosed themselves into an unusual adjournment for six or seven months."[11]

In August, angry farmers from fifty rural towns in Hampshire County met for three days in Hatfield protesting the "selfishness" of the delegates, the judges, and the lawyers and demanding that Massachusetts produce paper money. Even if their recommendation was approved, bellowed some of the protestors, it would take time to implement them and do little to rescue those faced with imminent bankruptcies.

Among the most shrill was Daniel Shays, a thirty-nine-year-old bankrupt farmer formerly a "brave and good soldier"[12] according to veteran Park Holland, who had served under him during the Revolution. By late August, Shays had rallied five hundred armed farmers who marched to Northampton where they stationed themselves outside the Court of Common Pleas to prevent it from convening.

Having intimidated its judges, Shays and his armed band then threatened the courts of Worcester, Concord, and Great Barrington. On September 26, they even stormed the Supreme Court at Springfield. From there the rebels were rumored to march upon Boston to force Massachusetts into revocation of its bankruptcy laws.

"We are now in a state of anarchy and ... confusion bordering on a civil war," James reported to John Adams. "The Massachusetts Assembly have set near a month without any ... wisdom ... to redress the unhappy situation."[13]

Finally, on November 8, in lieu of hard cash for back taxes, the delegates conceded that the farmers could pay their debts with produce such as potatoes, carrots, and wheat. On November 15, the assembly granted an eight-month extension on the collection of private debts. Two days later its delegates raised taxes on foreign luxuries, and, soon afterward, offered amnesty to the insurgents.

Such conciliations, the influential Justice Theodore Sedgwick of Stockbridge warned Governor Bowdoin, would only encourage the rebels. The surest way to quell the uprising was to raise a militia.

‹‹‹›››

From her "green parlor" on Neponset Hill, Mercy wrote Catharine Macaulay about the "tumults that have lately taken place in some of our counties... We have indeed been much alarmed at the... discontent, disorder and riot."

The chaos arose from the "burden of the late war and the pressure of... public and private debts, heightened by the injudicious conduct of [those] ... in the legislative and executive department, who feel little for the lower classes." She fervently hoped that those "disorders will soon be suppressed," followed by a "due subordination... on the one side, and levity and justice on the other."

Most disturbing to Mercy though was the reaction of "certain characters" within the government to "strengthen the hand of power and draw tight the reins of government,"[14] all too reminiscent of the tactics that had sparked America's break with Great Britain.

By January 1787, Shays and his men had returned to Springfield, where they plotted to seize the federal arsenal. Finally, on March 1, stalked by a four-thousand-person volunteer army supported by Governor Bowdoin but privately funded by Boston merchants, Shays and his men surrendered.

While the casualties were few, the confrontation between former fellow patriots had stunned the citizens of Massachusetts. "It was with no small grief that I now recognized in one of the dead, my old friend Spicer... a faithful soldier through the war... who... manifested much affection for me,"[15] General Benjamin Lincoln sadly recalled.

That spring, the Massachusetts legislature, horrified by the threat of civil war in America's cradle of liberty, convicted the rebels of treason. After a public protest, however, the perpetrators, among them Daniel Shays, were pardoned.

"The mild measures taken by the government were... proposed to bring these men to a sense of their duty and make them good citizens of the state," Park Holland, a commander in Bowdoin's militia, recalled forty years later. "We who had stood by the side of these men in severe battles with a powerful enemy, and witnessed their hardships... would much rather remember the good service they rendered their country."[16]

-<+>-

Unmentioned in Mercy's 1786 letter to Catharine Macaulay were the embarrassments surrounding her son Winslow. On November 2, 1786—the date the Connecticut Court of Claims finally scheduled the New Haven hearing—Winslow was ordered to prison. Somehow, either through bribes or chicanery, he subsequently "broke the goal aforesaid...made a willful and torturous escape from the custody of the sheriff."[17]

Once publicized in Massachusetts that Winslow—the Warrens' "debtor son"—was a fugitive from Connecticut, rumors began circulating that his father, James, sympathized with debtors, including the bankrupt farmers of Shays's Rebellion.

Ludicrous as such a leap was, Winslow's behavior provided James's political enemies with "proof." The elder Warren, they pointed out, had often denounced European luxuries, extolled the virtues of farming, and protested strong government control. Little did it seem to matter that his fourth son, Henry, fought in General Lincoln's militia against Shays's rebels—so bravely, as his commander General Lincoln explained, he had "gained the esteem of all."[18]

The rumors, nevertheless, persisted. At the height of Shays's Rebellion, a politically disillusioned Mercy lamented to John Adams that "[m]ankind, are governed less by reason than opinion. The caprice of the day, or the impulse of a moment will blow them about as with a whirlwind."[19]

In early January 1787, Mercy, apparently worrying that her long-delayed *History*, too, might suffer more from opinion than reason, asked Hannah Winthrop's stepson James, the librarian of Harvard College, to critique the early chapters.

Her *History*, Winthrop assured her in February, was "perspicuous and flowing. The facts are justly and methodically narrated. The characters, which indeed form the most difficult part of history, appear to be accurately defined...[and] perfectly just."

His main objection was Mercy's biased portrait of Thomas Hutchinson. While he agreed with her assessment of the former governor, "would it not be better to give him, on the credit of his own party, a little undeserved praise, to procure their judgment in favor of the work?"[20]

Simultaneous with Winthrop's observations, public opinion turned against Governor Bowdoin. At issue, as James explained to John that May, was the widespread conviction that the governor had dispersed, but not truly subdued the rebels. He especially objected to the tyrannical way the rebellion had been quelled. "For fear that Capt. Shays should destroy the [state] Constitution they [the leaders of Massachusetts] violated it themselves," James complained. Among his accusations was their temporary suspension of habeas corpus and prosecution of "some miserable scribblers [reporters]," who had penned "declarations of rebellion."[21]

In late 1786, during Shays's Rebellion, John sent James a copy of his new book, *A Defence of the Constitutions of Government of the United States.* While agreeing with nearly all of it, James objected to John's insistence that "the first magistrate must be set up very high in real power as well as in the opinion of the people."[22]

Having witnessed the alarming implications of Governor Bowdoin's rule, James distrusted absolute power and its symbols, which suggested the "pomp, parade, and magnificence of an European prince." Admittedly, in a crisis, "an addition of some real powers" might be necessary, but a governor should never have the right of a veto over the legislature, for that smacked of tyranny.

Others thought so, too, James explained. Governor Bowdoin's despotic measures had provoked new "general discontent," reflected in the "late elections" that returned the governorship to John Hancock.

Ironically, James admitted that he did not "regret the changes so much as I once should," for Hancock would likely govern more democratically than Bowdoin. Another surprise was "our old friend [Samuel] Adams," who, while again serving as lieutenant governor, "seems to have forsaken all his old principles and...become the most...despotic man in the Commonwealth."[23]

Had he read that remark, Sam would have denied it. From his perspective, Shays's Rebellion had been a parody of his cherished view of a republic of self-governing men. Appalled, Sam had consequently urged his protégé Bowdoin to inflict "just, condign punishment...on the detestable leaders of the banditti." Reasoning that "in monarchies the crime of treason and rebellion may...[be] pardoned or lightly punished," Sam believed that "the man who dares to rebel against the laws of a republic ought to suffer death."[24]

Coupled with those changes came new enthusiasm for James as a politician, and he was again elected to the state legislature. This time he accepted, if only because of his "dread of reviving the clamor of refusing everything." As he wrote John, "the duty of every man to go upon the deck when called upon in a storm, had induced me to accept."[25]

Having done so, James was again elected Speaker of the House.

The storm of Shays's Rebellion that impelled James to again "go upon deck"[26] blew far beyond the State of Massachusetts, sending winds of fear as far north as Vermont and as far south as Georgia, rattling the chimney stones and hearths of every home, hall, and court in America. In September 1786, while Shays rallied the disgruntled farmers against the courts, Congress had convened in Annapolis. On February 21, 1787, its delegates planned a meeting in Philadelphia for that May to refine the old Articles of Confederation. The thirteen states, as General Washington had nervously noted, were then held together by "a feeble thread"[27] vulnerable to making the new nation the "sport" of European nations.

To remedy that the states pledged to create a new federal union by electing seventy-four delegates to what was called the Constitutional Convention. Among the Massachusetts delegates was the Warrens' close friend Elbridge Gerry. While convinced that Shays's Rebellion symbolized democracy in the extreme, Gerry was no less suspicious of its opposite—despotism. Other delegates, hunkering down in steamy Philadelphia that May, were equally tenuous about the balance to be struck between personal freedoms, state rights, and the role of central government.

Negotiations were conducted in the strictest secrecy. Guards stood outside the doors of the State House where the delegates met. Workers piled dirt over the cobbled streets outside to muffle carriage traffic, as the delegates, sweltering in the soaring temperatures of a Philadelphia summer, were locked in debate.

"Indeed," as General Henry Knox grumbled to Mercy that summer, he wished to know about the debates, if only to anticipate "the complexion the remainder of our lives was likely to assume."[28]

While no less curious, Mercy spent her time writing Winslow's creditors for extensions, visiting Mary, the second wife of her brother Samuel Allyne, on the birth of a baby girl, and attending to her favorite niece, Sally Sever Russell, then dying of consumption.

On July 28, no longer able to contain her curiosity, Mercy wrote Ann, the wife of Elbridge Gerry, a delegate to the Constitutional Convention. Were the negotiators "yet locked up in silence and secrecy?" If so, Mercy stoically conceded, she, like the rest of "imperfect man" must thus wait until the "best systems of the wisest... are sufficiently ripened for the inspection of the vulgar eye."[29]

Four days later, seeking reassurance from another kindred spirit, she wrote Catharine Macaulay that "[t]he eyes of all Europe are upon them [the delegates]... God grant that a system may be devised that will give energy to law, and dignity to government... without leveling the fair fabric of a free, strong and national republic, beneath the splendid roof of royal or aristocratic pageantry."[30]

Few words were more distasteful to the Plymouth matron than "royal" or "aristocratic," in whose glittering European reflection, she sensed, stood Abigail and John Adams. While Mercy's 1785 congratulatory letter on John's appointment as first American minister to the Court of Great Britain extolled his "abilities and perseverance"[31] and expressed faith in his earlier patriotic ideals, Mercy was suspicious.

One of her letters to John had even raised the question. "Is it possible that, sir, after five or six years spent in the most splendid courts in Europe, [you] can look back and sigh for the retirement and simplicity of Pens Hill? If you really do I pronounce you a philosopher of the first magnitude, and if ever you voluntarily return to that style, I think you will... stand foremost in the list of genuine republicans."[32]

In reply, John had admitted that "fortune, and figure, birth and grace, titles and ribbons, that make impressions on courtiers," were "earnestly courted [at]... every ball, every entertainment, every horse race and gaming table" in Europe. Such activities, though, were accompanied by "incessant fatigue and chagrin, to the consumption of all his time and... inattention to business and neglect of all his duties... of which our country has no occasion and for which her humble minister has no ambition."[33]

Abigail, too, had reiterated that message. While Mercy may have imagined her friend living "at the height of prosperity, and swallowed up by the gayeties of Europe...the estimate is far from the truth," Abigail wrote on May 24, 1786. She was not "at all captivated, either with the manners or politics of Europe. I think our own country much the happiest spot upon the globe."[34]

On that same date, John again explained that their grandiose lifestyle—which included an elegant townhouse in London's Grosvenor Square maintained by eight servants, their handsome coach, and frequent appearances at the Court of St. James—was illusory. The mode in which he lived had been forced upon him as an American minister.

"If I were my own master...I should live in affluence indeed," John admitted, "but when you consider that I have a rank to support here that I hold in trust for others, and that this rank cannot be let down, without betraying that trust, you may depend upon it, I am driven to my wits' end for means."[35]

Earlier, Mercy's admiration had inspired her to dedicate *The Sack of Rome* to John, followed in 1787 by her request for him to arrange its live production in London. Initially her old mentor had been enthusiastic, but by year's end was discouraged. "It requires almost as much interest and intrigue to get a play acted as to be a member of Parliament," he explained. Moreover, the British had "a universal desire...to forget America...they cannot recollect it, without pain."

To mitigate Mercy's disappointment, John added, "Your annals, or history, I hope you will continue, for there are few persons possessed of more facts, or who can record them in a more agreeable manner. Yet let me not deceive you. America must support the publication of it. No other country will contribute much towards it."[36]

Gradually, John and Abigail's worldly perspective was unraveling their friendship with the Warrens, although neither couple would yet admit it.

Chatty as Abigail's infrequent letters to Mercy were—filled with news of Nabby's marriage to William Smith, Elizabeth Montagu's essays, gossip about the heir to the British throne, and, in May 1787, news that Nabby made her a grandmother—they inevitably included an apologetic paragraph about her preference for America.

"I long, my dear Madam, to return to my native land. My little cottage encompassed with my friends has more charm for me than the drawing room of St. James, where studied civility, and disguised coldness cover malignant hearts," Abigail assured Mercy. [37]

Doubtless Abigail was sincere but she was also self-protective, defending herself against envy on Mercy's part, an emotion the author once described as "a kind of canker worm that generally crawls round the loftiest branches."[38]

While Mercy and James would never admit it, that worm was already gnawing upon their own high-minded ideals.

16

"Too federal to talk freely"

IN AUGUST 1787, while awaiting news about the Constitution, Mercy wrote Catharine Macaulay that while "[e]very man is . . . convinced a strong efficient government is necessary," the form its leadership would take remained controversial. The patriots "wish to see a form established on the pure principles of republicanism" but others "secretly wish for aristocracy; while the young . . . cry . . . for monarchy."[1]

Among the drafters was the Warrens' frustrated ally Elbridge Gerry, who, having unsuccessfully voiced objections to the evolving document, refused to sign the final version on September 15. Ten days later a final version of the Constitution nevertheless arrived in Massachusetts for public inspection

Every citizen read the document "with attention," Mercy again wrote Catharine, then "solemnly folded the paper and kept his opinion to himself."

"Our situation is truly delicate . . . On the one hand, we stand in need of a strong federal government, founded on principles that will support the prosperity and union of the colonies. On the other, we have struggled for liberty."[2]

To the British, as Catharine explained in a letter that November, the Constitution seemed a document "grounded on simple democracy."[3] Disagreeing, Mercy clarified her objections in February 1788 by publishing a treatise called "Observations on the New Constitution, and on the Federal and State Conventions."

Bylined as "The Columbia Patriot, Sic Transit Gloria," Mercy's nineteen-page pamphlet pleaded for the preservation of "republican" values and assailed the federal system of checks and balances as a "many headed monster of such motley mixture, that its enemies cannot trace a feature of Democratic or Republican extract." The Constitution had overlooked the rights of the individual and those of individual states.

"All writers on government agree . . . that man is born free and possessed of certain unalienable rights—that government is instituted for the protection, safety, and happiness of the people," Mercy reminded her readers. Somehow though, the drafters of the Constitution had managed "to betray the people of the United States, into an acceptance of a most complicated system of government; marked on the one side with the *dark, secret* and *profound intrigues* of the statesman . . . practiced in . . . despotism; and on the other, with the ideal project of young ambition . . . to intoxicate the *inexperienced votary.*"

Specifically, she faulted the Constitution for the authority granted the executive branch of the government to the detriment of the "natural rights" of citizens. No provisions had been made for freedom of speech or freedom of the press. Nor had "limits" been placed upon the judiciary. The Supreme Federal Court was permitted an "unwarranted stretch of power over the liberty, life, and property" of citizens. Even trial by jury in civil suits, a hallowed right of British citizens, had been omitted.

Equally perilous was the way the drafters had "dangerously blended" the executive and legislative branches, ambiguously worded the rationale for a standing army, and disregarded fiscal "support of internal government" and "liquidation" of state debts.

The rights granted Congressional delegates to elect their own salaries— liberties likely to lead to a "drain for public monies"—was also dangerous. Provisions had been made neither for the rotation of those holding political office nor for limits upon their terms. Suspect, too, was the electoral college system, which was "nearly tantamount to the exclusion of the voice of the people." Those and other omissions, Mercy insisted, necessitated the addition of a "bill of rights to guard against the dangerous encroachments of power."[4]

In December 1791, ten of the objections Mercy so eloquently voiced in "Observations on the New Constitution" reappeared in the Bill of Rights.

For decades, it was assumed that the author of those "Observations" was Elbridge Gerry. One hundred and forty years later as legal scholar Charles Warren read Mercy's letter of May 1888 to Catharine Macaulay with its reference to her pamphlet, "Observations on the new Constitution," he realized his ancestor had authored it.

By autumn of 1787, when the State of Massachusetts called for electors to ratify the Constitution, Antifederalist broadsides had appeared that were attributed to those "abettors of anarchy and confusion,"[5] James Warren, Elbridge Gerry, and James Winthrop.

In seven essays bylined as "A Republican Federalist" and "Helvidius Priscus" (after a Roman stoic who opposed absolute power) that were published in the *Massachusetts Centinel,* James critiqued the drafters of the Constitution for disregarding their mandate to refine the Articles of Confederation and instead transforming it into a document establishing a strong federal union.

"Of all compacts, a constitution or frame of government is the most solemn and important," James warned. Its sole objective was "preservation of that property, which every individual of the community has, in his *life, liberty* and *estate.*"[6]

Such ideas, his enemies immediately retorted, tilted toward anarchy, such as that epitomized by Shays's Rebellion. "The object of the Antifederalists is not merely a rejection of the NEW PLAN but an abolition of all government,"[7] the *Massachusetts Centinel* reminded readers. During the subsequent smear campaign, neither James Warren nor Elbridge Gerry was elected to the state's three-hundred-fifty-five-member ratification committee.

Ironically, most members of the Massachusetts ratification committee were Antifederalists, who, thanks to the pleas of John Hancock and Sam Adams, voted by a slim margin on February 7 to ratify the Constitution. Attached to the committee's approval was a list of what Mercy once called *"necessary alterations"*[8]—the Conciliatory Proposition, containing nine amendments similar to the ones James and Elbridge Gerry had published in their protesting letters.

⋘⟶⟩⟩

"Niddy-noddy; Niddy-noddy/ two heads, one body!"[9] An eighteenth-century rhyme describing the reel that wound wool into skeins of yarn epitomized the indecision of other states. In farmhouse kitchens, city drawing rooms, and country inns, citizens debated that document for nearly a year.

Among the most persuasive arguments were those later known as the Federalist Papers, which appeared in New York newspapers in 1787 and 1788, bylined by "Publius" but alternately penned by Alexander Hamilton, James Madison, and John Jay.

Without a strong central government, the authors argued, the "insufficiency of the present Confederation to preserve that union," would leave the United States "vulnerable to anarchy and foreign intervention."[10] No less persuasive was an argument appearing in New York's November 3 *Independent Journal,* maintaining that representatives of the people would come from the nation's "most talented men" and probably be "more wise, systematical, and judicious than those of individual states."[11]

From Binfield, England, where an ailing Catharine Macaulay lived in retirement, she wrote Mercy in March 1788 about rumors that "the majority of States" favored the Constitution. "We are," she added sharply, "a little surprised here to find that the New England and Connecticut should be the earliest in aceeding."[12]

At that moment, three states were still needed for ratification. To dissuade them, the Antifederalists of Massachusetts widely distributed Mercy's newly published "Observations on the New Constitution" to the states. The most crucial was New York State, whose country committees received over sixteen hundred copies of the pamphlet. On April 2, the influential *New York Journal* and several other newspapers also reprinted it.

While an Albany committee agreed that "Observations on the New Constitution" was "well composed," they found its language "too sublime and florid for the common people."[13] Still, Mercy's treatise had revitalized the controversy, even to the point of disturbing members of the old Congress convened in the marble chambers of Manhattan's City Hall.

Among those curious about its authorship was Mercy's Federalist brother, Samuel Allyne Otis, then newly elected secretary of the senate. "I have heard in the circles here you, or Sister W. (Mercy) have written the 'Columbian Patriot,'" he wrote his brother-in-law James. "I suspect you."

Samuel's curiosity was piqued by his shallow pockets rather than from the deep wells of political philosophy. Having declared bankruptcy several years earlier but longing to reestablish his mercantile business, he believed that the establishment of a strong centralized government would "reanimate a dead mass of useless paper, and instantly make it an efficient capital."[14]

Nor was Samuel Allyne alone in his belief that a powerful central government would revive the economy and intimidate foreign nations from political manipulation. Convinced that "Observations on the New Constitution" flowed from the pen of James Warren—or possibly his allies Elbridge Gerry and James Winthrop—the Federalists of Massachusetts vowed to destroy Mercy's husband as a political influence. Surely, they believed, the author of that republican treatise could only be the still powerful old-line Speaker of the House, the same man who composed shrewdly sentimental pleas in publications such as the *Independent Chronicle* under the byline of Helvidius Priscus.

"Massachusetts has fought for her liberties...purchased them by the most costly sacrifices," that Antifederalist had written. "Let the youth of America, who are yet ignorant of the...causes that occasioned the dismemberment of the United States from the crown of Britain read...on the origin of government and the rights of human nature...let them examine the principles of the late glorious revolution."[15]

By winter of 1787–1788, after a cadre of representatives in the House, most of them farmers, fieldworkers, and tradesmen, nominated James for the lieutenant governorship, his enemies redoubled their efforts to paint him as a secret abettor of Shays's Rebellion.

"His emissaries were constantly engaged in attending the nocturnal scenes of the Star Chamber and...manufacturing speeches for the Antifederalist Junto,"[16] spewed the *Independent Chronicle* on January 3, 1788. Warren, opined the *Massachusetts Centinel,* had a "depraved heart," whose motives stemmed from "the gratification of malice and whose sole object is his private interest."[17]

Even the Adamses' brilliant eldest son, John Quincy, twenty, a Harvard graduate studying law in Boston, was persuaded. On April 25, after stopping for a brief visit at the Warrens' farm in Milton and finding Mercy at home alone, he wrote his father that James was not the same man his father once admired.

During John's years abroad, "the General's political character has undergone...a great alteration," the young man wrote. No longer was James admired by his former friends, for "the insurgent and Antifederal party... consider him...as their head...He has been charged with using his influence in favor of tender acts and paper money; and...secretly favored the insurrections."

Even his wife, Mercy, John Quincy added, seemed embittered and complained that her husband "had been abused shamefully." After that outburst, Mercy caught herself, became tight-lipped, and refused to further discuss the matter. Mrs. Warren, the youth concluded, "thought me too federal to talk freely with me."[18]

If little else, that portrait of Mercy's sudden restraint symbolized the depth of her disappointments—her dashed hopes for a democratic republic and dismay over the declining opportunities of her family. Not only were Winslow's hopes for a diplomatic appointment shattered, but even her son Henry's future was hurt by his parents' politics.

Having settled in Plymouth, the twenty-two-year-old aspired to an appointment as collector of impost and excise. Twice, James's supporters in the Massachusetts House had voted in Henry's favor but were defeated by what Mercy described as "violent opposition"[19] from the Senate.

In an argument years later, John Adams admitted to Mercy that while he still respected James, his political reputation was tarnished. "The conduct of General Warren at the time of Shays's Rebellion, whether truly or falsely represented, and his supposed...hostility to the federal Constitution had produced so determined a spirit against him that if Washington himself had nominated [him] to any office," John maintained, "he would...have been negatived by the Senate."[20]

Privately, James fumed to Elbridge Gerry, he was "surrounded by ill founded rumors." Nevertheless, he vowed that whatever happened, "my spirits shall never be affected."[21]

Soon after the June 1788 ratification of the Constitution, James thus graciously wrote George Washington that every citizen had a duty "to rejoice," over its acceptance and should cooperate "to carry it into operation." In turn, the Virginian replied that it was "no small pleasure to find that former friendships have not been destroyed by a difference of opinion."[22]

To the ascendant Federalists, nevertheless, James still seemed a dangerous man, a radical Whig whose passion for state and individual rights ignored the pressing reasons for a unifying federal system.

In time, years after ratification of the Bill of Rights, Mercy also accepted
the Constitution. The document, she admitted in her *History,* ultimately
proved more sound than during its initial unveiling.

"This instrument appeared to the public eye... doubtful in its origin,
dangerous in its aspect, and for a time very alarming to... men, who were
tremblingly alive on the smallest encroachment of rights and privileges...
But the system was adopted with expectations of amendment, and the
experiment proved salutary, and has... redounded... to the honor and interest of America... Perhaps genius has never devised a system more con-
genial to their wishes, or better adapted to the condition of man than the
American Constitution."[23]

On the eve of the Constitution's ratification, James sold the Hutchinson mansion on Neponset Hill. In June 1788, just before New Hampshire,
the ninth state, ratified that document into law, he and Mercy returned to
Plymouth.

If critics perceived that move as a sign of defeat, the Warrens considered
it a return to happier times. While at Milton, as Mercy once admitted to her
niece Sally Sever, she often daydreamed about Plymouth, walking mentally
through "every happy corner of a house where I have tasted... real felicity."[24] Mercy made no similar claims about the mansion in Milton.

The nearly sixty-year-old Mercy still believed life was to be savored—
especially her marriage to James of thirty-three years. As her poem "Extempore to a young Person beholding the motion of a Clock" once advised,
time passed so rapidly that it was important to avoid the world "with all its
snares"[25] that deprived one of joy.

Plymouth thus became the Warrens' sanctuary. No longer did Mercy
grumble, as eight years earlier, that the town was provincial. Now it seemed
a perfect venue for rest, reflection, and retreat. "We are again happily fixed
I believe for the remainder of life," she wrote Catharine in 1790. If only
they could "spend a few days together in... Plymouth beneath the shade of
retirement and philosophical contemplation."[26]

Another aspect of that shade of retirement, she wrote Winslow, then living in Boston and still in debt, concerned her writing. "We are now so much

out of the noise of politics . . . that I do not feel [it] . . . necessary . . . to write with that energy and pathos that such a subject requires."[27] Implied, too, was the cessation of her efforts to complete the *History*.

What, after all, was the point of describing a Revolution meant to create a democratic republic of free men that was destroyed by power-hungry men determined to create a new "aristocracy"?

For all the fiery Otis blood that ran through Mercy's veins and the fervor with which she had defended the rights of ordinary citizens, she no longer "dared . . . continue my observations on so bold a subject while the whole Continent was thrown in a ferment by a variation in political sentiment."[28]

After their 1789 return to America, John and Abigail Adams remained similarly mute. In anticipation of their arrival, Governor Hancock ordered lookouts to salute the famous couple with a cannonade when their ship, the *Lucretia*, entered Boston Harbor on June 17. As pealing church bells signaled their arrival, the Adamses stepped onto the gangplank of the Long Wharf before an admiring crowd and were rushed into Hancock's golden coach for an overnight stay on Beacon Hill.

The next morning, the embarrassed couple insisted upon hiring their own coach to return to Braintree, where they temporarily resided with Abigail's sister and brother-in-law Mary and Richard Cranch.

Mercy must have been thrilled at the news. Would her old friends still be as fond as the Warrens as before? Had their years in the courts of Europe changed them? Would they regard her and James as hopelessly provincial —especially compared to the foreign ministers and crowned heads of Europe and England? Did her friend Abigail still believe, as she had insisted to Mercy a year earlier, that her "little cottage, encompassed with my friends has more charms . . . than the drawing room of St. James."[29]

Or was the rumor Mercy heard that the Adamses had purchased a larger home along the Braintree coast a sign of their new fondness for aristocracy? Even Sam Adams had reported that John "had been corrupted by his residence in England."[30]

To John and Abigail such thoughts, had Mercy expressed them, would have seemed as distorted as the pompadours favored by stylish European women. Their purchase of the old Vassal-Borland property—as the old

Tory farmhouse, outbuildings, and eighty surrounding acres were known —was simply the fulfillment of a long-delayed dream.

"No employment however honorable, no course of life however brilliant, has such a luster in my imagination as absolutely a private life," John had written James from Paris. "My farm and my family glitter before my eyes every day and night."[31]

To the visitors who stopped at Braintree that summer, the Adamses seemed enchanted with their new role. Working in the garden, churning butter, and raising poultry, as Abigail wrote Foreign Minister Thomas Jefferson, held "more charms...than residing at the court of St. James's where I seldom meet with characters so inoffensive as my hens and chickens, or minds so well improved as my garden."[32]

Similar pastoral occupations engrossed John. The rustic character of the Vassal-Borland property, he happily wrote an English friend, epitomized "the farm of a patriot."[33]

Initially there were disappointments, among them unfinished repairs and the realization that the house was smaller than the one Abigail remembered—more a "wren's house"[34] than a proper setting for their new European furniture. Finally though, the Adamses moved in, seamlessly transformed, or so it seemed to outsiders, from the famous American minister and his lady into a New England farming couple.

Scattered about were mementos of their years abroad—John's elegant writing desk, handsome Dutch cabinets, and other European furnishings. In the garden, the cutting from an English red rose symbolic of the House of Lancaster was taking root near a white one for the House of York.

One of their first visitors was French writer J. P. Brissot, whom John proudly escorted around the property he dubbed "Peacefield," symbolizing retirement from public life. To the Frenchman, Adams embodied the neoclassical ideal of the Enlightenment, resembling "one of the generals and ambassadors of the golden ages of Rome and Greece."[35]

No less charmed was thirty-eight-year-old writer Judith Sargent Murray, who visited Peacefield that October during a honeymoon trip with her second husband, the English Universalist preacher John Murray. Four years earlier, while raising her first husband's niece, Judith published treatises on raising girls in the *Gentleman and Lady's Town & Country Magazine*.

Subsequent to meeting the Adamses, Judith reported that the "illustrious patriot and his truly amiable lady" had received the Murrays with open arms. Mr. Adams seemed benevolent but had "the marks of deep thinking," suggesting "the sage, the philosopher, the politician, and the man of unbending integrity."

As for Abigail, whose virtues European writers had already extolled, "It is evident the domestic as well as the more brilliant virtues are all her own— We were soon grouped in familiar chat."[36]

Similar reports of meetings and "familiar chat" are notably absent from the correspondence of Mercy and John Warren. Only one letter from that period remains in Mercy's papers, dated February 1789 and referring to John's loan of a volume of Gibbon's *Decline and Fall of the Roman Empire*.

In response, Mercy's former mentor explained that his ten months at Peacefield were "the sweetest morsel of my life," and that no "office in public life ... [could] furnish the entertainment and refreshment of the mountain ... meadow and the stream."[37]

Soon after the Adamses arrived in the United States, rumors had circulated that John would be nominated for a leading role in the new government—as a senator, governor, or vice president. In spite of an accompanying flurry of newspaper speculations, he and Abigail remained noncommittal, although Congress was already planning to nominate John for a prominent position.

By early November, in anticipation of Nabby's delivery of her baby, Abigail had rushed to New York—too late, as it happened, to be present at the birth of her second grandson, John Adams Smith.

Personal domestic events would not, however, fully explain the deteriorating relations between the Warrens and the Adamses. As Catharine Macaulay had warned Mercy in October 1788, John had become "a very warm Federalist and by what I have discerned of yours and Mr. Warren's political sentiments ... you will not agree quite so well on public matters as you did formerly."[38]

Initially, Mercy and James greeted the Adamses warmly, and by late summer they were socializing and visiting old friends together. On one occasion, after calling upon Hannah Winthrop in Cambridge, Mercy and John rode in Elbridge's carriage to his nearby home. As they chatted over tea about the ratification of the Constitution, John reprimanded Mercy for repeatedly hearkening back to American "virtue." American citizens, he snapped, were "alike all other people, and shall do like other nations, where all well-regulated governments are monarchic."

Wincing, Mercy retorted that "a limited monarchy might be the best government, but . . . it would be long before Americans would be reconciled to the idea of a king."

In spite of the tiff, she and James subsequently accepted an invitation for an overnight stay with the Adamses. At breakfast, the conversation again turned to monarchy—a subject that, or so Mercy later recalled, John seemed to favor, alongside "an order of nobility."

To that, James, defending his Antifederalist stance, had declared, "I am thankful that I am a plebian."

"No sir: you are one of the nobles," John retorted. "There has been a national aristocracy here ever since the country was settled—your family at Plymouth, Mrs. Warren's at Barnstable, and many others . . . that have kept up a distinction similar to nobility."

Somehow, the awkwardness of the moment passed, displaced by a moment of mirth. Afterward, the two men stood by the window and discussed the disposition of the southern states. Finally John—at least according to Mercy's recollection—exclaimed, "'They must have a master'; and added by a stamp . . . [of his] foot 'By God, they shall have a master.'" Later that evening, John even declared that he "wished to see a monarchy in this country, and an hereditary one too."

"And so do I too,"[39] Mercy declared sarcastically, or so she later claimed.

Whatever was actually said, the visit ended sourly. After that, James refused to write to John. In contrast, Mercy, hopeful of overlooking their political differences, attempted to maintain the friendship.

Politics, as she later insisted to General Henry Knox, should never get in the way of friendship. For that reason in early 1789, she had dallied with the idea of visiting the nation's temporary capital in Manhattan. "I still love my old friends, many of whom are collected at New York,"[40] Mercy wrote, mentioning Federalists George and Martha Washington.

In spite of Mercy's hopes, the political differences between the Warrens and the Adamses even affected their sons. In a letter of December 1788, Winslow wrote from Boston about a street encounter with a certain youth who had insulted his father, James. She hoped, Mercy replied, that the "pride of the young gentlemen of a certain family on whom ruin is pronounced, will lead them to preserve that integrity ... and ... [will] put them on a footing with those youths of another family who are soaring to imaginary distinctions of rank and honor that will not ... be peaceably enjoyed in this country."

The next evening Mercy added in a postscript that she could only laugh at the "greatest of men who at times are the sport of their own ambition and passionate fondness for distinction."

For the sake of peace, she advised Winslow, "this matter should for the present at least, pass off silently." After all, a "rupture with ___ would be a misfortune. I hope it will not take place. Why should it, for a difference in political sentiment?"[41]

PART IV

Penwoman to Posterity

17

"A sister's hand may wrest a female pen"

ON FEBRUARY 3, 1789, Mercy apologized to John for her tardy return of his volume of Gibbon's *Decline and Fall of the Roman Empire*. Hoping to heal their recent argument, she wished John continued respite from the "painful occupations of a public life" at Peacefield, but anticipated that he would soon be "immersed in...government and politics" once again. Perhaps he might still find time for the "entertainment of (a) friend, who though in private life, can never cease to wish for the welfare and peace of the United America."

Having learned on February 8 that Massachusetts and four other states voted for John as vice president, Mercy added a note to that letter confirming her opinion that he "ought to be called to this distinguished rank in government." She had only one objection, "the removal of valuable friends to such a distance." Her husband, James, she gingerly explained, would "make his own compliments and congratulations"[1] from Boston.

In spite of her flattering words, Mercy continued to brood about the new central government that she believed would become a monarchy in form, if not in name. Even Sam Adams who again seemed "just the easy friend he used to be," she unhappily confided to James, felt he "must be Federal, or nothing."[2]

Not, however, the Warrens. For the previous eight months, as she reported to Hannah Winthrop from Plymouth that winter, "[w]e are still, quiet, and passive, have little to do with either the political, the great or the little world."

Moreover, Mercy confessed, "The longer my pen lies still, the less disposed I am to use it . . . Perhaps . . . I have blotted paper enough already. But as politics are out of the question, all future compositions may be very harmless."[3]

In point of fact, Mercy was already wielding her pen in the "harmless" task of revising her poems and plays with the goal of publishing them in her own name.

By the early 1790s, a younger crop of female American writers had already begun to do just that. Among the most prominent were Judith Sargent Murray, Susanna Rowson, Sarah Wentworth Morton, and Hannah Adams, the first two whose works advocated rights for women.

Mercy's earlier works—the plays, poems, and essays that addressed the "masculine" politics of the Revolution and its alarming slide from old patriotic ideals—were addressed to a wider audience. Knowing that with the rise of the Federalists she had nothing to lose, Mercy thus decided to preserve her message in print, if only as a historical record for future generations.

James, meanwhile, still hoping to set the record straight about his own work during the Revolutionary era, spent time in Plymouth reviewing his accounts, hoping to collect the debts still owed him from the Navy Board. In 1788, he asked his brother-in-law and Congressional delegate, Samuel Allyne Otis, to help. Stymied by the unsettled bureaucracy of the young republic, Mercy's brother finally wrote, "I confess I know not how to get forward in the business."[4]

Those debts, as James wearily explained to Elbridge Gerry that same spring, came from his payment of "large sums due to many poor tradesmen whose families were suffering." Lacking government compensation, he had donated part of his Navy Board salary to the sailors so that they "might have a part of theirs" while he and his fellow directors "took our chances for the remainder."

Exacerbating the difficulties recouping those donations—an amount of some $80,000—had been the second treasury officer's refusal to carry James's records back to Congress. Never, James consequently grumbled to Elbridge, did he imagine it would be necessary for him to go to "the great expense of money and time to go to New York"[5] to seek reimbursement.

<<+>>

By March 1789, Vice President-Elect John Adams was also brooding over the problems of the new nation, albeit from a different perspective. Fearing that citizens might resist the authority of a centralized government, he asked Mercy's opinion if the "people of our united America find it much easier to institute authority than to yield obedience." Was there, he wondered, referring to Shays's Rebellion, "enough of the spirit of the union to insure obedience to the laws?"[6]

Inadvertently, John had touched a raw nerve. To Mercy, her mentor's endorsement of a strong central government was reprehensible. It was unlikely, she tartly replied, that "the people of America will be remarkably averse to ... obedience to the authority they have instituted."

Even so, "I am persuaded the new government will operate very quietly unless the reins are held too tight." After all, she wearily added, human beings "are much more prone to servile compliance to ... power, than to ... that freedom and independence."[7]

A month later, still ruminating over what she considered the likelihood of an American monarchy and the injustices wreaked upon her family—Winslow still struggling to remain out of debtor jail, Henry blocked from becoming Plymouth's customs collector, and the ruin of her husband James's reputation—Mercy wrote John Adams again. This time, ignoring her advice to Winslow about remaining discreetly silent, she penned what she admitted was a "very free letter."

Flattery was Mercy's first ploy. "You, my dear sir, have successfully surmounted all: you have baffled the intrigues of your foes: have reached the acme of applause, and are placed in a situation to do eminent service to your country, to establish your family and to assist most *essentially* your friends."

"Gen. Warren has unfortunately been the butt of party malice." Surprisingly, John either believed those "misrepresentations" or had been "impressed by the calumnies of open or disguised enemies to the prejudice of an old and tried friend ... whose zeal ... in the public cause you are acquainted with and whose integrity you never could suspect."

She could not understand "Mr. Adams' forgetfulness of, or indifference" toward "such an invariable friend ... whose patriotism has been unshaken and his virtue incorruptible; whose fortune had been impaired and whose family have personally suffered in the public cause."

Yet, Mercy continued, her ire rising with each word, "neither himself nor any one of a family of young gentlemen of promising expectations have sustained any office of honor or emolument since the commencement of the Constitution of Massachusetts."

Now, Mercy added, "at a time when you have it so much in your power to oblige without injustice to yourself, your family, or your country," she hoped John would "indulge the feelings of a friend and the patriot by an attention to interest of a gentleman [James.]"[8]

Still another version of that letter found in Mercy's papers—but possibly never sent—chastised John for his denial of help on Winslow's behalf. "I could scarcely believe... that your Excellency should give as a reason for declining to support his interest *a fear of injuring your own popularity*... I cannot suppose you could for a moment believe that my son joined in a rebellion against a government which his family were so instrumental in establishing."[9]

John received Mercy's letter in New York just a few weeks after his inauguration as vice president. In June, when Abigail arrived, he showed it to her. By July, Abigail confided to her sister Mary Cranch that she never met a lady so "equally ambitious, but I presume her pretensions and those of her family will fail, as I think they ought to if one quarter part is true which has been reported of them."

Yet Mercy's request was hardly a surprise. During her last visit to the Adamses' in Braintree, the author had voiced similarly "unbridled ambition" for her husband and sons. At the time, Abigail recalled, there had been no "alteration in Mr. A's conduct," toward the Warrens.

Her husband "dealt by them like a sincere friend and an honest man and their own hearts must approve his conduct, however, grating to their feelings," Abigail maintained. "I am most sincerely sorry for the cause. They were my old and dear friends for whom I once entertained the highest respect."[10]

By May 29, John had responded directly to Mercy. "There has never been on my part any failure of friendship to Mr. Warren or yourself," he asserted. "You are very much mistaken in your opinion of my situation. I have neither reached the acme of applause nor am I in a situation to establish my family or assist my friends."

After returning to the United States, he was "extremely mortified . . . to hear from all quarters the unpopularity of my friend Warren and his family," and other expressions of "public wrath." Admittedly, there were "many and great exaggerations and misrepresentations. But one thing is indubitable, that G[eneral] Warren did differ for a time from all his friends and did countenance measures that appear to me, as they did to those friends, extremely pernicious."

Mercy's letter of May 7 had mentioned that she felt "sure of our patronage," John added. He had none, but even if he did, "neither your children nor my own would be sure of it if I had it." To do so would "belie the whole course of my public and private conduct and all . . . maxims of my life, if I should ever consider public authority entrusted to me to be made subservient to my private views, or those of my family or friends."

Indeed, "I must say to you as to every one else, I am not the person to apply to. The Constitution has wisely made the President the judge in the first instance . . . Every application must be made to him . . . in writing."[11]

Stung by John's acidic tone but determined to help her sons, Mercy consequently made a desperate appeal to Henry Knox, President Washington's new secretary of war. Apologizing for making "applications for office," Mercy asked if he might arrange her son Henry's appointment as the customs collector for Plymouth. Knox's friend, General Benjamin Lincoln, under whom Henry had served as an aide-de-camp against the "insurgents of the western counties" of Massachusetts would attest to her son's character.

Perhaps, too, he might help Winslow "in the arrangement of the military department."[12]

Three weeks later, the secretary explained that while he would have enormous "satisfaction serving any of your family," he had no influence upon securing an appointment for young Henry and suggested that Mercy write to President Washington. Nor could he help Winslow obtain a military commission for "at present no new appointments can take place."[13]

Five days after Knox's letter, crowds of angry Frenchmen wielding knives, clubs, and guns and shouting "liberty, equality and fraternity," stormed the Bastille in Paris, igniting a civil uprising that would shatter the monarchy.

"What an astonishing revolution in France. Do you not tremble for the fate of the young hero [Lafayette] who has led the nation to such bold demands in favor of the rights of human nature?" Mercy wrote Henry Knox in autumn 1789. "By the tenure of their proposed constitution, it is evident the spirit of liberty was caught in America. Where, Sir, do you think the Marquis la Fayette imbibed those high ideas that have fired his ambition to make his country free?"

Was his "conduct tinctured with the spirit of seventy-seven?" Or, she added sarcastically, "the more enlightened and accommodating disposition of eighty-eight when most of our country men seemed convinced that republicanism is the ideal dream of the enthusiastic patriot."

Had Lafayette waited a decade, "our revolution, might . . . have exhibited a useful lesson." Frankly, she felt badly that the noble was "engaged in an enterprise of so much hazard to himself, and perhaps eventually of but little advantage to his nation."

Silence, Mercy then apologized, had been her original intent, but in spite of that vow, her "incautious pen . . . so easily glides into the slippery path of politics."[14]

In anticipation of President Washington's appearance in Boston in October 1789, James planned to meet him and renew their friendship. Just before Washington's arrival though, an influenza epidemic spreading through New England had "severely seized" James, which "still hangs heavily on myself and family," and ultimately prevented the reunion, as Mercy unhappily reported to Henry Knox. If properly treated, influenza was not fatal, simply one "among other infections of a physical and political nature that threaten our country."[15]

Among those infections was the national debt. By late March 1790, still hopeful of reimbursement from his Navy Board account, James rode two hundred miles to New York. Only later, after a "very fatiguing journey" along the muddy roads of a raw spring, as Mercy reported to Elbridge, did James discover that his efforts were fruitless.

On April 12, Alexander Hamilton, thirty-five, the new secretary of the treasury, had announced to the Speaker of the House of Representatives that once a settlement was determined "and the balance discharged, no claim for depreciation ought afterwards to be admitted."[16] To Mercy, Hamilton was dictating dangerous fiscal policies, among them setting state debts, creating a national bank, and pushing American Indians out of their lands —and all at the sacrifice of old patriots like James.

Subsequent to his return to Plymouth, James fell ill with "a very dangerous illness," complicated by a new attack of gout. Weeks after nursing her husband, Mercy reported to Elbridge Gerry that he was making a spirited recovery—that he would "kick away with one foot those appearances that have greatly alarmed my mind, as he does with the other, the unmerited abuse to . . . his property."

What still rankled James beyond the unpaid Navy Board debt was the time lost to his own business interests. Why, Mercy pondered, were the "plums of gratitude" granted only to the military? "Were not the patriots in the legislature and other departments as . . . necessary, as meritorious and as much endangered as those in the field . . . if a Warren sacrificed the happiness of domestic life and relinquished . . . business . . . is he not as much entitled to the consideration of his country . . . as a *Steuben* [German soldiers] or any other soldier . . . or foreign nobleman?"[17]

Sadly, America had forgotten those whose ideals had originally sparked the American Revolution—ideals that seemed to be fading with each passing year.

A day after writing Elbridge, Mercy received a harsh reminder of that tumultuous past when learning that her beloved patriotic friend Hannah Winthrop had died. While the widow had been ailing all spring and insisted that her illness was her last, no one had believed her, explained her stricken stepson James Winthrop. The idea of Hannah's demise was simply "too painful"[18] to contemplate.

During that same spring, Hannah's son had been searching for prepublication buyers, or subscribers, for Mercy's new volume of poems and plays. By March, Mercy had decided to dedicate the collection to George Washington.

The new president did not reply until June 4 and explained that while he "wished to avoid being drawn into public view more than was essentially necessary," being "sensible of the merits" of the writer, he could not "hesitate to accept the intended honor."[19]

Thrilled, Mercy later rode to Boston to finalize arrangements with patriotic printers Isaiah Andrews, publisher of the *Massachusetts Spy,* and his partner, Ebenezer Thomas. The resultant volume, *Poems, Dramatic and Miscellaneous,* featured eighteen of Mercy's poems, among them "The Squabble of the Sea Nymphs" and "The Genius of America weeping the absurd Follies of the day," as well as two of her post-Revolutionary plays —*The Ladies of Castile* and *The Sack of Rome.*

As a collection, Mercy's message—that despotism, the quest for absolute power, and political disloyalties could destroy a nation and an empire— would finally be preserved in hardcover.

Yet, even as Mercy arrived on Boston's Newbury Street near the churning presses of Isaiah Thomas's establishment, two thoughts nibbled at her: the book's likely reception in that "golden age of *federalism*"[20] and the health of her husband, who had remained in Plymouth nursing his gout.

Sensing Mercy's worry, James reported that his health was improved and he thought about her in Boston "busily engaged in the business of an author of great abilities, discernment & judgment." As usual, Mercy was probably punishing herself, "hunting for criticism and advice." Yet she need not worry. If only "you had half the good opinion of yourself that I have of you, you certainly would not feel half the anxiety you do now. Here the weather is fine & all nature in bloom. I long to pluck a rose & gather a plate of strawberries for my little angel but the distance is too great."[21]

Within a few days, Mercy returned to Plymouth and again was folded into James's affectionate arms. Regardless of the reaction to *Poems, Dramatic and Miscellaneous* after its September 1790 publication, Mercy found comfort in her husband's enduring love.

"Feeling much for the distresses of America, in the dark days of her affliction, a faithful record has been kept...through a period that has engaged the attention,... of the philosopher and the politician," explained Mercy's dedication to George Washington.

Above all, she hoped that the President would "continue to preside in the midst of your brethren until nature asks the aid of retirement" and that the characters described in *Poems, Dramatic and Miscellaneous* would be "faithfully transmitted to posterity."

While Mercy had finally published a collection of her works as Mrs. M. Warren, the handsome leather-bound volume was more than a "faithful record" of her literary reaction to the American Revolution: It was also a plea for the recognition of female writers.

The second half of *Poems, Dramatic and Miscellaneous* was consequently dedicated to the leader of Great Britain's female literati. Titled "To Mrs. Montague, Author, Observations on the Genius and Writings of Shakespeare" Mercy hoped that the noted British critic-essayist Elizabeth Montagu would "soften to the friend." If a "humbler muse at a distance," like herself, Mercy suggested, won the praise of Mrs. Montagu, whose "sister's hand may wrest a female pen/From the bold outrage of imperious men," she would allow herself "a poet's pride."[22] While repeatedly intimated in her more recent poems and plays, the dedication was Mercy's strongest statement yet that a woman's worldview demanded respect.

Published in the ascendant "federal" year of 1790, during her philosophical estrangement from John Adams, *Poems, Dramatic and Miscellaneous,* was Mercy's bid to be remembered as the forgotten conscience of the American Revolution. Accordingly, she sent copies of the volume to friends and acquaintances, among them George Washington, John Adams, Alexander Hamilton, and Paul Revere.

By November 4, Washington had thanked her for the "flattering expressions of regard" of her dedication. "From the reputation of its author, from the parts I have read, and from a general idea of the pieces, I am persuaded of its gracious and distinguished reception by the friends of virtue and science."[23]

Still seething over what she perceived as John's egregious attitude toward her family, Mercy had included a stinging note along with his copy suggesting that "the vice-president of the United States and his lady may have forgotten Mrs. Warren."[24]

By the end of 1790 she had not yet heard from Adams. As it happened, John had written on December 26 but his letter did not arrive until January. Within it, he confirmed receipt of *Poems, Dramatic and Miscellaneous* and mentioned that he had also received three other copies of her book that had arrived without an accompanying letter. Since he and Abigail had subscribed to Mercy's work, John believed the first three "might come from some bookseller, who in due time, will produce his account." Those extra copies, he diplomatically assured her, "will not be too many."

Some of the poems in her volume, John amiably continued, were familiar and some "read and esteemed some years ago. However foolishly some European writers may have sported with American reputation for genius, literature and science: I know not where they will find a female poet of their own to prefer to the ingenious author of these compositions."

As to the implication that as "vice president" he and Abigail had ignored her, John wrote, "I am ignorant, madam, of any foundation you may have for the distinction you make between the Vice President and Mr. Adams, or for an insinuation that either may have forgotten Mrs. Warren."[25] She, after all, owed John a letter.

Mollified though Mercy must have been by John's praise, she was upset that his letter had arrived unsealed—and hence open to anyone who might want to read it. He must, she decided, have done so deliberately. After thanking John for his "expressions of regard and esteem," she tactlessly mentioned that his letter arrived unsealed.

Had John done so because he was "apprehensive that your own reputation might suffer by an attention to any one of a family you *had been used to hear spoken off with respect and affection by all*"—the latter being John's critical words about James Warren. Indeed, she did owe John a letter but the comments in his last were "so irreconcilable with my former sentiment that I was impelled . . . to consider it . . . forbidding any further interruption."

Friendship was delicate, Mercy continued, and "easily wounded." While "I might, perhaps, feel too sensibly some former impressions," she would never treat a friend carelessly because of his "*ebullitions* of party or political malice."[26]

A month passed before John responded to Mercy's letter. The unsealed letter, he politely explained in a brief note on February 14, was unintentional and due to his secretary's carelessness.

Mercy's accusation that he was politically opportunistic, nevertheless, had cut deep into his self-image. Affronted, John then wrote a longer letter, insisting that neither "party nor political malice" was responsible.

"The expressions you allude to were the result of very sober reflection upon facts proved to me by the testimony of many witnesses . . . among whom were not a few of the best friends of General Warren. A civil war, Madam, is in my opinion a very serious thing. This country has once at least been within a hair's breadth of a very bloody one, nor is it likely to be soon so secure against the probability of another."

Twenty years ago, John observed, he socialized with several people who, since they no longer embraced "those principles and measures which appear . . . indispensable to preserve the liberty . . . of this people," he no longer shared the "same confidence"[27] with them as formerly.

For several days, that letter remained on John's desk. Some twenty-three years earlier, a young John had mused in his diary about the wisdom of displaying old wounds before an insolent public. If, he conjectured at that time, he took his withered old mare who had lost her tail and both ears and paraded her around town in a horse cart, onlookers would have snickered.

"But would all . . . their contempt and laughter tend to induce . . . a belief that an horse was not necessary to draw an horse cart, and that the cart may as well be put before the horse, as the horse before the cart?"[28]

In the end, John decided against sending his defensive letter to Mercy. A horse was still necessary to drive a cart, no matter who jeered at its appearance or imperfections.

18

"Alas, humiliated America!"

BY THE TIME MERCY WROTE her angry letter of January 14, 1791, to John Adams, she was nursing a new wound—the renewal of *Nicholas and Jacob Van Staphorsts* v. *Winslow Warren*. To Winslow's astonishment, Boston's new Federal Court had assumed the Connecticut case and had summoned him to trial in November 1790. The suit, one of the first on the U.S. Circuit Court docket, must have mortified Mercy, whose newly published *Poems, Dramatic and Miscellaneous* included one poem praising Winslow as a virtuous young man, "unshackled by the triple chains" of "folly pride, or pleasure's guilty scenes."[1]

In spite of judicial efforts to make Winslow a high-profile example to other scofflaws, he had the trial postponed until the spring. That winter he wrote to General Henry Knox, begging for a commission in the army.

The plea was well-timed, for by 1791, skirmishes with American Indians on America's western frontiers prompted President Washington to raise a second army, establishing a "strong...permanent military post"[2] near present-day Fort Wayne, Indiana. Like other debtors who joined the Second U.S. Regiment, Winslow's liabilities would thus be forgiven.

Upon hearing his plan, Mercy was horrified, not only by the prospect of Winslow at war but because she objected to the motive for that war. For decades she had considered the American Indians an "unhappy race of men hutted throughout the vast wilderness of America...original proprietors of the soil,"[3] whom, as she insisted in her *History*, were once again in 1791 victimized—and this time by Hamilton's "imperialistic" policies.

Knowing that her "moralizing strain"[4] annoyed her sons, Mercy thus kept her opinions to herself, even after Winslow announced his commission as a second lieutenant. Exacerbating her "maternal anxiety"[5] was her son's May 11 announcement that the court had just sentenced him to jail.

"Humanity has wept that the first victim of experiment in the United States was the son of General Warren and the nephew of the celebrated Mr. Otis," Mercy observed to General Knox. Corruption in the courts, she maintained in blind devotion to her favorite son, led a "prejudiced judge to gratify his vindictive passions"[6] upon Winslow with the same oppressive bias as that of Governor Hutchinson.

In contrast to Mercy's outbursts, her husband, James, retreated into silence. "Your father does not write, or does he often speak. I will not point you to the subjects of his contemplation. You know us both too well,"[7] she morosely wrote Winslow in his Boston cell.

Soon afterward, he wrote back, complaining that he was denied the privilege of exercising in the prison yard—a liberty traditionally accorded debtors in Great Britain. Even so, Winslow immediately rejected Mercy's offer to fly[8] to his side.

An eerie hush subsequently fell over the Warren household. How, James pondered, had it come to this—his son disgraced, his own name tarred as a traitor to Federalist America, his wife scorned for fidelity to the old patriotic ideals?

Mercy, in contrast, continued to attribute Winslow's imprisonment to Federalist corruption, coupled with the "vindictive spirit of his creditors." To her mind, Winslow's imprisonment was a harbinger of despotic government.

"Shall the citizens of America, be subjected to the severities of the Divan or the usages of the Bastille?" she histrionically wrote her beloved son on May 19. Was his cell "airy and comfortable?" she asked, advising him to "be careful of your diet." Perhaps, she might "send you a few cakes...would you laugh?"[9]

Ironically, the treatment Winslow received in prison forced him, perhaps for the first time in his life, to consider his plight in a broader political context. On May 19, the same day of Mercy's hysterical letter, Winslow wrote the Massachusetts legislature, complaining about the court's lack of distinction between debtors and felons. The "unhappy citizen who...fall[s] into this predicament" was then left to the "mercy of the law officer . . . confined in irons or cast into the dungeon with convicts under sentence of death; a condition scarcely preferable to that of the miserable tenants of the late Bastille of France."[10]

Soon afterward, perhaps through legislative intervention, rumor had it that Winslow would be released from prison to report for duty with the Second U.S. Regiment. In Plymouth, Mercy withered at the news. "The idea of going into the army has been painful for me *indeed,* but I hope for opportunities for conversing freely on that subject before you go,"[11] she wrote.

Such a discussion, Winslow tersely replied on June 2, was impossible. Then, just before Boston's *Independent Chronicle* published his letter to the legislature, Winslow insisted it was best[12] for him to leave immediately. Exactly why remains unclear.

In a gesture of love, Mercy, meanwhile, willed Winslow the copyright to *Poems, Dramatic and Miscellaneous.* She had, she plaintively added, in a reference to her sense of marginality, "nothing else I can so properly call my own."[13]

A month later, Mercy received a letter from Winslow in New York, apologizing for not answering "the 2 or 3 letters" he received before his departure. New York was "vastly superior to Boston . . . It is a new world—there is liberality, politeness of European towns, so much cleverness, civility . . . I wish to God you could visit . . . How much your merit would make you caressed!"

Promising to collect "anecdotes in the Indian country for your entertainment," Winslow giddily anticipated spending the next few years in "the most agreeable manner."[14] From Pennsylvania he wrote again, this time praising that state's leniency toward debtors, who were rarely held "in close confinement."[15] Ashamed, apparently, of his history, Winslow signed his letter in the name of his oldest brother, James, Jr.

General Arthur St. Clair, a Revolutionary War veteran with a dubious military reputation and the governor of the Northwest Territory, was commander of Winslow's regiment. By November 3, he had ordered his soldiers to camp near Fort Jefferson above a tributary of the Wabash River. Before dawn on November 4, the soldiers were jolted awake by howling hordes of tomahawk-yielding Miami and Shawnee natives.

"The sun had not yet risen when the army was thrown into a state of consternation by the yells of savages who advanced from all sides and ... commenced their fierce attack," wrote a survivor. "The savages seemed not to fear anything we could do," recalled another. "They could skip out of reach of bayonet and return ... The ground was literally covered with the dead."[16]

By morning, forty-six officers and six hundred of the army's fourteen hundred men lay dead as a dazed General St. Clair and his remaining men fled for their lives. Those captured were tortured, their mutilated bodies left upon the bloody battlefield for coyotes and vultures.

On December 17, Boston's *Columbian Sentinel* published an account about that battle to an appalled readership. Mercy already knew the worst. Among the slain officers was her beloved son Winslow Warren.

Her grief was boundless. "Oh, how I do regret that we did not all unite to prevent, if possible, our dear Winslow engaging in the late fatal expedition," Mercy wrote her son George in Maine. "For myself, I have never had a moment's quiet since I saw the direction that announced his appointment ... I can only sigh, alas! It is past, and the hard lesson of silent submission I must try to learn."[17]

Even her Federalist nephew, Harrison Gray Otis, had sympathized. "Good god, what a dismal stroke for poor Aunt Warren. It will kill her, I fear."[18]

And kill her it nearly did—especially after hearing rumors that General St. Clair's inept leadership had caused the military tragedy. Infuriated, Mercy poured her outrage into a treatise she intended to publish in the newspapers.

"Every man of understanding must be convinced that secret reasons of state and public necessity have prevented a Court of Inquiry into the conduct of General St. Clair of the fatal 4 of November," she carped. The government's "poor apologies are lost in ... painful emotions when they recollect their country involved in an expensive war ... their sons slaughtered by the hands of savages stimulated to cruelty ... by the wanton attempt of government to exterminate the simple tribes or drive them from their native inheritance."[19]

Ultimately, Mercy decided against publication. Instead, she preserved that bristling indictment of a duplicitous federal government in her private papers.

Years passed before Mercy recovered from Winslow's death. In her December 1793 letter to Elbridge Gerry she confessed that her "little talent for poetry" lay "buried in the grave of my dear children."[20]

While it was true, she admitted to Janet Montgomery, that she still had "a friend, the best of husbands, and other amiable...meritorious children," her "weak, my affectionate heart constantly wanders to the dreary wilderness and contemplates the dear remains that lie there."[21]

Observers like the French Duke de la Rochefoucault Liancourt, who visited the Warrens in the late 1790s, noted that while Mercy was lively and charming, she was obsessed with Winslow's death. Often she spoke his name, reread his letters, and gazed upon his portrait, which she prominently displayed in her North Street home.

The nights were especially difficult. As Mercy revealed in her poem "Written in Deep Affliction" about Winslow, she often prayed for acceptance of the loss of that "val'rous youth." Still the "moon's pale beams" often tempted her "to seek the solemn shade"[22] of death herself.

Preserved among Mercy's papers was a note from Alexander Hamilton written in July 1791 just after Winslow's departure. Composed with his usual gallantry, Hamilton praised the copy of *Poems, Dramatic and Miscellaneous* he had received the previous autumn.

"It is certain that in the Ladies of Castille, the sex will find a new occasion of triumph...Not being a poet myself, I am in the less danger of feeling mortification at the idea, that in the career of a dramatic composition at least, female genius in the United States has outstripped the male."[23]

Such words from the ambitious secretary of the treasury probably struck Mercy as sheer flattery, preserved as proof of the destruction of republican liberties by ambitious men like the hypocritical "little lion"[24] of New York.

No less unsettling was a 1790 publication by British statesman Edmund Burke, who once defended colonial America's protest against taxation. Now, however, Burke's treatise "Reflections on the French Revolution," proclaimed that revolution against a just, established government was foolhardy, that a "perfect democracy" was the "most shameless thing in the world." People, Burke contended, were inevitably ruled by "sordid selfish interest" and dangerously "prey to the ambitions of popular sycophants and courtly flatters." An enduring government, such as that of Great Britain, could "be only wrought by social means" over time "to produce that union of minds which alone can produce... [social] good."[25] Lamentably, the French revolutionaries failed to recognize that liberty was only one aspect of sound government.

In refutation, Catharine Macaulay wrote an opposing treatise, "Observations on the Reflections of the Right Hon. Edmund Burk," which praised the French for creating something "so *singular,* so *unique,* in that *perfect* unanimity in the people" that it "naturally excited the *surprise* and *admiration* of all men." Since government was merely a "contrivance of human wisdom to provide for human wants," the French revolutionaries were perfectly within their rights to reject "opinions by which they have [been] enslaved to *misery*" and assert their "natural right of forming a government for themselves."[26]

After reading both treatises, Mercy applauded Catharine and reminded her in a covert reference to John Adams that "some men of genius, professed republicans, who formerly shared the confidence of the people, are now...advocates for monarchy."[27] Moreover, Catharine's retort had arrived at the critical moment when the United States was to vote on ratification of the Bill of Rights. To enhance its passage, Mercy accordingly composed an introduction to Catharine's treatise and rushed both to her printer, Isaiah Thomas.

"Whatever convulsions may yet be occasioned by the revolution in France, it will doubtless be favorable to general liberty," she predicted in the introduction. Mr. Burke's critique had aided rather than abetted support by reviving "questions which have...lain dormant in England and have been almost forgotten, or artfully disguised in America."[28]

Had Catharine an opportunity to read Mercy's affirmation, she would likely have been pleased. But on June 22, 1791, while that pamphlet was still in press, the British historian died.

In Boston, where Catharine's friends remained unaware of her death, they cited the American reprint of "Observations" as proof of the importance of a Bill of Rights. Burke's *Reflections on the French Revolution,* as the Warrens' young friend James Winthrop contended, seemed a "dreadful heavy work" with little validity. Admittedly, as he wrote Mercy, the American version of revolution still required "vigilance ... against those ... attached to heredity distinctions," but he believed a republican democracy would ultimately prevail. [29]

Even before the December 21, 1791, ratification of the Bill of Rights, the Warrens had reason to rejoice. The event was the November 1 wedding of their fourth son, Henry, to a distant Plymouth relative. His bride, Mary, also called Polly, was the daughter of the late Pelham Winslow and the great-great-granddaughter of Governor Winslow, in whose North Street home Mercy and James dwelled.

In spite of the Winslow's Loyalist leanings, Mercy believed her daughter-in-law "the mistress of a good & affectionate heart." The reading of novels, she nevertheless warned, was frivolous. Moreover, she hoped that Polly would remain tidy and well-groomed for "nothing, [was] more disgusting than the appearance of a slatternly woman."[30]

Whatever faults Mercy found in Polly were dismissed when, a year later, she delivered a healthy girl named Marcia—a name that Mercy favored and often used to sign letters to friends. Flattered, reveling in her little namesake's lusty cries, she proudly reported to George that Marcia was "a very fine girl ... she is not tongue-tied as that is not a deficiency incident to the family on either side."[31]

Perhaps it was Henry's marriage, James's stoical acceptance of Winslow's death, or simply his retirement from public life, but whatever the cause, Mercy joyfully wrote George in February 1792 that his father had recovered his health and appeared remarkably "young, florid, and finely for a man of his years and sorrows."[32] The following winter James received another boost when his constituents in the House appointed him to the governor's advisory council.

During subsequent trips to Boston, James sent Mercy letters more suggestive of youthful passion than those of a husband of nearly forty years. "I constantly contemplate you," he wrote during the winter of 1793, imagining his wife at the breakfast table "with a cheerful & enchanting smile," followed by her "turning to literary pursuits." No husband, James assured her, "ever loved and respected a wife more."[33]

An enduring love, a long marriage, the comfort of Henry's family—including the 1795 birth of a grandson—became the highlights of Mercy's life. That Plymouth had embraced Federalism, leaving the Warrens with few like-minded neighbors and friends, was simply a disappointment to be endured.

More importantly, as Mercy insisted in November 1792 to James, Jr., who was then teaching school in nearby Hingham, was the family's commitment to republican ideals. "When you feel a little vexed that your father has lost his popularity—remember that he retains his integrity, that neither his public or private virtue has ever been shaken." While his "political opinions have differed . . . and he has had too much sincerity to conceal them—for this he has suffered—these are the sour grapes for which the children's teeth have been set on edge."[34]

Even that bitter legacy, as Mercy penned to an unidentified young woman, should not allow the aged—as she, then in her sixties, considered herself—to become "soured by defeated expectations." Older adults must not express "morose feelings towards the new generations," but "cherish with candor & good humor every spark of worth" in them, even if that spark was "different"[35] than their own.

Increasingly, tolerance for and education of youth became the threads that Mercy stitched into the frayed edges of her personal life with her grandchildren, the younger women who looked to her for advice, and a rising generation of female writers.

One of the most promising was Judith Sargent Murray, whose 1790 "Desultory Thoughts" and "On the Equality of the Sexes" advocated better education for women. That same year Catharine Macaulay's *Letters on Education* reiterated Murray's message, but both were eclipsed in 1792 by the publication of Mary Wollstonecraft's startling *Vindication of the Rights of Women*, which argued that women should be respected for their importance to the state as child-bearers, who, if properly educated, would not only educate their youngsters but become companions, rather than merely wives, to their men.

In comparison, Mercy's portraits of the abusive treatment frequently accorded women in her satirical plays seemed muted. Her private letters, nevertheless, often expressed her dissatisfaction about the widespread disrespect with which women were treated. During the Revolutionary era, she had complained about the refusal of Plymouth's male pilgrim descendants to include women in their annual Colony Club celebration and by 1792 repeated that affront to her brother Samuel Allyne. "Now they are regaling themselves at the old Colony Hall while their dames are left alone both... to reflect upon the difference between modern manners and the rigid virtues of their ancestors."[36]

The only remedy, Mercy confided to a young woman identified as Betsy, was to educate women like men.Mercy believed that once properly schooled, women could use their education to teach their children and organize their homes more efficiently.

"You are now free from those constant interruptions that necessarily occupy the mind of the wife, the mother, and the mistress," she reminded the young woman. Such tasks were relatively easy and could be accomplished in tandem with intellectual accomplishments, provided a woman had "a methodical and uniform plan of conduct, united with an industrious mind."[37]

Waiting for Mercy's own industrious mind in the second-story northeast room at North Street were piles of the still-unfinished manuscript of her *History*. By late March 1791, just before Winslow's trial, Mercy wrote Congressional delegate Elbridge Gerry a letter marked "*Secret* and *Confidential*."

"It is my purpose sir at the conclusion of a certain historical and biographical work to make a few strictures on the origin...nature, and the probable consequences of the new government," she explained. Worried that her reportage was incomplete, she asked Elbridge to provide descriptions of men such as Robert Morris, James Wilson, and Patrick Henry, as well as include any matters of "great consequences...not yet been recorded by other historians."

"You may think, sir, the business I am upon is a bold undertaking," she added, with the deference she formerly used with John Adams, explaining that the project was "for the amusement of myself...with a view of conveying to my children the causes of the struggle...the conduct and characters of the principal actors in the beginning of the revolution." If Elbridge did not respond, she would know that "I have gone out of my line."[38]

On April 3, 1791, Mercy sent a one-line note to Elbridge reiterating similar anxieties. Eight days later, Elbridge replied, assuring her that he would send along any important information.

Subsequent to Winslow's death, Mercy avoided her writing desk again. Only gradually, with the birth of Marcia, her husband James's return to health, and his appointment to the Governor's Council, would her literary appetites revive. First though, there were outings to be enjoyed—to West Barnstable, to Boston, to Cambridge, and finally to Watertown, where, James wrote Elbridge, he was overwhelmed with a "thousand memories" after seeing old friends, although few retained their former "noble spirit."[39]

If for the graying James the 1790s provided time for reflection, to Mercy they presented a new host of "maternal anxieties." Chief among them was her somber youngest son, George, by then a legislative delegate from Maine. (Abigail had observed that even in childhood George had a "grave senatorial"[40] expression.) Extravagant like his brother Winslow and contentious like his uncle Jemmy, George worried Mercy from afar—especially after learning about his large home and extensive land holdings. By November 1792, Mercy, convinced that George was living beyond his means, announced she "could not bear the thought of your being in debt to any man."[41] Disconcerting, too, were descriptions of George's quarrels with friends, neighbors, and even his minister. "Is it not best you should concede a little?"[42] the famously stubborn Mercy suggested in March 1795.

That same spring, the word "concession" was sharply questioned in coffeehouses, taverns, and hearths after news arrived about John Jay's new treaty with Great Britain meant to quell the rumblings of a new war, precipitated by the French Revolution and its aftermath.

Ironically, in the first days of the Revolution, Americans, and especially the Antifederalists or republicans, were so enthralled that they greeted one another as "Citizen" and "Citizeness," sported tricolor cockade hats, and sang liberty songs. Civic feasts, celebrating the new "democratic-republican spirit" then sweeping Europe soon appeared in the United States as well, most famously one in Boston where a thousand-pound ox was roasted, labeled "Aristocracy," and served to citizens.

In contrast were ensuing arguments between the Federalists and republicans in Washington's cabinet over national policy. So bitterly did Alexander Hamilton, secretary of the treasury, quarrel with Thomas Jefferson, secretary of state, that an exasperated Washington complained their "dissension" was "harrowing our vitals."[43] After 1793, the bloodshed and factionalism of the French Revolution led the frightened Federalists to denigrate the republicans as "Jacobins," extreme leftists willing to sacrifice an orderly government to free-wheeling liberties. The republicans, in turn, sneered at Hamiltonian Federalists as blind-sighted "monocrats" in favor of absolute rule.

When though, in 1793 Robespierre and his followers seized control of the French Committee of Public Safety, executed Louis XVI, and placed thousands of heads under the blade of the guillotine, many republicans, including Mercy and James Warren, recoiled.

The Reign of Terror was so ghastly, Mercy opined in her sweeping *History,* that "[d]ecency, humanity, and every thing else respected in civil society, disappeared ... [into] pandemonium. Thus was republicanism disgraced by the demoralization of the people and a cloud of infidelity darkened the hemisphere of France."[44]

In reaction, the Federalists leaned toward Great Britain during its war with France. The British, meanwhile, bent on coercing the United States to take their side, repeatedly seized American ships in neutral waters. In the spring of 1794, Washington consequently dispatched Chief Justice John Jay to England to negotiate a treaty.

That mission, the Warrens and their fellow republicans grumbled, was one more example of Federalist complicity with oppression, leading to reconciliation with the same tyrannical nation from whom the American colonies once broke.

No less disquieting to the republicans were reports from Pennsylvania during the summer of 1794 about farmers near Pittsburgh who protested Hamilton's excise tax on whiskey. Traditionally, to ease transportation for their grain, farmers had fermented it into whiskey before transporting it across the Allegheny Mountains. Now, having paid those taxes for three years, they howled it was unfair.

To publicize their complaint, the protestors stopped the U.S. mail at gunpoint, shut down the courts, and even threatened to storm Pittsburgh. Mindful of Shays's Rebellion, Washington nervously summoned militias from Pennsylvania and nearby states, resulting in a force of fifteen thousand men. Twenty men, finally, were captured, marched down Philadelphia's Market Street, and, as after Shays's Rebellion, pardoned.

The heavy-handed suppression of the whiskey rebellion, Mercy insisted in her *History*, was motivated less by the "honor of the national character" than by a mindful gesture of the "supreme power of the first magistrate," and the establishment of a "standing army and other projects approaching ... despotic sway."[45]

Predictably, Jay's return in the spring of 1795 with a treaty with Great Britain provoked a violent public reaction. Citizens rioted in towns from Maine to South Carolina. John Jay was burned in effigy. Hamilton, allied with Jay, was stoned in the streets. In Boston, angry Antifederalists stormed the homes of wealthy Federalists while Sam Adams, then the governor of Massachusetts, yawned it was only boys having "water melon frolics."[46] The treaty, the republicans bellowed, was a betrayal of America's early friendship with France as well as a concession to British power. Had nothing been gained from the long years of the American Revolution—except the titular creation of a new government whose leaders had monarchial appetites of their own?

"Alas, humiliated America!"[47] Mercy lamented in black and white to George that July. Only twenty years had passed since the American Revolution, but little, it seemed, had changed.

19

A Sea Change in Party Politics

NEITHER THE PERSONAL nor the political differences separating the Warrens and the Adamses would permanently alienate Mercy and Abigail. In August 1796, Mercy received a visit "unexpected,—friendly, politic or accidental I know not what,"[1] from Abigail, accompanied by her own sister-in-law Mary Otis, wife of Samuel Allyne.

It had been eight years since Mercy and Abigail had seen each other. During that time, each had aged and become grandmothers. Mercy, gray-haired and nearing seventy, was still lively and well informed. Abigail, no longer slender, was fifty-one years old.

Once again, Abigail chatted with James, whom, as French émigré Duke de la Rochefoucault Liancourt had recently noted, seemed an "old, grey-headed man."[2] On a lighter note, Abigail delighted in her conversation with the Warrens' three-and-a-half-year-old granddaughter, Marcia.

Abigail seemed "clever,"[3] Mercy later confided to George, which in eighteenth-century parlance meant agreeable and cheerful. Not yet was she "fastened up hand and foot and tongue,"[4] as John warned Abigail she must be if he became president.

A few weeks later, when Washington announced his retirement, that became a possibility. Yet the following February 1797, when Adams's election to the U.S. presidency was announced, he was already brooding over the nation's problems. Foremost among these was French hostility to the Jay Treaty. "I never in my life felt such an awful weight of obligation...to the public,"[5] he confided to Elbridge Gerry.

In her congratulatory letter to Abigail upon John's election, Mercy insinuated that her friend had finally attained her dream of a crown. Piqued, Abigail penned a sharp reply on Inauguration Day, March 4, from Quincy, where she remained to avoid a winter journey to Philadelphia. The recent election was the "unsolicited gift, of a free and enlightened people," she asserted, which "calls for every exertion of the head, and every virtue of the heart, to do justice to so sacred a trust.

"As to a crown, my dear madam," Abigail added, "I will not deny, that there is one which I aspire after, and in a country where envy can never enter . . . I shall esteem myself peculiarly fortunate, if at the close of my public life, I can retire, esteemed beloved and equally respected with my predecessor."[6]

Humbled by Abigail's forthright reply, Mercy replied, "I merely wish you may obtain that *crown* which you had made the ultimatum of your wishes. I am confident there is none other worth pursuing." Fervently, she hoped that "God grant he [John] may be the instrument in the hand of Providence to preserve the United States from war or from slavery," and asked Abigail to remind John of his "tried friends at Plymouth."[7]

In reply the new first lady triumphantly reminded Mercy of the years they "trod together, through one gloomy scene of war, havoc and desolation; and we have seen our country rise superior to oppression and despotism, and take its rank among the nations."[8]

Such memories, Abigail declared, were not lightly held. Even if politics had alienated their husbands, she and Mercy would remain friends.

Several days later, Mercy expressed condolences to Abigail on the recent death of John's eighty-nine-year-old mother and of a niece. For months she received no answer, for Abigail was then traveling to Nabby and her young children in isolated New York, followed by a visit to Charles and his family. Immediately upon her arrival in Philadelphia, Abigail was swept into a dizzying whirl of duties as first lady. Her aunt Tufts, Abigail wearily wrote to her sister Mary, once "styled my situation, splendid misery." She was "not far from truth."[9]

In September 1797, when Mercy heard about the Adamses' return to Quincy from Philadelphia, she invited them to Plymouth. On October 1, Abigail replied thanking Mercy for her last two letters, which she had "no right to expect," but considered a "pledge of a friendship . . . which I hope will endure with our lives however we may dissent upon some subjects." Accepting Mercy's invitation "would have given both Mr. Adams and myself great pleasure," but she and John were about to return to yellow-fever-riddled Philadelphia.

A "certain clamor will be raised if Congress are convened at any other place," Abigail noted, implying that was one more obstacle her husband faced deciding "what is best and most for the good of the Country."[10]

During the two years subsequent to the Jay Treaty, the question of what was most for the good of the country evolved into a shrill national debate—especially after the French began seizing American ships on the high seas. Determined to settle the dispute, President Adams appointed three ministers to France—Charles Pinckney, John Marshall, and his old Massachusetts friend Elbridge Gerry.

"For the sake of the rising generation I am very glad we have so skilful a *political doctor* commissioned to the honor," Mercy enthusiastically wrote Elbridge in July. "At all events, we must avoid war."[11]

Whatever conciliations Elbridge and his fellow ministers intended, however, were soon dashed. After a brief meeting with Charles Maurice de Talleyrand-Périgord, France's cagey foreign minister, the American trio were referred to his three representatives—identified in official dispatches as "X, Y and Z." Talleyrand would meet with the Americans again, they explained—but only after the Americans paid $250,000, granted France a twelve-million-dollar loan, and received an apology from President Adams.

Outraged, the American ministers had refused and were soon supported by an irate Congress clamoring for war. Newspapers joined the uproar. "Millions for Defense, but not one cent for tribute,"[12] trumpeted their headlines. Alarmed, the republicans counseled caution. In Philadelphia, John Adams wavered, calling for a buildup of the military, but took no other action.

By April 25, Abigail angrily reported to Mercy that "the olive branch, tendered to our Gallic allies ... has been rejected with scorn." All attempts at negotiations were "useless," unless attended by the "power of Midas."

Most terrifying of all was the French "boast of a powerful party in this country ... sowing the seeds of vice, irreligion, corruption, and sedition."

She was writing, Abigail observed, "with the freedom and confidence of an old friend, who, I am sure, will unite with me in sincere, and ardent wishes, for the peace... of our common country."

Her husband, "the president," she added decorously, "desires me to present to Genll. Warren the remembrance of an old friend who would be much more at his ease, and happier in cultivating the useful science of agriculture with him, than in the arduous... task assigned."[13]

To that, Mercy had politely replied. Embarrassed that she and her son Henry had signed a letter supporting John's diplomatic efforts with France but that her husband, James, had refused, Mercy excused his silence on his old vow to "answer to no being below the *supreme.*"[14]

Silence, as Mercy grimly confided to her son George, "is the only medium of safety for those who have an opinion of their own that does not exactly square with the enthusiasms of the time."[15]

Mercy's letter to Abigail was "a kind of apology"[16] for James, she confided to her sister Mary. Determined, nevertheless, to indicate that he was an exception to the public, Abigail's letter of June 17 talked about the "testimonials" for John that "poured in from all quarters of the union."[17]

A day later Congress passed the first of four laws designed to protect the country from internal foes. Each, as the republicans later reminded fellow Americans, President Adams had signed. Known as the Alien and Sedition Acts, the first, the Naturalization Act of June 18, raised the residency requirement for citizenship from five to fourteen years. A week later Congress passed the Alien Act, allowing deportation of those considered "dangerous to the peace and safety of the United States."[18] The third, the Alien Enemies Act, empowered the president to imprison foreigners considered enemies of the state. The last, and perhaps most notorious of all, was the Sedition Act of July 14, designed to punish those guilty of treasonable activities, criminalizing "false, scandalous and malicious... writings against the government of the United States... the Congress... or the President."[19]

The resultant Alien and Sedition Act, republican Vice President Thomas Jefferson grumbled to James Madison, were "so palpably in the teeth of the Constitution as to... pay no respect to it."[20]

Just as Jefferson feared, twenty-five Antifederalist newspapers were closed and their publishers arrested. Among the imprisoned was Benjamin Franklin's grandson, Benjamin Franklin Bache, editor of Philadelphia's *Democrat-Republican Aurora,* who had jeered at his former friend Adams as a "President by Three Votes,"[21] and a leader slavishly obedient to Hamilton and Federalist war mongers.

"Despotism ... while it is gaining ground, will suffer men to think, say, or write what they please," Mercy had warned a decade earlier in "Observations on the New Constitution." Once a ruler established "arbitrary power," certain "unjust ... restrictions may take place," among them an ominous "*imprimateur* on the press" designed to silence an "injured and oppressed people."[22]

Tyranny, or so it seemed to Mercy and other republicans, had thus slyly snaked its way into Congress, pierced the Bill of Rights, and venomously directed how America was to be ruled.

After visiting Mercy and James at their North Street home in the mid-1790s, Rochefoucault scribbled a few notes in his travel diary. His witty and charming hostess, he noted, "has written a history of the American revolution, which her husband and she have with great prudence, resolved not to send to the press while they live."

Mercy's manuscript, the Warrens had explained, would be published after their deaths, for only then "would the truth be safely declared."[23]

Nearly simultaneous with the French émigré's visit, Hannah Adams, a forty-one-year-old distant cousin of John Adams living in Dedham, Massachusetts, searched for a publisher for her own account of the Revolution. Her goal, like everything the shy author published, including her guidebook, *Alphabetical Compendium of the Various Sects Which Have Appeared from the Beginning of the Christian Era to the Present Day,* was to be "useful"—which in the eighteenth-century sense was meant to justify her life as a single woman.

With its reliance upon state archives and newspapers, Hannah's 1798 *A Summary History of New England* spanned a broader topic than its title suggested, and essentially was a chronological account of America from the seventeenth-century arrival of the *Mayflower* through the Revolution and ratification of the Constitution. Thematically, Hannah linked those events to the virtues of the early New Englanders, whose quest for liberty inspired their arrival in North America.

Pitting European greed, avarice, and religious oppression against New World freedoms and religious tolerance, *A Summary History* celebrated the enterprising American character and its centralized government, which Hannah hailed as a unique blend of Federalist and republican principles.

The publication of *A Summary History* probably caught Mercy by surprise. While less detailed and written in plainer prose than Mercy's lofty style, Hannah's account had preempted her unpublished *History*. Her own work, Mercy implied seven years later when the first of her three-volume *History of the Rise, Progress and Termination of the American Revolution* rolled off the press, was more authoritative because it was based on eyewitness accounts and experiences as well as published documents.

She was, as Mercy reminded readers in its introduction, "connected by nature, friendship, and every social tie, with many of the first patriots, and most influential characters on the continent; in the habits of... epistolary intercourse with several gentlemen employed abroad in the most distinguished stations, and with others since elevated to the highest grades of rank... I had the best means of information, through a long period that the colonies were in suspense, waiting the operation of foreign courts, and the success of their own enterprising spirit."[24]

In August 1798, as the Adamses returned to Quincy from Philadelphia, where a severe yellow fever epidemic raged, Abigail became feverish, took to her bed, and remained there for three months. "The illness of our dear mother has cast a gloom over the face of everything here, and it scarce seems like home without her enlivening cheerfulness,"[25] Nabby, having returned home with her daughter Caroline, gloomily wrote her brother John Quincy that September.

Possibly Abigail had fallen victim to the yellow fever that raged through Philadelphia every summer or, as some historians surmised, suffered from malaria.

By late autumn, disease and the threat of death also loomed over the Warrens. Gradually, Mercy's poor eyesight had worsened, even though she still scratched out letters to George in Maine. Only rarely, though, did she and James have an opportunity to see George when he traveled the rough roads from Maine to Boston where he served in the Massachusetts House.

In 1797, Mercy finally begged James to escort her to Maine but he had refused. "I tell him he is not too old for such a journey,"[26] Mercy later explained to George. Yet, in his defense, as Rochefoucault had observed, James looked old and seemed in "very feeble health."[27]

Paradoxically, it was George's health, rather than James's, that soon became a family concern. In late 1799, George sent Mercy a letter mentioning that he had been ill, but was recuperating. Several weeks later George wrote again, explaining he was stricken, and this time so severely that he had canceled a trip to Boston.

"Alas, what can we do?"[28] Mercy wrote, offering to send confections, oranges, lemons, tamarinds—anything to boost his health. Nothing was needed, George assured her. Then his letters stopped.

Frightened, Mercy dispatched a message to her son Henry, then in Boston where he served as clerk of the legislature, that she was worried about "a person to the eastward whose happiness I have much at heart and whom I have expected to see [or receive his letters] for the last three stages [coaches].

"I dare not ask. Your total silence is enough to convince me that you are afraid of giving trouble to your Mother if you name him [George]. You must have heard something."[29]

The something, as Mercy suspected, was George's rapidly deteriorating health, which had so alarmed his friends that they rushed him to Augusta for tapping—the era's traditional bloodletting "cure." Someone from the family must ride to George at once, Mercy insisted. But who? Much as she longed to, she could not hazard such a trip in the harsh winter weather. Henry, unable to leave the legislature, frantically searched for a substitute.

One of George's local friends, meanwhile, volunteered to brave the icy roads to Augusta. There, after attending to the bedridden George, his friend returned to Mercy and James with loving messages. By March, Henry finally rode to Maine—too late, as it happened, to offer his brother any comfort. On February 5, 1800, the Warrens' youngest son, thirty-three-year-old George Warren, had died.

<+->

By spring of 1800, three of Mercy's five sons were gone, leaving only her crippled eldest, James, Jr., and her fourth child, Henry. Struck by the personal tragedies that had befallen the Warrens, Samuel Allyne Otis addressed a condolence letter to Mercy as his "afflicted sister."[30] The salutation was fitting, Mercy replied.

"The waves have rolled upon me, the billows are repeatedly broken over me, yet I am not sunk down," she penned. "Shall I complain that I have never been suffered to catch the last accents of my dying friends and children? No," she replied, citing the Scripture. "He who knoweth my frame, knoweth what is fittest for me."[31]

Among Mercy's letters was a document the Warrens received that same year from the U.S. government testifying that James, Jr., as a wounded veteran of the Revolutionary War, was entitled to a lifelong pension. Soon afterward, the forty-four-year-old amputee moved back to Plymouth, compelled perhaps to return by the untimely death of his brother George, the publication of Hannah Adams's *A Summary History*, and Mercy's failing eyesight, and opened a school of his own.

During the ascendant years of Federalism of the 1790s, Mercy had complained that "virulence of party spirit shuts up the avenues of just information," and prevented "truth" from getting "fair play." Given the animosity between the Federalists and Democratic-Republicans, as the patriotic party was often called, the "annalist," or historian, might just as well confine her *History* "to the cabinet," where it would become nothing more than "a pleasant amusement to her children."[32]

By 1800, however, certain positive changes in "party spirit" toward the republicans had brightened Mercy's view and even inspired her to again consider publishing her *History*. In that spirit, she expanded her work into a third volume on the years subsequent to the Revolution with the aid of her new secretary, James, Jr.,

Politically, the moment was apt. With the turn of the century, a sea change was occurring in American politics, one whose stormy passage had already crashed over John Adams's presidency, swamping his Federalist allies and leaving the traces of a new republican era in its ebb.

France and its tumults—including Napoleon's war against Great Britain and Europe—had provided the prevailing winds, the old struggle between the Federalists and republicans became its anchor points, and Adams's determination to avoid war was the undertow that prevented him from fastening firmly to one side or the other of the bobbing political ballast.

When, on Monday, February 18, 1799, John Adams asked Vice President Jefferson to nominate William Vans Murray to negotiate with the French, the Federalists and republicans were both stunned. Merely eight months earlier, Adams had approved a standing army to protect the United States from French attack. A few weeks later, he also signed the Alien and Sedition Acts.

The Federalists, and especially Hamilton, felt betrayed. Adams, nevertheless, dispatched three new ministers to France on October 19 in spite of reports that the French Directory had been shattered. Three weeks later, thirty-year-old General Napoleon Bonaparte assumed the role of First Consul of France and the greater part of Europe.

"Great revolutions ever produce excesses and miseries at which humanity revolts," Mercy admitted in her *History*. But the American Revolution was an exception. Its success, in contrast to the French experiment, could be attributed to its citizens' "strict adherence to the principles of the revolution, and the practice of every public, social and domestic virtue."[33]

Mercy's optimism reflected the republicans' rising hopes. While prior to the election of 1801, the Federalists had attacked Thomas Jefferson for impracticality—as a dreamer, a deist, and a libertine, a man, sneered Hamilton, who was an "atheist in religion and a fanatic in politics,"[34]—even he, like his Federalist advocates, preferred the tall Virginian to John Adams. By the end of his presidential term, Adams was regarded as a vain, cowardly leader who had hedged his bets with France.

The republicans objected to John Adams on other grounds, as a "monarchist" and Anglophile and, worst of all, a disloyal patriot who shattered their civil rights with passage of the Alien and Sedition Acts.

On October 3, 1800, John's peace treaty with France was signed and became the most proud accomplishment of his presidency. Jefferson, nevertheless, defeated Adams in February 1801 by eight electoral college votes—73 to 65.

"I was turned out of office, degraded and disgraced by my country; and I was glad of it," John subsequently asserted in his private writings. "I felt no disgrace . . . I thought my duty to my country ought to prevail over every person and party consideration."[35]

The era of Federalist control over which John Adams had so uncomfortably ruled came to an end.

The Warrens were thrilled. It was fitting that the new president, as Mercy observed in her *History,* was Thomas Jefferson, whose "elegant and energetic pen,"[36] had written the Declaration of Independence.

To James, the election signaled a renaissance of the old patriotic ideals. "I . . . sincerely congratulate you, on your elevation to the first magistry of the union, and the triumph of virtue over the most malignant, virulent and slanderous party that perhaps ever existed in any country," he wrote Jefferson on March 4, 1800. "Driven myself from active scenes of political life . . . I have sat like a man under the shade of tree unnoticed, I have seen principles sacrificed to ambition, and consistency of sentiment to the interest of the moment."[37]

With the advent of Jefferson's administration, favors long denied the Warrens' sons suddenly arrived. James, Jr., was appointed postmaster of Plymouth and Henry became collector of the Pport.

"Sir: You have gratified me exceedingly by appointing my son the collector of this district," James duly thanked Jefferson. "You have done one of my family the honor to hold an office under a man whose person and administration we all respect, and . . . given him an opportunity to indulge . . . his intention to serve the cause of Republicanism."[38]

Symbolic of those ideals was Jefferson's cancellation of the Alien and Sedition Acts.

While 1801 was a bright year for republicans, it literally became darker for Mercy because of painful attacks upon her eyes. Forced to lie in a shuttered room, the seventy-three-year-old author depended increasingly upon James, Jr., for help with the final draft of *The History of the Rise, Progress and Termination of the American Revolution.* Rather than a sweeping account of Revolutionary battles, Mercy's *History*, as its subtitle "Interspersed with Biographical, Political, and Moral Observations," implied, focused upon the personalities of the nation's leaders.

Acknowledging in the final chapter that there had been "some agitation of spirits between existing parties," Mercy hoped it would "evaporate," and that the "present representative government may stand for ages a luminous monument of republican wisdom, virtue and integrity."

To achieve that, she reminded readers that "the elective franchise is in their own hands; that it ought not to be abused, either for personal gratifications, or the indulgence of partisan acrimony." Above all, "[t]he principles of the revolution ought ever to be the pole-star of the statesman, respected by the rising generation."[39]

Such statements, Mercy realized even before publication of the *History*, was bound to rankle the Federalists who continued to dominate New England.

By 1802, still fretting about the *History*'s probable reception, Mercy consulted her friend Dr. James Freeman, the Unitarian minister of Boston's King's Chapel. Warming to her and her project, the clergyman advised her on the book's design and format and urged her to arrange a list of subscribers.

Still another year would pass and little was accomplished. Diplomatically, Dr. Freeman assured Mercy that the *History* would be a great success, especially since it was the only eyewitness account of the Revolution written from a republican perspective. There was no time to waste. Other histories, besides Hannah Adams's *Summary History of New England*, the minister reminded her, were already published, among them the popular 1789 *History of the American Revolution* by a southern Federalist, David Ramsay.

A letter dated August 30, 1803, from Quincy may have provided the final goad. From his farm, Peacefield, the retired John Adams wrote that his family brooded "in great affliction . . . for more than three months on account of the dangerous illness of our friend and my companion," Abigail, who again suffered recurrent fevers. While claiming that morning that she felt better than in weeks, Abigail was convinced that her illness was fatal.

"The day is far spent with us all," John observed. "It can not be long before we must exchange this theatre for some other. I hope it will be one, in which there are no politicks."[40]

20

"In the spirit of friendship"

"THOUGH IN HER INFANTILE STATE, the young republic of America exhibits the happiest prospect,"[1] a septuagenarian Mercy triumphantly penned on the last page of her *History of the Rise, Progress and Termination of the American Revolution*. On December 21, 1804, she and James signed an agreement with Boston publisher Ebenezer Larkin to print fifteen hundred copies of the book in a three-volume set of approximately four hundred pages each.

Within a few months, Larkin, worrying over the *History*'s female authorship and lackluster advance sales, suggested he print only one thousand copies.

Mercy objected and redoubled her efforts to compile a list of subscribers. Among the most prominent was President Jefferson, who recommended the *History* to his cabinet and expressed hope for "great satisfaction that Mrs. Warren's attention" to the Revolution would prove "equally useful for our country and honorable to herself."[2]

Other potential subscribers were less enthusiastic. On June 1, 1805, Mercy's literary colleague Judith Sargent Murray explained that while she was pleased to subscribe, her friends had balked.

Readers, already familiar with Englishman William Gordon's 1788 *History of the Rise, Progress, and Establishment of the Independence of the United States of America* and Southerner David Ramsay's 1789 *History of the American Revolution*, had recently been reading Chief Justice John Marshall's 1804 *The Life of George Washington*. In spite of its Federalist slant, Judith explained that Marshall's work "forestalls, if not wholly precludes, the utility of this history."

Mercy's well-known republican views were another obstacle. Unfortunately, "Genius is not possessed by the multitude," Judith reminded Mercy, especially in the "commercial country" of America, where "a taste for literature"[3] remained undeveloped.

In spite of its lukewarm reception, fifteen hundred copies of *The History of the Rise, Progress and Termination of the American Revolution* were finally printed at a cost of $2,882 and sold at $2 per three-volume set, or $0.69 per volume. An account of the new nation from the arrival of the first settlers to the turn of the nineteenth century written in Mercy's characteristically high-toned prose, the *History* celebrated the triumph of republicanism and suggested that providence had guided the nation to protect the rights of the ordinary citizen.

Reactions to the 1805 first volume of Mercy's *History* drifted in only slowly. From Pennsylvania, septuagenarian John Dickinson praised her mention of his contribution, cherished especially for having been written by the sister of his "highly valued friend James Otis."[4]

By April 1806, President Jefferson also thanked Mercy for his copy, assuring her that he anticipated it must include certain facts "not before given to the public."[5]

Yet, even after February 4, 1807, when James Winthrop pronounced the *History* a "well digested and polished narrative"[6] save for a few inaccuracies, Mercy nervously hoped to hear from John Adams.

With trepidation, she finally opened a letter from Abigail on March 9, 1807, that discussed another siege of poor health but praised Mercy's last letter written "in the style of...[her] ancient friendship." She hoped, Abigail added, they might enjoy a "still closer and more cordial union in the world of spirits to which we are hastening."

After writing about her family, Abigail conveyed the Adamses' regards to Mercy's eighty-one-year-old husband, James, who "enjoys so much health at his advanced period of life. We shall always be happy to hear of the welfare of friends whom we have loved from our early years."[7]

A monumental silence in Quincy thus surrounded the publication of Mercy's *History*. Had John or Abigail read it, they seemed reluctant to render an opinion.

~<~<~>~>~

"We are all republicans—we are federalists...I know, indeed, that some honest men fear that a republican government cannot be strong...But would the honest patriot...abandon a government which has so far kept us free and firm, on the...fear that this government, the world's best hope, may...want energy to preserve itself?" Thomas Jefferson asked constituents in his March 4, 1801, inaugural address. .

"I trust not," he added, urging Americans to embrace their respective "federal and republican principles, our attachment to our union and representative government."[8]

Six years later the ongoing war between Great Britain and France finally forced America's first republican (in the sense of one who advocated for a republic rather than a monarchy) president to a new appreciation of those "federal principles." By then, Great Britain, disgruntled with American neutrality, was capturing its privateers on the high seas. On June 30, 1807, the argument came to a head when officers of the *Leopard*, a British man-of-war, claimed that the American frigate the *Chesapeake* harbored deserters. Their men fired, resulting in the deaths of three sailors.

America was horrified, especially in view of the controversial peace the Federalists had previously achieved with the Jay Treaty of 1794.

Subsequent to his 1801 retirement to Peacefield, John Adams, meanwhile, vented his disillusionment with politics in his autobiography. By the time of the *Leopard* attack, the former president had, moreover, nearly finished reading Mercy's *History*.

On Saturday, July 11, he coldly wrote "Mrs. Warren" in a "spirit of friendship, that you may have an opportunity in the same spirit to correct"[9] several mistakes. The first was Mercy's comment in volume three, page 393, that "Mr. Adams, his passion and prejudices were sometimes too strong for his sagacity and judgment."

Never, John retorted, had he "taken one public step or performed one public act from passion or prejudice, or from any other motive than the public good."

Had he ever "acted from passion or prejudice, from interest...or avarice, the public affairs of this country would have been in a much less

prosperous condition than they are." Mercy, therefore, should particular-
ize[10] her accusations.

Unfair, too, was her accusation that he had failed to negotiate "a treaty of
commerce with England" in the last year of the Revolution. While committed to doing so, the treaty was never completed because the British ministry
claimed a formal "treaty of peace" was not yet executed.

Mercy's dates about John's appointment in England, moreover, were incorrect, having lasted less than three years—not the four or five noted in
her *History*. Outrageous, too, was her assertion that "nothing had been
done" during his stay.

"The truth is, a great deal was done, and will appear to the world, if
ever my letters to Congress and their instructions...be published," John
seethed.

Most despicable was Mercy's crack that "[u]nfortunately for himself and
his country, he became so enamored with the British Constitution and the
government...that a partiality for monarchy appeared, which was incon-
sistent with his former professions of republicanism."

"Despotism, absolute monarchy, absolute aristocracy and absolute
democracy I have uniformly detested through my whole life," John maintained. Absolute power in any form "was tyranny...A mixed government
is the only one that can preserve liberty."

No less malicious was Mercy's footnote on page 394 accusing John of
suggesting that it might be "necessary to adopt an hereditary monarchy in
the United States." That, he fumed, "is going the utmost length...though I
could name to you men in high rank...and popularity with the present predominant party [republican], who have gone much further."[11] He would
thus wait "with impatience your answer."

Sourly, John concluded his letter with "regards to the General, and believe me still your friend though with some grievances to complain of."[12]

Mercy received John's ranting letter on July 16. Surprise, anger, and in-
dignation broke over her as she read his critique, shattering her already
insecure view of her life's work. Fearful that republicanism was threatened
and unwilling to admit that her derogatory remarks about John's iconoclas-
tic politics were personally fueled, Mercy impulsively replied that same day.

Nothing in her *History*, she retorted "should occasion a resentment...

prevent his old style of address to Mrs. Warren, or give the semblance of an 'old friend being hastily converted into an enemy.'" John's accusations that her account suffered a "want of veracity" and arose from "a malignancy of heart" must have been prompted by the "irritations of the times or some other cause," she wrote, insinuating that the ascendancy of the republicans, Jefferson's reelection, and the sudden threat of war with Great Britain had provoked him

Otherwise, she tactlessly added, echoing Abigail's occasional reprimand to John about his irascible tendencies, he would never have written such a letter.

Her *History*, Mercy asserted, was composed "with impartiality, to state facts correctly, and to draw characters with truth and candor." After all, she wrote, quoting John's letter of March 1775, "the faithful historian delineates characters truly, let the censure fall where it will."

Not only had she composed John's "character," thoughtfully, but assumed he would be "relieved by such a candid scrutiny of his life" and the mistakes to which "all are liable." His "natural irritability of temper" was no "impeachment of character," merely a reflection of the popular opinion that John had evolved from "a firm republican. . . [to]an advocate for monarchic government."

She had other objections as well, but since John intended to send her "further commentaries" in the so-called spirit of friendship,[13] Mercy would await his response.

So it was that a bitter verbal duel commenced—one in which Mercy defended her *History* against what John considered a damming analysis of his character preserved in perpetuity in hardcover. Reminiscent of the Greek and Shakespearean tragedies that the pair had so often admired, the graying former friends clashed in sixteen letters over interpretations of their lives using quill pens and paper in lieu of swords, determined to preserve their honor to the death.

Four days later John wrote again, slashing away at Mercy's insinuation that he had "relinquished the republican system," and insisting that his earlier *A Defence of the Constitutions of Government of the United States* had been a model for the U.S. Constitution.

The word "republic" John exhorted in his twenty-page letter was an inexact term, signifying "every actual and every possible government among men—that of Constantinople as well as that of Geneva." Its simplest definition was a government exclusive of "despotisms and simple monarchies." The Constitution did not even indicate that citizens were entitled to a "free republican government" because that term was "so loose."[14]

Nor did John's tirade end there. On July 27, even after acknowledging that "[a] man never looks so silly as when he is talking or writing concerning himself," John assailed "Mrs. Warren's severity" for compelling him to "pouring out all myself" in self-defense.

To prove it John sent a detailed account of his quarrels with royal representatives in Massachusetts between 1761 and 1774 that Mercy had omitted. Surely he "ought not to have been shoved off the theatre and kept behind the screen for fourteen years"[15] in her *History*.

The next day, even before receiving John's third letter, Mercy expressed disgust over his July 10 tirade. "My threat of existence in this evanescent state is too far spent for me to enter on political discussion," Mercy wearily observed, but believed it her duty to correct the "unfounded charges" and "repel the assertions that my pen has been guided by a malignant heart." She had not intentionally ignored John's contributions to key pre-Revolutionary events, but accorded her friend as much space in the *History* as she had other patriots.

John's critique, moreover, was written in a "rambling manner... [with] angry and indigested letters," leaving her unable to "know where to begin my remarks."

Perhaps, Mercy tartly suggested, she had inadvertently wounded his famous vanity. "Had not Mr. Adams been suffering under suspicions that his fame had not been sufficiently attended to, or that his character was not invulnerable, he would not have put such a perverse construction upon every passage where he is named."[16]

That same day, John raged in a fourth letter about the details of his missions in France and Holland, enclosing within it a copy of his letter to Sam Adams explaining his disputes with Vergennes and Franklin.

Still smarting from Mercy's comment that he favored "monarchic principles," John asserted that while perhaps "indispensable... in the great nations of Europe," he believed them "wholly inadmissible in America." Nor, he declared, had he been "mortified" upon returning to the United States as a commissioner. "With how much apparent delight do you insert that word 'mortified'! Instead of being retired, I was...forming a constitution...for Massachusetts which finally made the Constitution of the United States."[17]

If "anger is a short madness"[18] as Horace, one of the Enlightenment's admired classical poets observed, Mercy and John's argument illustrated that insanity in black and white.

John's fifth letter of July 30 listed other errors in Mercy's *History* about his foreign assignments. Her analysis, he sneered, read more like a "satirical poem than a grave history," and her comment that he favored the "trappings of nobility" was a slur meant "to gratify the prejudices of the present ruling party in America."[19]

Even before receiving that letter, Mercy wrote that John seemed determined to "misconstrue every expression of mine wherever you, sir, are introduced in my History." Among those was his "resentment" of her use of the word "mortified"—a word John had used himself to describe his experiences in France.

Ridiculous, too, was John's accusation that Mercy and her "party" were responsible for an "inundation of atheism, deism, annihilation, gambling, contempt of marriage and the Sabbath."[20] Yet that was no more ludicrous than his comments that Mrs. Warren "does not know her own meaning" about "republicanism" and even the "celebrated Mrs. Macaulay knew nothing about government." Both statements were meant to defend his accusation that "it is presumption in a lady to write a history with so little information as Mrs. Warren has."

How paradoxical for a man who once deeply admired her work! As proof, Mercy cited John's March 15, 1775, letter to her husband, praising her as an "incomparable satirist," and asking James to remind her that "God Almighty" had "instructed her with powers for the good of the world... that, instead of being a fault to use them, it would be criminal to neglect them."[21]

Nothing, it seemed, could settle the argument. Two days later John penned a sixth letter, listing still other errors about his Dutch ambassadorship. Particularly irksome was her comment that "Mr. Adams had never enjoyed himself so well as while residing in the Dutch Republic." That was hardly the case, John bristled, for in Holland he had suffered an illness "the most severe that I ever experienced."

Mercy's remark that John's "genius was not altogether calculated for a court life amidst the conviviality and gayety of Parisian taste" was another affront. Where could she have obtained that information—other than from malicious newspaper reports? "Mrs. Warren, you have exposed yourself to eternal ridicule by this very ladylike, I will not say, insinuation."[22]

What enraged John most was the malevolence with which she portrayed his character. "I cannot but admire the wonderful fluency and the dear delight with which those soft expressions 'not beloved,' 'thwarted,' 'ridiculed,' 'viewed with jealousy,' 'hatred,' 'frigidity and warmth,' are rolled along by Mrs. Warren, and applied to her old friend who has been all his lifetime, more tender of her reputation and that of her husband, than his own. What have I done to deserve this?"[23]

Four days later, an exasperated Mercy reiterated her previous message— that she "did not know how to satisfy the demands you make upon my time and patience, without entering in discussions which at this late day I have no wish to call up."[24]

As she parried her way through John's attack in a subsequent letter of her own, Mercy proved her point that "Mr. Adams' genius was not altogether calculated for a court life." From their long friendship, she knew that "his plain manners and unpolished habits" were ill-suited to the "conviviality and gayety of Parisian taste." John had even admitted "in France he was never happy."[25]

Should she, Mercy posed in the most cynical passage in the patriots' paper war, rewrite her *History* to satisfy him by "contradicting her former assertions"?

If so, "[s]he must tell the world that Mr. Adams was no monarchist; that he had no partiality for the habits, manners, or government of England; that he was a man of fashion, that his polite accomplishments, rendered him completely qualified for the refinements of Parisian taste; that he had neither frigidity nor warmth of temper, that his passions were always on a due equipoise; that he was beloved by every man, woman, and child in France, that he had neither ambition, nor pride of talents . . .that he was ever hated by courtiers and partisans."

While John might consider that "a very pleasant portrait... I doubt whether the world would receive it as a better likeness than the one drawn in the 'copious stream of Mrs. Warren's historical eloquence.'"[26]

The absurdity of Mercy's solution did little to cool John's rage. A day later he penned his seventh letter, flailing at Mercy's intention to "wink him out of sight... represent him in an odious light... degrade him below his station."[27] In a torrent of ink John defended his efforts in France, jeered at Mercy's understanding of "republicanism," and described himself "the father of it in this State in 1779."

Her thirty-first chapter, he carped, "is like mustard after dinner, as our friends the French say."[28]

A week later Mercy replied. "Angry as you have appeared in your late correspondence, your integrity or industry, your moral or religious character, has never been impeached." She never intended to "write a panegyric on your life and character, though fully sensible of your virtues and your services."[29] Should he desire such an account, John should write his own memoir.

Perhaps, she added, "mustard after dinner is not more disgusting to any palate than the vinegar and nitre which so plentifully seasons all your pages while writing in the 'spirit of friendship.'"[30]

Above all, she longed to be "relieved from a correspondence so repugnant to my feelings." Nor did her "feeble health" allow her to continue the exhausting work of answering John's abusive letters. [31]

Once the floodgates of John's wrath were opened, they were impossible to stem. That same day he wrote again accusing the Warrens of malice. While Mercy had evolved from a friend into a "bitter enemy," he would not allow her errors to "go down to posterity uncorrected." Of course, if "Mrs. Warren is determined to be enrolled in the glorious list of libelers of John Adams, she is welcome." Most of them, John predicted after naming his enemies in his letter, "have come to a bad end, and the rest will follow."[32]

On August 17, John dashed off still another letter, lambasting Mercy for mistakes in volume one. A ninth letter followed on August 19, asserting he was more responsible for "three great subjects, a Declaration of Independence, a Confederation of the States, and treaties with foreign powers"[33] than any other patriot.

Two days later, in his tenth letter, John excoriated Mercy for her comment on page 393 of volume three that "pride of talents and much ambition, were, undoubtedly, combined in the character of the President who immediately succeeded General Washington." That president, of course, was him.

Never had he allowed himself such self-flattery. He had an "open disposition," knew his talents were mediocre, but had "run through more and greater dangers" and "made greater sacrifices than any man among my contemporaries...in the service of my country."[34] While Hamilton had accused him of pride for achieving peace with France, he never expected such meanness from Mrs. Warren "or any of her party." Whatever peace America now enjoyed, John sneered, was "the source of all the triumphs of your party."[35]

After countless pages of self-defense, Adams added that he could critique Mercy's *History* still more, but having generally expressed his view, that "this letter will be the last."

In a final rapier thrust, John claimed that if he had read her *History* without knowing its author, he would have associated it with a mocking stanza from a Pope poem, where a fishwife named Obloquy taught Slander,

> With Envy (spitting cat), dread foe to peace,
> Like a curs'd cur, Malice before her clatters,
> And, vexing ev'ry wight, tears clothes and all to tatters.

Of course, John sardonically concluded, while "Mrs. Warren's egregious errors must be corrected, I cannot, and will not, apply these lines to her."[36]

Eight days later, Mercy replied with her sixth and final letter, declaring that "ten long letters of accusation and reproach, of interrogation and retrospection, within the terms of a few weeks" was simply too much.

"It is impossible to pass over in silence your tenth letter, though you say it is your last," she wrote. The past two were "the top stone of insolent composition... wound up with the most finished abuse and affrontive language that your genius... could furnish. To this you have subjoined a curious selection of poetry from Pope's alley. But it was a miserable subterfuge, to cover your own malignancy... with different ink... that 'you cannot nor will not apply these lines to Mrs. Warren.'"[37]

Several pages followed in which Mercy admitted that John had rendered "many important services for our country," but noted that he had wavered between various concepts regarding government. Sometimes he expressed "despair of the Commonwealth, at others... assert jocosely that *liberty-pole government was the best government in the world.*" At other times, John praised the "divine science of politics," and "systems productive of the great good to mankind," yet then insisted that "*self-love was the sole principle of human action.*"

Having reflected his political evolution, Mercy was unjustly accused of having a "malignant heart" merely for "telling the truth: that... Mr. Adams was in favor of a monarchic government" as was "generally believed through the United States."

John's reaction, she maintained, was likely prompted by his desire for her "to draw an *immaculate* character"[38] regardless of her vow to provide a historically balanced picture.

Earlier, John had admitted he was writing his memoirs "'because nobody else could do it.'" Should he do so, producing a work that even he had admitted would be "voluminous," he would have to include "every trivial suggestion" from "friends or foes."[39]

Equally unrealistic were John's attempts to drag the entire Warren family into a political conspiracy against him. "This is a bold and unfounded assertion. The *Warren family* at the period to which you allude were too deeply immersed in domestic affliction of the most poignant nature to pay much attention to the party contests," Mercy reminded him. The Warrens had never attacked John; moreover, Mercy had always remained "attentive and affectionate "to his children... and to this my beloved friend Mrs. Adams will attest."

How then could he accuse her of writing her *History* to the "taste of the nineteenth century... to gratify the passions, prejudices, and feelings of the party predominate?"

Not only was the *History* thirty-five years in the making, but John often urged her to "continue her annals," insisting that "no one had more authentic materials, and that . . . no one that would do it better."[40]

Now, judging from his tirade, Mercy believed that if anyone should suspect a conspiracy, it was she. For months she had suspected that "there has been a combination to sink into oblivion or to destroy the validity of a late History of the revolution; but until recently I did not suspect that Mr. Adams had any hand in the authorcide."

Should there be another edition of her *History,* Mercy conceded that if she had made any errors about John, she would correct them. Henceforth she would no longer write him. "The lines with which you concluded your late correspondence cap the climax of rancor, indecency, and vulgarism. Yet, as an old friend, I pity you; as a Christian, I forgive you; but there must be some acknowledgment of your injurious treatment or some advances to conciliation, to which my mind is ever open, before I can again feel that respect and affection towards Mr. Adams which once existed in the bosom of MERCY WARREN."[41]

21

"Blessed are the peacemakers!"

"WITH FRANCE WE ARE IN no immediate danger of war," President Jefferson assured Charles Cotesworth Pinckney, his former rival on March 30, 1808. "The immediate danger with England, is postponed for this year ...by the embargo."[1]

That embargo, the Non-Importation Act of December 1807, ordered a cessation of trade with foreign nations to prevent French and British attacks upon American ships on the high seas. While Jefferson hoped diplomatic negotiations would end the hostilities, the act, meanwhile, would protect American vessels from "the insanity of Europe."[2]

The cure, much like the harsh "physicks" doctors administered to patients, soon proved as disastrous as the disease. Predictably, the American economy, which heavily depended upon overseas commerce, had withered. In harbors from Maine to South Carolina, frigates and clipper ships rocked restlessly at anchor, their rigging covered in canvas bags that angry Federalists dubbed "Madison nightcaps," after America's secretary of state. The nation's once-lively coastal ports were stilled, reminders of the British blockade of Boston Harbor forty years earlier.

By late spring, a fuming cadre of Northern ship owners, merchants, and Southern planters blamed the republicans for the economic downturn. Among the most vocal were residents of Plymouth whose lucrative foreign trade had produced nearly $100,000 in annual revenues a few years earlier.

The Warrens, nevertheless, staunchly supported Jefferson's embargo even when James lost money from overseas investments and Henry, Plymouth's tax collector, was abused for monitoring the destination of its ships.

In his farewell address to Congress on November 8, a disheartened Jefferson reluctantly admitted that "the suspension of our foreign commerce...and the consequent losses and sacrifices of our citizens" had become "subjects of just concern."[3]

In Plymouth, meanwhile, Mercy's eighty-two-year-old husband was dying. "I do not expect ever to recover more health; the season of the year is against it, my age is against it," James wrote a friend. "I have had a long life and have enjoyed a thousand blessings. I have uniformly endeavored to do my duty...If death should make its approach this day, I should not be alarmed."[4]

On November 28, 1808, James Warren passed away. With the loss of her husband of fifty-four years, the "first friend of her heart," Mercy sank into grief. By December 8, she had composed an acrostic poem praising James as a "patriot firm," a "steady and constant" friend with "many virtues" which appeared in Boston's *Independent Chronicle*. A man with:

> A judgment sound and understanding clear,
> Replete with knowledge and a heart sincere,
> Rejoicing most when most mankind are bless'd,
> Ever with generous heart aids the distress'd
> No more I'll say but time shall tell the rest.[5]

Today visitors who walk through the venerable graveyard looming over Plymouth center can read Mercy's epitaph for James: "Mark the perfect man, and behold the upright: for the end of that man is peace."

By early 1809, Mercy heard rumors about a Federalist secession planned by influential New Englanders, among them her Federalist nephew, Harrison Grey Otis, president of the Massachusetts Senate. Neither grief nor old age had yet stifled Mercy's patriotism. "What," she demanded of the forty-four-year-old Harrison, "are you about?"

His reply was as urbane as the curtains lining his handsome Beacon Hill mansion. "There was no one of your political party, who I would prefer for a confessor to your much respected self," Harrison conceded, but "it certainly must occur to you that if I have really turned conspirator against the State, I ought not to put it...in your power to hang me."

After all, Mercy's nephew added, "My respect and affection for you, are so utterly at variance with [your] . . . political views and party attachment . . . that I have for twenty years, studiously evaded all discussions." Henceforth, his conversations with his aunt would center upon "tenderness, consolation and respectful love."[6]

By March 1809 Mercy's "political views" and "party attachment" nevertheless remained dominant. As the new president, James Madison, proudly claimed in his inaugural address, the "benign influences of our republican institutions" and the "maintenance of peace with all nations" had produced "unrivaled growth of our faculties and resources."[7]

So popular was Madison that even former Federalist John Quincy Adams joined a republican caucus to elect him. Simultaneously, his father, John, had become disillusioned with Federalism. Subsequent to the death of Boston orator Fisher Ames, his Federalist advocates had hosted an enormous funeral. "The aristocratical tricks, the *coup de theatre,* played in the funerals of Washington, Hamilton and Ames," John grumbled to his friend Dr. Benjamin Rush, were "calculated like drums and trumpets and fifes in an army to drown the unpopularity of speculations, banks, paper money and mushroom fortunes."[8]

Ironically, during the first years of Madison's administration, Adams thus edged closer to republicanism than Mercy had predicted while writing her *History.* John's accusations about her harsh portrait, nevertheless, continued to gnaw at her, especially after reading an 1807 review from a Christian journal called the *Panoplist.*

Mrs. Warren's *History,* that reviewer sneered, was the product of "a mind that had not yielded to the assertion that all political attentions lay outside the road of female life." Indeed, "every page affords a proof of this."[9]

Few women "have hitherto ventured to appear before the public in the character of historians." While the author's account of events "during the revolution is both interesting and entertaining, and will be read with pleasure by those . . . satisfied without entering into the minutiae of cruelty and carnage . . . she seems to have occasionally forgotten . . . she was writing the history of the American Revolution, and . . . introduced narratives . . . which had no connection."

As was customary for reviews of that era, the *Panoplist,* focusing upon the *History*'s conformity to the "proper" British standards of English rather than the work's literary qualities, critiqued Mercy for the incorrect use of certain words, and the "introduction of others totally unknown to the English language," such as "benevolent" and "innumerable."[10]

Readers may occasionally be "charmed with elegant expression" the reviewer grudgingly admitted, but just as frequently would be "disgusted" by the "heavy sentence, rendered tedious, and almost unintelligible by parentheses."

Especially the reviewer objected to the literary "freedom ... in some instances which a gentlemen would not, perhaps, have ... produced." Among these was Mrs. Warren's noncommittal statement about General Washington, that "'further strictures on his character and conduct shall be left to future historians, after time has mollified, the passions and prejudices of the present generation'" Equally inappropriate was her neutral statement about President Adams, that "[t]he administration of ... [Washington's] immediate successor we shall also leave."

Sniffing as if to clear away the scent of female authorship, the *Panoplist* concluded that it could not "bestow unqualified commendation of the work" but "we have derived considerable pleasure, and we hope, some profit, for a careful perusal of it."[11]

Three years later, the Worcester's Jeffersonian *National Aegis* refuted the *Panoplist* in a seven-part series praising Mercy's "full ... accurate, and ... animated picture" of the Revolution, emanating "from the enlightened sensibility of the painter."[12] Instead of condemning the author as a woman, the *Aegis* declared that Mercy's *History* "exalts the character of the female and the human intellect," proving to foreign nations that Americans "can adore her loveliness and & personal graces without denying her the additional advantages of intellectual improvements."

Unfortunately, in spite of praise for Mercy's execution of the "sacred obligation of a historian" and "strict adherence to every minutiae of truth,"[13] the *Aegis* had a far smaller readership than the *Panoplist*.

Even as a widow in her eighties, Mercy immersed herself in a series of intellectually challenging projects. Encouraged by James Winthrop, the white-haired Plymouth author delved into biblical prophecies of a New Coming, read the theories of Newton and papers of patriot John Dickinson, learned about Hinduism, and even studied Russian. One summer, after exchanging letters with a horticulturist who cultivated a passion flower, she received a pressed blossom.

In spite of those interests, Mercy continued to brood over her estrangement from John. Finally in 1812, perhaps having learned about his recent reconciliation with Thomas Jefferson, she asked Elbridge Gerry to attempt a similar rapprochement.

To others, nevertheless, the octogenarian author of Plymouth had become a patriotic icon, one of the last eyewitnesses to the Revolution, who, in spite of her years, remained erect, vibrant, and well-informed. An avid follower of local and national politics, Mercy was thrilled about the news of Elbridge's 1812 election as governor of Massachusetts.

When though, a few months later on June 18, James Madison declared war upon Great Britain, the Federalists of Massachusetts hotly protested. "Organize a *peace party* throughout your country...Express your sentiments without fear, and let the sound of your disapprobation of this war be loud and deep,"[14] declared a Federalist delegate in the Massachusetts House.

In Plymouth, Mercy reacted stoically, claiming that at eighty-four years of age, she did not "feel nor fear much from the world," even though she had "much at stake as regards my children, my friends, my country and posterity."[15]

On the evening of August 5 Mercy's stoicism was tested when republican Congressman Charles Turner, Jr., walking toward North Street to visit "Madame Warren," was assaulted by a group of Federalists. Hearing the commotion outside, James, Jr., had opened the door to the street and dragged the bloodied congressman into the Warren home.

The next day, rumors about the incident swept through Plymouth, as citizens lamented the outbreak of party violence on the steps of the home of the revered historian of the American Revolution. While Mercy did not record the incident, it undoubtedly reminded her of the old bitterness between Plymouth's patriots and Tories.

By September, news of that disturbance and the resultant court case had prompted Abigail Adams to visit Plymouth, accompanied by her forty-seven-year-old daughter, Nabby, and her eighteen-year-old granddaughter, Caroline.

After sixteen years, Mercy and Abigail must have gazed upon each other with wonder. Nor could Mercy's greeting to Nabby—newly arrived from upstate New York "in all the dust and heat"[16] and suffering from a worrisome lump in her breast—have been less poignant. For hours the old friends chatted, catching up on events barely mentioned in their letters before politics had silenced their pens. Happily they realized that they agreed upon many issues, including the evils of political parties, the benefits of republicanism, and support for the war against Great Britain.

In a gesture of friendship, Mercy presented Abigail with a lock of her hair. Several days later, she wrote, "Blessed are the peacemakers!"[17] anticipating that the long years of alienation from John, too, had ended.

By mid-December, however, Elbridge expressed his doubts. Earlier that month during a "very agreeable" visit with the Adamses at Peacefield, he mentioned to Abigail Mercy's hope for a reconciliation with John. Uneasily, she explained that her husband did "not regret this circumstance" and even believed "he had gone too far in his advances" to Mercy.

Still Elbridge remained optimistic, assuring Mercy that if he sensed "any future prospect of restoring mutual friendship," he would pursue[18] it.

Elbridge's overture may have made an impact, for two weeks later Mercy received a letter from Abigail. Enclosed was a handkerchief pin set with pearls and a matching ring containing strands of Mercy's hair interwoven with those of the Adamses.

"I forward to you a token of love and friendship. I hope it will not be the less valuable to you, for combining with a lock of my own hair, that of your ancient friend's at his request,"[19] Abigail explained.

Thrilled, Mercy wrote back, thanking her for that "*token of love and friendship* . . . I shall with pleasure wear the ring as a valuable expression of your regard; nor will it be the less valued for combining with ours a lock of hair from the venerable and patriotic head of the late President of the United States. This, being at his own request, enhances its worth . . . an assurance that he can never forget former amities."[20]

Thereafter, the two women continued to correspond. On April 9, 1813, Abigail wrote, "I cannot let my son pass through Plymouth without stopping to inquire after your health and that of your family!" Then, as in former years, she elicited Mercy's views of the "great and important events" and begged her to write "to give pleasure to her assured friend."[21]

Inevitably, John continued to ruminate upon Mercy's *History*. On April 17, he explained to Elbridge Gerry, by then vice president under Madison, that he was researching the latter's recommendation to the 1775 Massachusetts General Assembly for a continental navy. One of the first places John looked for a copy of Gerry's proposal was in Mercy's *History*.

Indeed, the first volume mentioned that bill but, John complained, Mercy should have "at least inserted your law, which is certainly one of the most important documents in the history of the world, in her Appendix... But no: the above paragraph is all she says."

The omission typified Mercy's flawed historical account. "Had that law been... drawn by her brother, her father, or her husband, her reader would have been favored with a more ample detail," he opined. "But I presume this was written after she had conceived the horror of a navy... and after she had acquired the habit of concording with my enemies, in condemning me."

Equally careless was Mercy's cursory mention of the 1798 Proceedings of Congress that established a navy during John's administration. "Is it not strange, that one of the boldest, more dangerous and most important measures... in the history of the New World, the commencement of an independent naval military power should be thus carelessly and confusedly hurried over?"

Obviously, "History is not the province of the ladies," John declared. While the three volumes contained "many facts, worthy of preservation," it suffered from "little passions and prejudices, want of information... frequent partiality."[22]

Diplomatically, Elbridge suggested that John should write his own history of the Revolution. "If I was only thirty, I would not undertake an history of the Revolution in less than twenty years," John retorted. Now, at seventy-seven, such a task was impossible.

Even so, he intended to put a "few facts... upon paper" especially since, a few days earlier, with the news of the death of Dr. Benjamin Rush, he had received "an awful warning to do it soon." Other old patriots were also dead. "How few remain. Three in Massachusetts I believe are a majority of the surviving signers of a Declaration [of Independence]."[23]

In contrast to John's obduracy, Abigail continued her friendship with Mercy. Having thanked her on July 11, 1813, for her congratulations on John Quincy Adams's appointment to negotiate with Great Britain, Abigail expressed her sorrow for the Federalist "party violence" directed at Mercy's son Henry as collector of the port of Plymouth. She also reported the alarming news that Nabby, suffering from a second siege of breast cancer, had resolved to make an arduous three-hundred-mile carriage ride to Quincy with her daughter, Caroline, and son, John.

"God tempers the wind to the shorn lamb . . . all our troubles in the life are no doubt designed for salutary purposes,"[24] Abigail maintained.

On August 15, 1813, after returning to Quincy to be nursed by her parents, Nabby passed away. In reply to Mercy's condolences, Abigail praised her daughter's "patience, submission, and resignation" and thanked her friend for inviting her and Caroline to visit Plymouth, but explained she was "more wedded to home than ever, and could not leave the bereaved father a prey to solitude." Caroline, however, would visit along with another Adams granddaughter, seventeen-year-old Susanna, the oldest child of her late son, Charles, who would enjoy "being noticed by a lady so . . . justly respected as the venerated friend of many years."[25]

Like the threads of finely woven linen, the warp and woof of friendship uniting the Warrens and Adams through successive generations was once again seamlessly bound.

Nabby's death had so deeply affected her father, John, that he was again moved to forgive old wounds. On September 1, 1813, he finally wrote Mercy. Enclosed in his letter was one from Governor Thomas McKean of Pennsylvania, a delegate of the Stamp Act Congress, containing a reminiscence about Jemmy as its "boldest and best speaker."[26]

Equally flattering was John's second attachment—a copy of his "Dialogue of the Dead," concerning the death of Benjamin Franklin, written in 1789 while attending Congress in New York.

Thrilled, Mercy replied on September 12 that she was "much gratified by seeing your signature affixed to a letter addressed to Mm. Warren," as well as "by the marks of your attention manifest in the interesting enclosures . . . one of which deeply affected me as a sister."

Her delay in responding, Mercy explained, was a result of her ongoing eye problems and delighted distraction entertaining the Adamses' grand-daughters. "Lovely Girls! Sent by Providence to support the pillow of age, while nightly recollecting the tomb that encloses the most amiable of daughters."[27]

By November 24, John wrote again, affirming his opinion that Governor McKean's letter was an accurate recollection of Jemmy. "I know not, Madam, what your father, your husband, or your father would think of these times," John added. "An entire separation, in government at least, between America and Europe seems to be commencing."[28]

A month later Mercy gratefully assured John that she was one "who, through a long life, has not been insensible of the worth of friendship." She, too, found it impossible to correspond "without recollecting past time, when my father, my husband, my brother and yourself were united . . . to emancipate their country from the yoke of foreign domination."[29]

By 1814 increasingly warm letters passed between Plymouth and Quincy. In one of March 31, Mercy confided that though her life was "smoothed by the intercourse with a number of sensible, pious, elegant correspondents," she was especially "satisfied . . . to receive letters from a gentleman with whom I have corresponded for near half a century" and find the "same flow of esteem, friendship and confidence which used to drop profusely from his pen."[30]

By then, the health of the nearly eighty-six-year-old Mercy was failing. As James, Jr., often wrote his Otis relatives, things were as usual in Plymouth, "my mother feeble."[31] Knowing that, Mercy's only living brother, seventy-four-year-old Samuel Allyne, who still served as secretary to the U.S. Senate, visited Plymouth on his way to Washington.

As he said goodbye, Samuel Allyne riveted his eyes upon Mercy and backed away from the front door as if fixing her face in his memory. It would be the last time they met. Soon after Samuel Allyne arrived in Washington, he suddenly died.

From Quincy on May 5, Abigail dutifully sent sympathies, reminding

Mercy that her brother had passed away "with the love, respect, and esteem of his country, having for twenty-five years exhibited, a striking example of attention and punctuality." Should "we live to old age . . . string after string is severed from the heart until . . . we have scarcely anything left to resign, but breath."[32]

If nothing else, Samuel Allyne's death intensified Mercy's longing to cling to those strings as long as possible. Was she doing so, she wondered to Samuel Allyne's widow, Mary, "because I am about to leave them, or . . . because the circle is so circumscribed?"[33]

By July 10, 1814, having learned of John's illness that spring, Mercy longed to see him. "What think you, sir, of a little jaunt to Plymouth in company with Mrs. Adams and my sweet Caroline?" she wrote that day. "The ride might contribute to your health and to that of my long tried friend, your excellent partner." Such a visit would enable them to have a discussion that was impossible to fulfill in letters.

Nor was that all. Mercy had a question that, she apologetically admitted, John "might deem impertinent. Do you remember who was the author of a little pamphlet entitled the *Group?* To your hand it was committed by the writer. You brought it forward to the public eye."

She mentioned *The Group,* Mercy explained, because a friend visiting the Boston Athenaeum spotted the pamphlet and discovered that a certain Samuel Barrett claimed its authorship.

Fuming, Mercy asked John if "you please, give a written testimony contradictory of this false assertion. You and Mr. Gerry are the only surviving gentlemen that I recollect, who know anything of the character, . . . the movements, and a thousand circumstances that . . . occupied the . . . patriots who struggled and suffered in the cause of their country from 1765 to 1783.

"Am I mistaken . . . that the generations of men . . . since . . . have been too notoriously negligent in their inquiries relative to the principles and the foundation of the rights and liberties acquired by the labors and blood of their ancestors?"[34]

On August 4 Mercy again wrote to John with her usual persistence. "If the author of the 'Group' ever deserved half the encomiums you have lavished on her talent, it ought to be rescued from oblivion. I know of no one living who can or will do this but yourself."[35]

Intuitively, John knew that to be true. Appalled by the plagiarism of Mercy's most famous play, John subsequently rode into Boston. "I have certified in the book in the Athenaeum that to my certain knowledge, The Group was written by Mrs. Warren,"[36] he proudly announced to his old friend on August 17, 1814.

Today visitors to the Boston Athenaeum can see that copy of *The Group* with John Adams's confirming statement scrawled upon it.

In that same letter, John thanked Mercy for her invitation to visit Plymouth. Indeed, he had been ill most of the winter. "Head loaded, eyes almost blind, horrid churchyard cough! High fever!"[37] as he had described his ailments to a friend. While finally recovered, his advanced age, the seventy-nine-year-old explained, made him unwilling to "sleep out of his own bed, for any office the King could have given him."

John was, nevertheless, willing to share his view of current political developments. "If the war continues between Great Britain and the United States, as I believe it will, it will soon rekindle the flames of Europe."[38]

At that very moment the flames of that war were threatening the United States. On August 24, the British burned Washington then seized part of Maine. Terrified, the residents of Boston stockpiled weapons and trained militias—just as their fathers had forty years earlier.

On Thursday evening, October 6, Mercy received a visit from Sarah Cary, a friend she had not seen in twenty-one years. As Mrs. Cary wrote her own son Henry, the mental faculties of her eighty-six-year-old hostess were "unimpaired," and she conversed "with the same vicacity" as in former years.

Seated in a red damask easy chair, Mercy was "dressed in a gown of black satin, a mob cap tied under the chin & a small snug black bonnet with a little green curtain to shade her eyes, which, have failed her very much of late years." Mercy's fingers were adorned with rings, "chiefly mourning ones" but she especially cherished one "lately received from the former Pt. [President] Adams with his, & his wife's hair."[39]

A week later on October 13, Mercy entertained other guests from Boston. In the middle of the night she awoke "suddenly and violently attacked" with pain. For five days she suffered, but on Monday morning the 17 rose and briefly appeared at the breakfast table.

Two nights later on Wednesday, October 19, at two a.m., Mercy quietly passed away. "She expired with great calmness & perfect recollection of mind," her son Henry recalled. "And thus the *last* frail reed is broken."[40]

The events recorded by that "frail reed" were among the most extraordinary in history, ones whose monumental importance are still echoed in the neoclassical poems, fiery satirical plays, Bill of Rights, and lofty phrases of Mercy's eyewitness account of the American Revolution. In spite of its flaws, *The Rise, Progress and Termination of the American Revolution* is a unique record of one colonial woman's lifelong effort to capture history as she had lived and witnessed it through the glorious ideals of the early patriots.

ONE OF THE REWARDS in writing about Mrs. Warren's life were the many individuals I met whose guidance and expertise were indispensable to the research and completion of the manuscript. While it is impossible to name all the librarians, historical experts, archivists, and museum curators who helped, I am grateful to all of them.

I am indebted to Peter Drummey, librarian of the Massachusetts Historical Society, for his helpful suggestions and overview of the primary sources on Mercy Otis Warren and suggestions for other resources and archives, and to reference librarians Kim Nusco, Carolle Morini, and Elaine Grublin. Architect and preservation planner Frederic Detwiller of New England Landmarks graciously shared new information about the Edmund Fowle House, the Watertown headquarters for the Executive Committee of the Provincial Congress, where Mrs. Warren occasionally lived with her husband, James, in 1775. Joyce Kelly of the Watertown Historical Society provided additional information on that site.

Thanks to a Creative Artists and Writers Fellowship at the American Antiquarian Society, I spent a month researching the Revolutionary era and its impact upon Massachusetts. There, I am indebted to outreach director, James Moran; research librarian Joanne Chaison; Marie Lamoureax, then head of research services; and Tom Knoles, curator of manuscripts, for their enthusiasm on behalf of the project and suggestions for research.

Lee Reagan, local history librarian at Plymouth Public Library, enthusiastically provided key facts about the town during the Revolutionary era, suggested local experts, and facilitated my introduction to important local sites. Peggy Baker, director of Pilgrim Hall Museum and Library, directed me to the invaluable *Warren Family Letters and Papers, 1763–1814* and suggested other research sources.

With special thanks to Elizabeth Creeden, an expert in colonial era needlework, for her keen interest in the project and guidance, which greatly enhanced my understanding of eighteenth-century domestic arts. I am also grateful to Dorothea Anderson and Joan Smith for their tour of the Warren homestead and farm near the Eel River and to Harold Moody, Jr., for showing me the hidden corners of the Winslow-Warren house in downtown Plymouth.

In West Barnstable, Massachusetts, I am indebted to local historians Nancy and Paul Shoemaker for taking me through the former Otis property, gravesites, and surrounding community and their ongoing enthusiasm for the project. Through their help Gabrielle Black donated a copy of the will of James Otis, Sr., and Audrey Loughnane provided a history of the 2001 dedication of the Mercy Otis Statue at the Barnstable Court House. My heartfelt appreciation to Lou Cataldo, archivist of the town of Barnstable, for abiding ongoing interest in my work and information on Mrs. Warren's life.

As a Manhattan resident, I spent months working in the New York Public Library's Humanities and Social Sciences Library, where Wayne Furman, director of special collections, extended my tenure in the Allen Room and offered valuable suggestions for accessing library resources. Many other talented librarians aided my research, especially David Smith, whose unflagging attention to my requests for information and books enhanced my research.

Thanks are also due to Jennifer Lee of the rare book room and manuscript division of the Butler Library at Columbia University for her assistance with the Otis Family Papers. University of Mississippi historian Sheila Skemp read a draft of the manuscript and offered valuable suggestions. I also appreciate the several conversations I had with Ray Raphael about Mrs. Warren and her era. I thank Joann Rosoff for her careful perusal of the manuscript.

My literary agent, Patty Moosbrugger, believed in the project from the start and has remained a source of encouragement through the writing and publication process. My editor, Gayatri Patnaik, at Beacon Press, meticulously followed the evolving manuscript from first draft through its final form and eased the inevitable challenges along the way.

Above all, I wish to thank my husband, Bill Stetson, for his abiding interest in the book, critical comments on various drafts of the manuscript, patient tours of historical sites, and good-humored understanding of the long hours I spent at the computer in the "northeast" corner of my Manhattan writing room. For that and so much more, I thank him.

Frequently cited works and individuals are identified in the notes by the following abbreviations:

AAS	American Antiquarian Society
AFC	Adams Family Correspondence
GOP	Gay-Otis Papers, Rare Book and Manuscript Library, Butler Library Columbia University
JAD	Diary and Autobiography of John Adams
CMOW	Correspondence with Mercy Otis Warren, Massachusetts Historical Society
MWH	*History of the Rise, Progress and Termination of the American Revolution.*
MWP	Mercy Otis Warren Papers, Massachusetts Historical Society
MWLB	Mercy Warren Letterbook, Massachusetts Historical Society
OFP	Otis Family Papers, Rare Book and Manuscript Library, Butler Library Columbia University
WFLP	Warren Family Letters and Papers, 1763–1814, Archives, Pilgrim Hall Museum

AA	Abigail Adams
EG	Elbridge Gerry
HFW	Hannah Fayerweather Winthrop
HK	Henry Knox
HW	Henry Warren
JA	John Adams
JO	"Jemmy," James "the Patriot" Otis, Jr.
JW	James Warren
JWIN	James Winthrop, Jr.
GW	George Warren
MOW	Mercy Otis Warren
SA	Samuel Adams
SO	Samuel Allyne Otis
WW	Winslow Warren

Preface

1. JA to MOW, *WAL*, II, 131, March 18, 1780.
2. AA to MOW, WFLP, April 19, 1776.
3. Arthur Lee to JW, *WAL*, II, 144, Oct. 30, 1780.
4. MWH, III, 696.
5. Ellet, I, "Mercy Warren," n. 4.
6. Stanton, I, 32.
7. MWLB, 113–15.
8. MOW to Elizabeth (Otis) Brown, WFLP, 1781.
9. AA to JA, *AFC*, I, 370, March 31, 1776.

CHAPTER 1

A Pen As Explosive As Gunpowder

1. WFLP, Dec. 22, 1773.
2. Anthony, 76.
3. *AFC*, I, 93, Jan. 19, 1774.
4. WFLP, April 9, 1774.
5. Ibid.
6. Tudor, 76–77.
7. Wroth and Zobel, II, 106–7.
8. *WAL*, II, 80, Dec.15, 1778.
9. WFLP, April 1773.
10. MWLB, 115.
11. MWLB, 43, March 18, 1779.
12. Waters, 72.
13. *MWH*, I, 33.
14. *JAD*, I, 227, June 8, 1762.
15. Hayes, "Private Poems," 210.
16. MOW to JW, MWLB, Feb. 1775.
17. MWLB, 1774.
18. Gardiner, 201.
19. *WAL*, II, 1, Jan. 2, 1778.
20. *MWH*, I, 13.
21. Waters, 110.

22. Ibid., 112.
23. Sigmund, 53.
24. Tudor, 9.
25. *WAL*, I, 61, June 18, 1775.
26. Tudor, 40.

CHAPTER 2

Fires, Civil and Domestic

1. Franklin, *Poor Richard's Almanack*.
2. Kerber, 26.
3. WFLP, June 6, 1779.
4. Ibid., April 5, 1778.
5. *AFC*, I, 182, Jan. 28, 1775.
6. MWLB, 485, Nov. 11, 1791.
7. Ibid., May 17, 1763.
8. *WAL*, I, 44, April 6, 1775.
9. WFLP, Aug. 9, 1775.
10. Gardiner, 10.
11. WFLP, Jan. 1776.
12. Ibid., Dec. 2, 1775.
13. Ibid., June 16, 1775.
14. Ibid., Sept.13, 1775.
15. Ibid., Sept.21, 1775.
16. MOW to JW, Ibid., May 17, 1763.
17. *WAL*, II, 115, Aug. 6, 1779.
18. Ibid.
19. Hayes, "Private Poems," 205.
20. Hutchinson, *History*, II, 342.
21. *MWH*, I, 45–46.
22. Tudor, 303.
23. *MWH*, I, 25.
24. Hutchinson, *History*, III, 63.
25. Ibid.
26. Ibid., 64.
27. Ibid., 199.
28. Waters, 123.
29. Tudor, 76–77.
30. Wroth and Zobel, 121–44.
31. *MWH*, I, 28.

32. CMOW, Feb. 1773.
33. Ibid., Oct. 12, 1779.
34. *AFC*, I, 48, Sept. 30, 1764.
35. Ibid., 83, May 1772.
36. Otis, *Vindication of the Conduct*, 18.
37. *MWH*, I, 28.
38. Fritz, 53.
39. *JAD*, I, 271, Dec. 23, 1765.
40. Van Doren, 334.
41. *MWH*, I, 17.
42. Ibid.
43. Mullet, 323–57.
44. *Boston Gazette*, May 13, 1765.
45. Hibbert, 3.
46. Ibid., 3.
47. Ibid., 92.

CHAPTER 3
"Neither the pen nor the tongue of a lawyer"

1. Wells, 107–8.
2. Hayes, "Private Poems," 218.
3. *WAL*, I, 1–2, April 11, 1766.
4. Van Doren, 354.
5. *Boston Gazette*, May 19, 1766.
6. *MWH*, I, 26.
7. CMOW, Sept. 6, 1769.
8. Hayes, "Private Poems," 206.
9. *WAL*, II, 85, Jan. 17, 1779.
10. *MWH*, I, 27.
11. *WAL*, I, 4, Dec. 5, 1768.
12. Beach, 144.
13. Barck and Lefler, 536.
14. Blecki, 172.
15. Moore, 50.
16. *Boston Evening Post*, May 29, 1769.
17. Moore, 44–47.
18. CMOW, Feb. 1773.

19. *Royal American Magazine*, I, (June 1774): 233–34.
20. Ibid.
21. Barck and Lefler, 538.
22. *MWH*, I, 38.
23. Ibid., 35.
24. CMOW, Sept. 6, 1769.
25. Wells, 231.
26. *JAD*, I, 349, Jan. 16, 1770.
27. Fritz, 83.
28. Hosmer, 48, n. 1.
29. Sibley and Shipton, II, 277.
30. *JAD*, I, 343, Sept. 2, 1769.
31. *Boston Gazette*, Sept. 4, 1769.
32. Ibid.
33. Ibid., Sept.18, 1769.
34. Ibid., Sept. 25, 1769.
35. Anthony, 70.
36. WFLP, 1770.
37. Sibley and Shipton, 280.
38. *JAD*, I, 348, Jan. 16, 1770.
39. Ibid., 350.
40. Miller, 219.
41. *JAD*, I, 349.
42. Anthony, 73.
43. Hayes, "Private Poems," 213.
44. *JAD*, II, 15, May 22, 1771.
45. Hutchinson, *Diary*, 65, n.
46. *WAL*, I, 9, March 25, 1771.
47. *JAD*, II, 14, May 15, 1771.
48. CMOW, Jan. 1, 1772.
49. *MWH*, 50.
50. CMOW, March 1774.

CHAPTER 4
The Patriots' Secret Pen

1. CMOW, June 22, 1772.
2. Shipton, 514.
3. *MWH*, I, 55.
4. *Boston Gazette*, Oct. 12, 1772.

5. Wells, I, 497.
6. Barck and Lefler, 346.
7. *WAL*, I, 11–12, Nov. 4, 1772.
8. Ibid., 12, Nov. 27, 1772.
9. Ibid., 14, Dec. 9, 1772.
10. Barck and Lefler, 547.
11. Hosmer, 250.
12. *JAD*, II, 202, March 4, 1773.
13. *WAL*, I, 27, April 27, 1769.
14. WFLP, June 9, 1773.
15. *JAD*, II, 360, Aug. 9, 1770.
16. Warren, *Poems*, 228.
17. Franklin, 8–9, 26, 32.
18. CMOW, Nov. 10, 1773.
19. WFLP, June 6, 1779.
20. Weales, 107.
21. Anthony, 84.
22. *AFC*, I, 88, Dec. 5, 1773.
23. *WAL*, I, 14, Nov. 27, 1772.
24. Hutchinson, *Diary*, I, 15.
25. Ibid., 16.
26. "To W.B. Esq.," *Boston Gazette*, Jan. 4, 1773.
27. *JAD*, II, 78, March 4, 1773.
28. Van Doren, 443.
29. *MWH*, I, 56.
30. Ibid., 352–53.
31. Ibid., 56.
32. *JAD*, II, 81, April 24, 1773.
33. JA to AA, *AFC*, I, 123, July 4, 1774.
34. WFLP, Feb. 1773.
35. Hayes, "The Defeat," 457.
36. *Boston Gazette*, July 19, 1773.
37. CMOW, Nov. 5, 1771.
38. *AFC*, I, 85, July 16, 1773.
39. Ibid., 47.
40. *FC*, I, 87, July 25, 1773.
41. Ibid., 86.
42. WFLP, 1773.
43. Ibid., May 17, 1763.

44. MWLB, 451.
45. Fielding, xi, 59.
46. Blecki, 247.
47. Barck and Lefler, 549–50.
48. Moore, 56–57.
49. *Boston Evening Post*, Dec. 20, 1773.
50. Blecki, 63–64.
51. *Boston Evening Post*, Nov. 8, 1773.
52. *WAL*, I, 18, Dec. 5, 1773.
53. Wells, II, 122.
54. *JAD*, II, 85–86, Dec. 17, 1773.
55. *AFC*, I, 92–93, Jan.18, 1774.
56 *WAL*, I, 21, Jan. 3, 1774.
57. *AFC*, I, 99, Feb. 27, 1774.
58. WFLP, April 9, 1774.

CHAPTER 5
"No one has at stake a larger share of domestic felicity"

1. *AFC*, I, 91, Jan. 19, 1774.
2. Hibbert, 21.
3. *Boston Gazette*, 3, Jan. 24, 1774.
4. WFLP, April 22, 1772.
5. *AFC*, I, 98, Feb. 1774.
6. Ibid., 299, Feb. 27, 1774.
7. MOW to AA, WFLP, Feb. 1774.
8. *WAL*, I, 46, April 6, 1775.
9. CMOW, March 1774.
10. "Extract of a Letter from London" *Boston Evening Post*, Feb. 15, 1774.
11. Ibid., Feb. 19, 1774.
12. Van Doren, 482.
13. *WAL*, I, 23, Jan. 3, 1774.
14. *JAD*, II, 93.
15. Hibbert, 21.
16. *WAL*, I, 24, March 31, 1774.
17. Commager and Cantor, I, 71.
18. *MWH*, I, 79.

19. Gerlach, 87.
20. *Boston Gazette*, May 16, 1774.
21. Koch and Peden, 282.
22. Barck and Lefler, 555.
23. LaFeber, 17.
24. WFLP, May 14, 1774.
25. *AFC*, I, 108, May 17, 1774.
26. *MWH*, I, 80.
27. Hutchinson, *Diary*, 109.
28. Ibid., 130–31.
29. *JAD*, II, 97, June 25, 1774.
30. "Parliament Blockading,"
    Boston Gazette, May 16, 1774.
31. Barck and Lefler, 556.
32. *MWH*, I, 88 & 87.
33. Ibid., 88, n. 1.
34. *WAL*, I, 26, May 21, 1774.
35. *JAD*, II, 96.
36. WFLP, July 14, 1774.
37. *WAL*, I, 22, Jan. 3, 1774.
38. *AFC*, I, 138–39, Aug. 9, 1774.
39. WFLP, Aug. 1774.
40. Ibid., Oct. 14, 1774.
41. Ibid.
42. MOW to HFW, WFLP, 1774.
43. MOW to JW, Ibid.
44. *AFC*, I, 151, Sept. 14, 1774.
45. JA to AA, Ibid., 150, Sept. 8,
    1774.
46. Ibid., 155, Sept. 14, 1774.
47. *JAD*, II, 134.
48. Ibid., 150.
49. WFLP, 1774.
50. Ibid., Sept. 11, 1774.
51. Ibid., Dec. 29, 1774.
52. Ibid., 1774.
53. Franklin, 2–3.
54. Ibid., 5–6.
55. Ibid., 15.
56. Ibid., 9, 20, 22.
57. Ibid., 22.

CHAPTER 6
"Perhaps the whole land be involved in blood"

1. WFLP, 1774.
2. *AFC*, I, 185, Feb. 3, 1775.
3. *WAL*, I, 136, Jan, 17, 1775.
4. Ibid., 37–38, Jan. 30, 1775.
5. WFLP, March 15, 1775.
6. *WAL*, I, 43–44, March 15, 1775.
7. Maier, 285.
8. Barck and Lefler, 565.
9. Ibid.
10. Hibbert, 27.
11. WFLP, Jan. 3, 1775.
12. *AFC*, I, 182, Jan. 28, 1775.
13. *AFC*, I, 179–80, Jan. 25, 1775.
14. WFLP, Feb. 1775.
15. Ibid., March 1775.
16. *WAL*, I, 45, April 6, 1775.
17. *MWH*, I, 103–4.
18. Salisbury Family Papers, box 3,
    folder 3, April 20, 1775, AAS.
19. WFLP, April 1775.
20. Parkman Family Papers, Diary
    of Breck Parkman. April 27,
    1775, AAS.
21. CMOW, April 1775.
22. WFLP, April 1775.
23. Ibid., May 3, 1775.
24. *AFC*, I, May 2, 1775.
25. *WAL*, I, 49, n. 2.
26. Hutchinson, *Diary*, 526.
27. *MWH*, I, 106.
28. *AFC*, I, 190, May 2, 1775.
29. *AFC*, I, 191, May 2, 1775.
30. *AFC*, I, 198–99, May 15, 1775.
31. WFLP, June 16, 1775.

CHAPTER 7
Reporter of Revolutionary Events

1. *WAL*, I, 59, June 18, 1775.

2. Brooks, 151.
3. Commager and Morris, 126.
4. Ibid., 132.
5. *WAL*, I, 59, June 18, 1775.
6. Commager and Morris, 133–34.
7. *WAL*, I, 59–60, June 18, 1775.
8. *MWH*, I, 120–22.
9. AA to JA, *AFC*, I, 260, July 24, 1775.
10. French, 336.
11. AA to JA, *AFC*, I, 261, July 25, 1775.
12. *WAL*, I, 66, June 27, 1775.
13. Ibid., 68, June 27, 1775.
14. Ibid., 71–72, July 5, 1775.
15. Ibid., 88, July 23, 1775.
16. *MWH*, I, 129.
17. *WAL*, I, 77, July 7, 1775.
18. CMOW, Aug. 17, 1775.
19. *WAL*, I, 200, Jan. 8, 1776.
20. WFLP, July 1775.
21. *WAL*, I, 91, July 30, 1775.
22. Ibid., 78, July 7, 1775.
23. Ibid., 103–4, Aug. 17, 1775.
24. JW to MOW, WFLP, Aug. 9, 1775.
25. *AFC*, I, 274–75, Aug. 26, 1775.
26. MWLB, Aug. 1775.
27. *WAL*, 106–7, Sept. 4, 1775.
28. WFLP, Sept. 13, 1775.
29. *WAL*, I, 107–8.
30. WFLP, Sept. 21, 1775.
31. Ibid., Sept. 13, 1775.
32. *AFC*, II, 274, Aug. 26, 1775.
33. WFLP, Aug. 17, 1775.
34. Ibid., Sept. 28, 1775.
35. *WAL*, I, 115, Sept. 16, 1775.
36. WFLP, Oct. 22, 1775.
37. Ibid.
38. WFLP, Oct. 22, 1775.

CHAPTER 8
A Still Calm Within,
Violent Concussions Without

1. *MWH*, I, 4.
2. CMOW, Sept. 30, 1775.
3. *AFC*, II, 301, Oct. 19, 1775.
4. *WAL*, I, 184, Nov. 14, 1775.
5. Ibid., 179, Nov. 1775.
6. *AFC*, I, 338–39, Dec. 11, 1775.
7. WFLP, Dec. 2, 1775.
8. Ibid.
9. Ibid., Dec. 5, 1775.
10. Ibid., Nov. 28, 1775.
11. Ibid., Dec. 24, 1775.
12. Ibid., Jan. 1776.
13. *WAL*, I, 201, Jan. 8, 1776.
14. French, 634.
15. Commager and Morris, 166.
16. *MWH*, I, 142.
17. WFLP, Jan. 20, 1776.
18. *AFC*, I, 353, March 2, 1776.
19. Fleming, 181.
20. Ibid.
21. Gardiner, 8.
22. WFLP, March 8, 1776.
23. Franklin, 5, 7–8, 17–18.
24. WFLP, March 10, 1776.
25. Fleming, 184.
26. WFLP, March 23, 1776.
27. Ibid., April 3, 1776.
28. Fleming, 187.
29. *WAL*, I, 217, March 30, 1776.
30. WFLP, March 23, 1776.

CHAPTER 9
"Ladies are the greatest politicians"

1. *WAL*, I, 217–19, March 30, 1776.
2. Ibid., 228, April 16, 1776.
3. Ibid., 228–29, April 17, 1776.
4. WFLP, April 19, 1776.

5. *AFC*, I, 396–97, April 27, 1776.
6. *WAL*, I, 221, April 16, 1776.
7. *AFC*, I, 397, April 27, 1776.
8. Ibid., 370, March 31, 1776.
9. Ibid., 397, April 27, 1776.
10. Butterfield, *Book of Abigail and John*, 121–23.
11. *AFC*, I, 397, April 27, 1776.
12. Brown, 242.
13. *AFC*, I, 418, May 27, 1776.
14. Ibid., II, 2, 13, June 16, 1776.
15. Ibid., I, 418, May 27, 1776.
16. CMOW, Nov. 5, 1771.
17. WFLP, July 16, 1773.
18. Gardiner, 39.
19. WFLP, June 1776.
20. *AFC*, II, 2, 79–80, Aug. 5, 1776.
21. *WAL*, I, 240, May 8, 1776.
22. Charles Francis Adams, *Familiar Letters*, 178.
23. *AFC*, II, 99, Aug.18, 1776, I, 245.
24. *WAL*, I, 251, May 20, 1776.
25. Gardiner, 38.
26. *WAL*, I, 259, July 10, 1776.
27. Ibid., 261, July 17, 1776.
28. *AFC*, II, 29–30, July 5, 1776.
29. *WAL*, I, 261, July 17, 1776.
30. *AFC*, II, 57, July 22, 1776.
31. *MWH*, I, 170.
32. *WAL*, I, 263–64, July 24, 1776.
33. Ibid., 265, July 27, 1776.
34. WAL, I, 264, July 2, 1776.
35. Ibid., 268, Aug. 11, 1776.
36. *AFC*, II, 67, July 29, 1776.
37. Ibid., 118, Sept.4, 1776.
38. Franklin, 213–14.
39. WFLP, Sept.15, 1776.

CHAPTER 10
"The hand often shrunk back from the task"

1. *WAL*, I, 274, Sept. 19, 1776.
2. Shipton, 522.
3. WFLP, Nov. 21, 1776.
4. *AFC*, II, 142–43, Dec. 1, 1776.
5. WFLP, Dec. 4, 1776.
6. *MWH*, xliii.
7. WFLP, Dec. 4, 1776.
8. *MWH*, xliii.
9. Ibid., 184.
10. WFLP, Dec. 26, 1776.
11. Ibid., postscript, Dec. 31, 1776.
12. *AFC*, II, II, 150, Jan.? 1777.
13. WFLP, April 19, 1776.
14. *AFC*, I, 150, Jan? 1777.
15. Ibid., March 1, 1777.
16. WFLP, Feb. 1, 1777.
17. Ibid., Feb. 15, 1777, Ibid.
18. *WAL*, I, 324–25, May 6, 1777.
19. Ibid., 327, 1777.
20. WFLP, June 14, 1777.
21. *AFC*, II, 264, June 14, 1777.
22. Ibid., 276, July 7, 1777.
23. Ibid., 312, ante Aug. 1777.
24. Ibid., 313, Aug.14, 1777.
25. Shipton, 521.
26. Gardiner, 51, 58.
27. *AFC*, II, 166–67, March 1, 1777.
28. Ibid., 312, July 7, 1777.
29. Ibid., 313, ante Aug. 14, 1777.
30. Ibid., 172, March 8, 1777.
31. WFLP, 1777.
32. Ibid., April 29, 1777.
33. *MWH*, II, 249.
34. *WAL*, II, 451–52, Nov. 11, 1777.
35. *WAL*, II, 1–2, Jan. 2, 1778.
36. WFLP, March 10, 1776.
37. *WAL*, II, 16, June 2, 1778.
38. Ibid., 13, May 31, 1778.

39. Unger, 261.
40. *WAL*, II, 41, Aug. 18, 1778.
41. Ibid., 16–17, June 2, 1778.

CHAPTER 11
"War has ever been unfriendly to virtue"

1. *AFC*, II, 143, Dec. 1, 1776.
2. Ibid., III, 152, Jan. 19, 1779.
3. WFLP, 1778, n.
4. *WAL*, II, 82–83, Dec. 16, 1778.
5. Ibid., 81, Dec. 15, 1778.
6. Ibid., 85–86, Jan. 19, 1779.
7. *AFC*, III, 154, post Jan. 22, 1779.
8. Ibid., 160, Feb. 7, 1779.
9. Ibid., 188, March 15, 1779.
10. Ibid., 190, March 19, 1779.
11. Ibid., 194, April 8, 1779.
12. Ibid., 289, Feb. 28, 1780.
13. *WAL*, II, 165, Jan. 8, 1781.
14. *AFC*, III, 189, March 15, 1779.
15. *WAL*, II, 131, March 18, 1780.
16. Ibid., 20, June 7, 1778.
17. Ibid., 8–9, May 8, 1778.
18. Ibid., 26, June 26, 1778.
19. Ibid., 60, Oct. 25, 1778.
20. Ibid., 66, Nov. 9, 1778.
21. *WAL*, II, 54, Oct. 15, 1778.
22. Franklin. 246, 249n.
23. Warren, *Poems*, 246.
24. Franklin, 5, 15.
25. *WAL*, II, 102, June 6, 1779.
26. Franklin, 212.
27. Gardiner, 135.
28. *WAL*, II, 104–5, June 13, 1779.
29. Ibid., 114, July 29, 1779.
30. Ibid., 120, Sept. 1779?
31. Franklin, 232–34.
32. WFLP, Dec. 4, 1779.
33. Waingrow, I, 193.
34. Chesterfield, 112–13, 122.
35. WFLP, Dec. 1779.

36. Chesterfield, 133.
37. WFLP, Dec. 1779.
38. *WAL*, II, 128–29, Feb. 28, 1780.
39. Ibid., 105, June 13, 1779.
40. *WAL*, II, 59–60, Oct. 25, 1778.
41. *MWH*, II, 389–90.
42. *WAL*, II, 105, June 13, 1779.
43. Ibid., 121–22, Dec. 1779.
44. Shipton, 523.
45. *WAL*, II, 49, Sept. 30, 1778.
46. Ibid., 20, June 7, 1778.
47. Ibid., 139, Sept. 17, 1780.
48. WFLP, Nov.16, 1780.
49. *WAL*, II, 145, Nov. 2, 1780.
50. WFLP, March 12, 1780.
51. Ibid., March 15, 1780.
52. Ibid., March 25, 1780.
53. Ibid., March 26, 1780.

CHAPTER 12
Views from Neponset Hill

1. WFLP, April 2, 1780.
2. *WAL*, II, 132, April 2, 1780.
3. WFLP, note of April 6 in letter of April 11, 1780.
4. Ibid., May 18, 1780.
5. Cotton Tufts to JA, *AFC*, III, 386, July 25, 1780.
6. Moore, *Diary*, 805–6.
7. Pynchon, 63.
8. Cotton Tufts to JA, *AFC*, III, 386–87, July 25, 1780.
9. WFLP, June 3, 1780.
10. Ibid., Aug. 20, 1780.
11. Ibid., Aug. 29, 1780.
12. Ibid., Sept.1, 1780.
13. Ibid., Sept.1, 1780.
14. *WAL*, II, 144, Oct. 30, 1780.
15. Ibid., Dec. 9, 1780.
16. Fritz, 195.
17. WFLP, Nov. 20, 1780.

18. Fritz, 196–97.
19. WFLP, Dec. 1780.
20. CMOW, Jan. 2, 1781.
21. *AFC*, IV, 41–42, Dec. 21, 1781.
22. WFLP, June 3, 1781.
23. Ibid., Jan. 27, 1781.
24. *AFC*, I, 102, Feb. 27, 1774.
25. WFLP, Jan. 1781.
26. Ibid., March 4, 1781.
27. WFLP, June 3, 1781.
28. *AFC*, IV, Intro., iv.
29. *WAL*, II, 181, Oct. 24, 1782.
30. WFLP, June 15, 1781.
31. Ibid., Sept. 28, 1781.
32. Ibid.
33. Ibid., Nov. 17, 1781.
34. *AFC*, V, 446, Sept. 5, 1784.
35. CMOW, Jan. 16, 1782.
36. WFLP, Oct. 1782.
37. *MWH*, III, 474.
38. Ibid., 482.

CHAPTER 13
Hope Is an Airy Queen

1. WFLP, Dec. 1781.
2. Ibid., Nov. 17, 1781.
3. Ibid., Dec. 13, 1781.
4. Warren, *Poems*, 221.
5. WFLP, Dec. 1781.
6. Ibid., March 2, 1782.
7. *WAL*, II, 183, Nov. 1, 1782.
8. Ibid., 178, Oct. 7, 1782.
9. Ibid., 175, July 2, 1782.
10. Ibid., 178, Oct. 7, 1782.
11. Ibid., 183, Nov. 1, 1782.
12. Ibid., 176–77, Aug.19, 1782.
13. Ibid., 180, Oct. 24, 1782.
14. WFLP, Oct. 25, 1782.
15. *AFC*, IV, 328, June 17, 1782.
16. *WAL*, II, 131, March 18, 1780.
17. Ibid., 188, Jan. 29, 1783.

18. Ibid., 189, n. 1, Jan. 29, 1783.
19. Ibid., JA to MOW, 189, Jan. 31, 1783.
20. Ibid., JW to SA, 145, Nov. 2, 1780.
21. Tudor, 483–86.
22. Ibid., 483.
23. *WAL*, II, 224.
24. Otis, *Genealogical Memoir*, 103.
25. WFLP, June 8, 1783.
26. Ibid., May 19, 1783.
27. Ibid.
28. Ibid., May 18, 1783.
29. Ibid.
30. *MWH*, II, 600.
31. *WAL*, II, 229, Oct. 27, 1783.
32. Fritz, 220.
33. Warren, *Poems*, 195.
34. Unger, 302.
35. Gardiner, 175.
36. WFLP, April 28, 1783.
37. *WAL*, II, 219, June 24, 1783.
38. Warren, *Poems*, intro.
39. Ibid., 127, 143, 144.
40. Ibid., 108, 117.
41. Gardiner, 177.
42. WFLP, Jan. 5, 1784.
43. Ibid., March 24, 1784.
44. Ibid., May 2, 1784.
45. Raymond, 150–52.
46. WFLP, July 17, 1784.
47. Ibid., June 29, 1784.

CHAPTER 14
The Public Is a Monster Seldom Guided by Reason

1. Hill, 117.
2. Ibid.
3. Ibid., 118.
4. Ibid.
5. WFLP, April 27, 1785.

6. *AFC,* VI, 140, May 10, 1785.
7. WFLP, Nov. 10, 1784.
8. Ibid., Dec. 13, 1784.
9. Ibid., April 27, 1785.
10. Ibid., Nov. 10, 1784.
11. Ibid., second letter of Nov. 10, 1784.
12. Gardiner, 182.
13. WFLP, Nov. 7, 1784.
14. SO to Joseph Otis, April 10, 1785, OFP 289.
15. WFLP, Aug. 28, 1785.
16. Davies, 221.
17. WFLP, March 7, 1785.
18. *Massachusetts Centinel,* Jan. 26, 1785.
19. WFLP, March 7, 1785
20. *Sans Souci,* 4, 11–124.
21. *Massachusetts Centinel,* Jan. 19, 1785.
22. WFLP, April 27, 1785.
23. Ibid., Feb. 18, 1765.
24. Ibid., March 7, 1785.
25. Ibid., Feb. 18, 1785.
26. Ibid., March 7, 1785.
27. *WAL,* II, 257–58, July 15, 1785.
28. Ibid., 257, June 9, 1785.
29. *Boston Gazette,* Feb. 14, 1785.
30. WFLP, Feb. 26, 1785.
31. Cushing, IV, 316.
32. *MWH,* 651.
33. WFLP, Oct. 31, 1784.
34. Ibid.
35. Ibid., April 30, 1785.
36. Warren, *Poems,* 9–11.
37. Ibid., 33, 49.
38. Ibid., 96.
39. WFLP, Aug. 28, 1785.
40. Ibid., Aug. 22, 1785.
41. Ibid., Dec. 29, 1785.

CHAPTER 15
"The fair fabric of a free, strong and national republic"

1. WFLP, 1786.
2. *WAL,* II, 188, Jan. 29, 1783.
3. Gardiner, 195.
4. *WAL,* II, 270–71, March 6, 1786.
5. Fritz, 238.
6. CMOW, March 23, 1786.
7. AA to MOW, *WAL,* II, 274, May 24, 1786.
8. Ibid., 272–73, April 30, 1785.
9. Ibid., 276, May 24, 1786.
10. Ibid., 277, July 4, 1786.
11. Ibid., 278–79, Oct. 22, 1786.
12. Holland, 540.
13. *WAL,* II, 278, Oct. 22, 1786.
14. MOW to CM, WFLP, 1786.
15. Holland, 539.
16. Ibid., 542.
17. Fritz, 239.
18. WFLP, March 12, 1787.
19. Ibid., Dec. 1786.
20. *WAL,* II, 282, Feb. 26, 1787.
21. Ibid., 292, May 18, 1787.
22. Ibid., 281, Jan. 9, 1787.
23. Ibid., 291–93, May 18, 1787.
24. Wells, 246.
25. *WAL,* II, 293, May 18, 1787.
26. Ibid.
27. Bobrick, 488–89.
28. *WAL,* II, 297, Aug. 21, 1787.
29. Gardiner, 202.
30. WFLP, Aug. 2, 1787.
31. *WAL,* II, 260, Sept. 1785.
32. Ibid., 253, April 27, 1785.
33. Ibid., 255, May 6, 1785.
34. Ibid., 274, May 24, 1786.
35. Ibid., 275.
36. Ibid., 301, Dec. 25, 1787.

37. Ibid., 287, May 24, 1787.
38. MOW to JA, Ibid., 260,
    Sept. 1785.

CHAPTER 16
"Too federal to talk freely"

1. WFLP, Aug. 2, 1787.
2. Ibid., Sept. 28, 1787.
3. *WAL*, II, 299, Nov. 1787.
4. Storing, IV, 275, 274–79.
5. Gardiner, 206.
6. Storing, IV, 172.
7. *Massachusetts Centinel*, Nov. 28, 1787.
8. WFLP, Dec. 18, 1787.
9. Ulrich, 179.
10. Wright, 92.
11. Federalist Paper Number 3. The Same Subject Continued (Concerning Dangers from Foreign Force and Influence), *Independent Journal*, Nov. 3, 1787.
12. *WAL*, II, 302, March 2, 1788.
13. *Proceedings*, Oct. 1930–June 1932, LXIV, 1932, 144.
14. WFLP, April 24, 1788.
15. Storing, 4, 153–54.
16. *Proceedings*, Oct. 1930–June 1932, LXIV, 1932, 155–56.
17. Ibid., 158.
18. John Quincy Adams, 128.
19. WFLP, Feb. 25, 1788.
20. Charles Adams, *Correspondence*, 476.
21. Gardiner, 210.
22. Shipton, 531.
23. *MWH*, III, 663, 693.
24. WFLP, Dec. 1781.
25. Hayes, "Private Poems," 204–5.

26. MOW to CM, MWLB, 29, May 31, 1790.
27. WFLP, "at Boston, 1788."
28. Ibid.
29. *WAL*, II, 290, May 14, 1787.
30. Charles Adams, *Correspondence*, 335.
31. *WAL* II, 206, April 9, 1783.
32. Cappon, 227–28.
33. McCullough, 391.
34. Ibid., 39.
35. de Warville, 102.
36. Murray, *Three Essays*, 4.
37. *WAL*, II, 305, March 2, 1789.
38. Ibid., 304, Oct. 29, 1788.
39. Charles Adams, *Correspondence*, 361–62.
40. *WAL*, II, 306–7, March 9, 1789.
41. WFLP, Dec. 8, 1788.

CHAPTER 17
"A sister's hand may wrest a female pen"

1. WFLP, Feb. 3, 1789.
2. Ibid., Jan. 25, 1788.
3. Ibid., Feb. 6, 1789.
4. Ibid., April 4, 1788.
5. Gardiner, 223.
6. *WAL*, II, 305–6, March 2, 1789.
7. Ibid., 309, April 2, 1789.
8. Ibid., 311, May 7, 1789.
9. MWLB, 202, May 8, 1789.
10. Stewart Mitchell, *New Letters*, 16.
11. *WAL*, II, 313–14, May 29, 1789.
12. Ibid., 315, June 18, 1789.
13. Ibid., 317, July 9, 1789.
14. WFLP, 1789.
15. Ibid.
16. Gardiner, 238, 240, n. 3.

17. Ibid., 238.
18. *WAL,* II, 320–21, July 13, 1790.
19. Ibid., 318, June 4, 1790.
20. Proceedings, Oct. 1930–1932, LXIV, 1932, 164.
21. MWP, June 28, 1790.
22. Warren, *Poems,* v, 181–82.
23. Ibid., Nov. 4, 1790.
24. *WAL,* II, 323, Sept. 24, 1790.
25. Ibid., 324, Dec. 26, 1790.
26. Ibid., 325, Jan. 14, 1791.
27. Ibid., 325–26, n. 1, Feb. 14, 1791.
28. *JAD,* I, 300, Dec. 31, 1760.

CHAPTER 18
"Alas, humiliated America!"

1. Warren, *Poems,* 221.
2. Battin, S6.
3. *MWH,* II, 284.
4. WFLP, Sept. 12, 1784.
5. MWLB, 395, Feb. 1792.
6. Ibid., 478, June 30, 1791.
7. Ibid., 324, June 10, 1791.
8. Ibid., 320, May 18, 1791.
9. Ibid., 322, June 10, 1791.
10. *Independent Chronicle,* June 10, 1791.
11. MWLB, 322, May 18, 1791.
12. Ibid., June 10, 1791.
13. Ibid., 324, June 10, 1791.
14. Ibid., July 9, 1791.
15. Ibid., July 22, 1791.
16. Battin, SU6.
17. MWLB, 303, Jan. 15, 1792.
18. Morison, *Harrison Gray Otis,* 66.
19. MWP.
20. MWLB, 472, Dec. 25, 1793.
21. Ibid., 53, April 1792.
22. Hayes, "Private Poems," 220–21.
23. *WAL,* II, 326, July 1, 1791.

24. Chernow, 83.
25. Burke, 95.
26. Macaulay, *Observations,* 10, 19, 14.
27. MWLB, 29, May 31, 1791.
28. Warren, intro. in Macaulay's *Observations.*
29. *WAL,* II, 327, Aug.3, 1791.
30. MWLB, 485, Nov. 11, 1791.
31. Ibid., 395, Oct. 5, 1792.
32. Ibid., Feb. 1792.
33. Ibid., Feb. 18, 1793.
34. Ibid., 224, Nov. 11, 1792.
35. Brown, 301.
36. MWLB, Dec. 22, 1792.
37. Ibid., 117.
38. Gardiner, 246–47.
39. Ibid., 251.
40. *AFC,* III, 79, Dec. 10, 1779.
41. MWLB, 413, Nov. 1793.
42. Ibid., 418, March 22, 1795.
43. Rhodehamel, 817 & 819.
44. *MWH,* III, 683.
45. Ibid., 672.
46. Miller, 396.
47. MWLB, 419, July 17, 1795.

CHAPTER 19
A Sea Change in Party Politics

1. MWLB, 426, Nov. 10, 1796.
2. Ibid.
3. Rochefoucault, 2, 257.
4. Smith, 2, 916.
5. *WAL,* II, 331, Feb. 20, 1797.
6. Ibid., 332, March 4, 1797.
7. MWLB, 147, April 1797.
8. *WAL,* II, 339, July 17, 1798.
9. Stewart Mitchell, *New Letters,* 90.
10. *WAL,* II, 333–34, Oct. 1, 1797.
11. MWLB, 473, July 1797.

12. Cunningham, 215.
13. *WAL*, II, 336–38, April 25, 1797.
14. MWLB, 144, May 1798.
15. Ibid., 431, June 18, 1797.
16. Stewart Mitchell, *New Letters*, 188.
17. *WAL*, II, 341, June 17, 1798.
18. Commager and Cantor, 176.
19. Ibid., 178.
20. Cunningham, 215.
21. *Aurora*, May 19, 1797.
22. Storing, 4, 276.
23. Rochefoucault, 2, 258.
24. MWH, xli, I.
25. JA to John Quincy Adams, Sept. 28, 1798, Adams family papers, MHS.
26 MWLB, 431, June 18, 1797.
27. Rochefoucault, 2, 258.
28. MWLB, 442, Jan. 17, 1800.
29. Anthony, 200–1.
30. MWLB, 1800.
31. Ibid., March 23, 1800.
32. Anthony, 203.
33. *MWH*, III, 694.
34. Chernow, 609.
35. Charles Francis Adams, *Works of John Adams*, 10, 153–54.
36. *MWH*, III, 631.
37. JW to Thomas Jefferson, MWP, March 4, 1801.
38. Ibid., 1801.
39. *MWH*, III, 696.
40. *WAL*, II, 344, Aug. 30, 1803.

CHAPTER 20
"In the spirit of friendship"

1. MWH, III, 698.
2. *WAL*, II, 345, Feb. 8, 1805.
3. Ibid., 346, June 1, 1805.
4. Ibid., 347, March 9, 1805.

5. Ibid., 348, April 1806.
6. Ibid., 350, Feb. 4, 1807.
7. Ibid., 352–54, March 9, 1807.
8. Koch and Peden, 298–99.
9. Charles Francis Adams, *Correspondence*, 21,321.
10. Ibid., 321–22.
11. Ibid., 323–26.
12. Ibid., 328.
13. Ibid., 328–30.
14. Ibid., 353–55.
15. Ibid., 358.
16. Ibid., 358–60.
17. Ibid., 376.
18. Horace, *Epistles*, I, II, 46–71.
19. Charles Frances Adams, *Correspondence*, 393.
20. Ibid., 394–96.
21. Ibid., 398–99.
22. Ibid., 407.
23. Ibid., 411.
24. Ibid., 416.
25. Ibid., 420.
26. Ibid., 422–23.
27. Ibid., 425.
28. Ibid., 432.
29. Ibid., 448.
30. Ibid., 451.
31. Ibid., 456.
32. Ibid., 463–64.
33. Ibid., 465.
34. Ibid., 469.
35. Ibid., 470–71.
36. Ibid., 478.
37. Ibid., 479–80.
38. Ibid., 484.
39. Ibid., 486–87.
40. Ibid., 489–90.
41. Ibid., 489–91.

CHAPTER 21
"Blessed are the peacemakers!"

1. Koch and Peden, 537.
2. Cunningham, 315.
3. Koch and Peden, 321.
4. MWP, 1808.
5. *Independent Chronicle,* Dec. 8, 1808.
6. Harrison Gray Otis to MOW, *WAL,* II, 361–62, Feb. 4, 1809.
7. Lott, 30.
8. Grant, 435.
9. "History of the Rise, Progress and Termination of the Revolution,'" in *The Panoplist,* vol. 2, 580, 1807.
10. Ibid., 381.
11. Ibid., 431–32.
12. "Remarks on the History of the Rise, Progress and Termination of the American Revolution," *National Aegis,* Jan. 17, 1810.
13. Ibid., Jan. 10, 1810.
14. Morison, *Harrison Gray Otis,* 326.
15. MWP, 314, Aug. 16, 1812.
16. Smith, II, 1100.
17. MWP, Sept. 1, 1812.
18. WAL, II, 373–74, Dec. 17, 1812.
19. *Collections,* 5th series, IV, appendix, 502.
20. Ibid.
21. *WAL,* II, 377, April 9, 1813.
22. Ibid., 378–80, April 17, 1813.
23. Ibid., 381–82, April 26, 1813.
24. Ibid., 383, July 11, 1813.
25. Ibid., 385–86, Sept. 5, 1813.
26. Ibid., n. 3, 386, Aug. 20, 1813.
27. *WAL,* II, 386–87, Sept. 12, 1813.
28. Ibid., 388, Nov. 24, 1813.
29. Ibid., 388–89, Dec. 22, 1813.
30. Ibid., 390, March 31, 1814.
31. James Warren, Jr., to Maria Otis Colby, May 9, 1814, GOP Papers.
32. *WAL,* II, 392, May 5, 1814.
33. MWP, Aug. 16, 1814.
34. *WAL,* II, 394–95, July 10, 1814.
35. *Collections,* 5th series, IV, 509.
36. *WAL,* II, 396, Aug. 17, 1814.
37. Smith, II, 1114.
38. *WAL,* II, 396, Aug. 17, 1814.
39. Sarah Cary to Henry Cary, Oct. 10, 1814, Carey Family Papers, III, MHS.
40. HW to Maria Otis Colby, Oct. 19, 1814, GOP.

Adams, Charles Francis, ed. *Correspondence between John Adams and Mercy Warren, Relating to her "History of the American Revolution."* New York: Arno Press, 1972.

Adams, Charles Francis. *Familiar Letters of John Adams and His Wife, Abigail Adams, During the Revolution, with a Memoir of Mrs. Adams.* Freeport, N.Y.: Books for Libraries Press, 1970.

_____. *The Works of John Adams. Second President of the United States with a Life of the Author, Notes and Illustrations by his grandson Charles Francis Adams.* 10 vols. Boston: Little, Brown and Company, 1850–1856.

Adams, Hannah. *Summary History of New England from the First Settlement at Plymouth to the Acceptance of the Federal Constitution Comprehending a General Sketch of the American War.* Dedham: Printed for the author by H. Mann and J. H. Adams, 1799.

Adams Family Papers, Massachusetts Historical Society.

Adams, John Quincy. *Life in a New England Town: 1787, 1788, Diary of John Quincy Adams.* Boston: Little, Brown and Company, 1903.

Addison, Joseph. *Cato: A Tragedy in Five Acts.* Printed from the acting copy, with remarks, biographical and critical, by D.—G. London: John Cumberland, 1829?

Allan, Herbert Sanford. *John Hancock: Patriot in Purple.* New York: Macmillan Company, 1948.

Anthony, Katharine. *First Lady of the American Revolution: The Life of Mercy Otis Warren.* Garden City, N.Y.: Doubleday & Company, 1958.

Anthony, Susan B., Elizabeth Cady Stanton, and Matilda Joslyn Gage, eds. *History of Woman Suffrage.* 3 vols. Rochester, N.Y: Charles Mann, 1889.

Bailyn, Bernard, ed., with the assistance of Jane N. Garrett. *Pamphlets of the American Revolution; 1750–1776.* Cambridge, Mass.: Belknap Press, Harvard University Press, 1965.

Bailyn, Bernard. *The Ordeal of Thomas Hutchinson.* Cambridge, Mass.: Belknap Press, Harvard University Press, 1974.

Barck, Oscar Theodore, Jr., and Hugh Talmage Lefler. *Colonial America.* New York: Macmillan Company, 1958.

Battin, Richard. "Early America's Bloodiest Battles." *The News-Sentinel,* 17 Sept. 1994.

Beach, Stewart. *Samuel Adams: The Fateful Years, 1764–1776.* New York: Dodd, Mead and Co., 1965.

Berkin, Carol. *Revolutionary Mothers: Women in the Struggle for America's Independence.* New York: Alfred A. Knopf, 2005.

Blecki, Catherine La Courreye, and Karin A. Wulf, eds. *Milcah. Martha Moore's Commonplace Book from Revolutionary America.* University Park, Pa.: Pennsylvania State University Press, 1997.

Bobrick, Benson. *Angel in the Whirlwind: The Triumph of the American Revolution.* New York: Simon & Schuster, 1997.

Boston Evening Post (December 20, 1772): 12.

Boston Gazette and Country Journal.

Brink, J. R., ed. *Female Scholars: A Tradition of Learned Women Before 1800.* Montreal: Eden Press Women's Publications, 1980.

Brissot de Warville, J. *New Travels in the United States of America, 1788.* trans. Mara Soceanu Vamos and Durand Echeverria. Ed. Durand Echeverria. Cambridge, Mass.: Belknap Press, Harvard University Press, 1964.

Brooks, Victor. *The Boston Campaign: April 1775 to March 1776.* Conshocken, Pa: Combined Pub., 1999.

Brown, Alice. *Mercy Warren: Women of Colonial and Revolutionary Times.* New York: Charles Scribner's Sons, 1896.

Brumgardt, John. *The Revolutionary Era.* Cambridge, Mass.: Riverside Press, 1975.

Bruns, Roger. *Towards a More Perfect Union: The Creation of the United States Constitution.* Washington, DC: Published for the National Archives and Records Administration by the National Archives Trust Fund Board, 1986.

Burke, Edmund, the Right Hon. *Reflections on the French Revolution.* London: Revived Apollo Press, 1814.

Butterfield, L. H., and D. Garrett Wendell, eds. *Adams Family Correspondence.* 8 vols. Cambridge, Mass.: Belknap Press, Harvard University Press, 1963.

Butterfield, L. H., Marc Friedlander, and Mary-Jo Kline, eds. *The Book of Abigail and John: Selected Letters of the Adams Family 1762–1784.* Cambridge, Mass.: Harvard University Press, 1975.

Butterfield, L. H., ed., Leonard C. Faber and Wendell D. Garrett, asst. eds. *Diary and Autobiography of John Adams.* 5 vols. Cambridge, Mass.: Belknap Press, Harvard University Press, 1961–66.

Campbell, Frederick Hollister. "Mrs. Warren's Revolution: Mercy Otis Warren's Perceptions of the American Revolution, Before, During and After the Event." Ph.D. diss., University of Colorado, 1993.

Cappon, Lester J., ed. *The Adams-Jefferson Letters: The Complete Correspondence Between Thomas Jefferson and Abigail and John Adams.* Chapel Hill: Published for the Institute of Early American History and Culture at Williamsburg, Virginia, by the University of North Carolina Press, 1959.

Cary Family Papers III, Massachusetts Historical Society.

Casper, Scott E., Joanne D. Chaison, and Jeffrey D. Groves. "Publishing the American Revolution." *Perspectives on American Book History, Artifacts and Commentary.* Amherst: University of Massachusetts Press, 2002.

Chernow, Ronald. *Alexander Hamilton.* New York: Penguin Press, 2004.

Chesterfield, Lord, and Philip Dormer Stanhope. *Letters, Sentences and Maxims.* New York and London: G. P. Putnam's Sons, 1888.

Cohen, Lester H. "Explaining the Revolution: Ideology and Ethics in Mercy Otis Warren's Historical Theory." *William and Mary Quarterly* 37, no. 2 (April 1980): 200–18.

_____. *The Revolutionary Histories: Contemporary Narratives of the American Revolution.* Ithaca: Cornell University Press, 1980.

Collections of the Massachusetts Historical Society.

Commager, Henry Steele, and Morris R. Richard. *The Spirit of "Seventy-Six": The Story of the American Revolution As Told by Participants.* Indianapolis: Bobbs-Merrill, 1958.

Commager, Henry Steele, and Milton Cantor, eds. *Documents of American History.* Englewood Cliffs, N.J.: Prentice Hall, 1998.

Correspondence with Mercy Otis Warren, Massachusetts Historical Society.

Cott, Nancy F. *The Bonds of Womanhood: "Women's Sphere" in New England, 1780–1835.* New Haven: Yale University Press, 1977.

Cunningham, Noble E. *In Pursuit of Reason: The Life of Thomas Jefferson.* Baton Rouge: Louisiana State University Press, 1987.

Cushing, Harry Alonzo, ed. *The Writings of Sam Adams.* 4 vols. New York: Octagon Books, 1968.

Davies, Kate. *Catharine Macaulay and Mercy Otis Warren: The Revolutionary Atlantic and the Politics of Gender.* New York: Oxford University Press, 2005.

Davis, William T. *Ancient Landmarks of Plymouth.* Boston: Damrell & Upham, the Corner Bookstore, 1887.

_____. *History of the Town of Plymouth: With a Sketch of the Origin and Growth of Separatism.* Philadelphia: J. W. Lewis & Co., 1885

_____. *Plymouth Memories of an Octogenarian.* Plymouth: Memorial Press, 1906.

DePauw, Linda Grant, and Conover Hunt. *"Remember the Ladies": Women in America 1750–1815.* New York: Viking Press, 1976.

Deyo, Simeon L., ed. *History of Barnstable County, Massachusetts 1620–1890.* New York: H. W Blake & Co., 1890.

Dunn, Susan. *Sister Revolutions: French Lightening, American Light.* New York: Faber and Faber, 1999.

Ellet, Elizabeth. *Women of the American Revolution.* 3 vols. New York: Baker & Scribner, 1848.

"Extract of a Letter from London, March 28, 1766." *The Boston Gazette and Country Journal,* 19 May 1766.

Fairclough, H. Rushton, trans. *Horace: Satires, Epistles and Arts Poetica,* Cambridge Mass.: Harvard University Press, 1929.

Ferguson, E. James. "The Nationalists of 1781–1783 and the Economic Interpretation of the Constitution." *Journal of American History* LVI (Sept. 1969): 241–61.

_____. *The Power of the Purse: A History of American Public Finance, 1776–1790.* Chapel Hill, N.C.: University of North Carolina Press, 1961.

Fielding, Henry. *Love in Several Masques, A comedy as it is acted at the Theatre-Royal, by His Majesty's servants.* London: Printed for John Watts, 1728.

Fischer, David Hackett. *Washington's Crossing.* Oxford, New York: Oxford University Press, 2004.

Fitzpatrick, John C., ed. *The Writings of George Washington from the Original Manuscript Sources, 1745–1799.* Vol. 31. Westport, Conn.: Greenwood Press, 1970.

Fleming, Thomas. *1776: Year of Illusions.* New York: W. W. Norton & Company, Inc., 1975.

Forbes, Esther. *Paul Revere and the World He Lived In.* Boston: Houghton Mifflin Company, 1942.

Franklin, Benjamin. *Poor Richard's Almanack, being the choicest morsels of wisdome, written during the years of the Almanack's publicaton/ by that well-known savant, Dr. Benjamin Franklin of Philadelphia.* Mount Vernon, N.Y.: Peter Pauper Press, 194-?

Franklin, Benjamin V. *The Plays and Poems of Mercy Otis Warren.* Delmar, N.Y.: Scholars' Facsimiles & Reprints, 1980.

French, Allen. *The First Year of the American Revolution*. Boston: Houghton Mifflin Company, 1934.

Fritz, Jean. *Cast for a Revolution 1728–1814*. Boston: Houghton Mifflin Company, 1972.

Gardiner, Harvey C., ed. *A Study in Dissent: The Warren-Gerry Correspondence 1776–1792*. Carbondale: Southern Illinois University Press, 1968.

Gay-Otis Papers, Rare Book and Manuscript Library, Butler Library, Columbia University

Gelles, Edith B. *Portia: The World of Abigail Adams*. Bloomington, Indiana: Indiana University Press, 1995.

George, Carol, ed. *Remember the Ladies. New Perspectives on Women in American History: Essays in Honor of Nelson Manfred Blake*. Syracuse: Syracuse University Press, 1975.

Gerlach, Don R. "Memoranda and Documents: A Note on the Quarterly Act of 1774." *New England Quarterly* XXXIX (March 1966): 80–88.

Grafton, John, ed. *The Declaration of Independence and Other Great Documents of American History, 1775–1865*. Mineola, N.Y.: Dover Publications, 2000.

Grant, James. *John Adams: Party of One*. New York: Farrar, Straus and Giroux, 2005.

Green, Samuel. *James Otis's Argument Against the Writs of Assistance 1761: Remarks Made Before the Massachusetts Historical Society, December 11, 1890*. Cambridge, Mass.: John Wilson and Son University Press, 1890.

Hackett, David, and Sharon M. Harris, eds. *Selected Writings of Judith Sargent Murray: Women Writers in English 1350–1850*. New York, Oxford: Oxford University Press, 1995.

Hayes, Edmund M. "Mercy Otis Warren: The Defeat." *New England Quarterly* 49, (September 1976): 440–58.

————. "Mercy Otis Warren Versus Lord Chesterfield 1779." *William and Mary Quarterly* XL (October 1983): 616–21.

————. "The Private Poems of Mercy Otis Warren." *New England Quarterly* LIV (June 1981): 199–224.

Hayes, Kevin J. *A Colonial Woman's Bookshelf*. Knoxville, TN: University of Tennessee Press, 1996.

Hibbert, Christopher. *Redcoats and Rebels: The American Revolution Through British Eyes*. New York: Avon Books, 1990.

Hill, Bridget. *The Republican Virago: The Life and Times of Catharine Macaulay*. Oxford, New York: Clarendon Press, 1992.

Holland, Park. "Reminiscences of Shays's Rebellion," *New England Magazine* 23, no. 5 (Jan 1901): 540.

Hosmer, James Kendall. *The Life of Thomas Hutchinson, Royal Governor of the Province of Massachusetts Bay.* Boston, New York: Houghton Mifflin Company, 1896.

Hutcheson, Maud Macdonald. "Mercy Warren 1728–1814." The *William and Mary Quarterly* 10 (July 1953): 378–402.

Hutchinson, Peter Orlando. *The Diary and Letters of His Excellency Thomas Hutchinson, Esq.* Boston, New York: Houghton Mifflin Company, 1884.

Hutchinson, Thomas. *The History of the Colony and Province of Massachusetts-Bay.* Edited from the authors' own copies of volumes I and II and from his manuscript of volume III, with a memoir and additional notes by Lawrene Shaw Mayo. Cambridge, Mass.: Harvard University Press, 1936.

Kaye, Harvey J. *Thomas Paine and the Promise of America.* New York: Hill & Wang, 2005.

Kerber, Linda K. *Women of the Republic: Intellect and Ideology in Revolutionary America.* Chapel Hill: Institute of Early American History and Culture by the University of North Carolina Press, 1980.

Knight, Russell, ed. *Elbridge Gerry's Letterbook: Paris 1797–1798.* Salem, Mass.: Essex Institute, 1966.

Koch, Adrienne, and William Peden, eds. *The Life and Selected Works of Thomas Jefferson.* New York: Random House, 1993.

La Rochefoucault Liancourt, Francois-Alexandre-Frederic, duc de, 1747–1827. *Travels through the United States, the country of the Iroquois and Upper Canada, in the years 1795, 1796, and 1797; with an authentic account of Lower Canada.* By the Duke de la Rochefoucault Liancourt. London: Printed for R. Phillips; sold by T. Hurst and J. Wallis and Carpenter and Co., 1799.

Laska, Vera O. *Remember the Ladies: Outstanding Women of the America Revolution.* Commonwealth of Massachusetts Bicentennial Commissions Publications, May 1976.

LeFeber, Walter. *The American Age: United States Foreign Policy at Home and Abroad since 1750.* New York: W. W. Norton & Company, 1989.

Lott, Davis Newton. *The Presidents Speak: The Inaugural Addresses of the American Presidents.* New York: Henry Holt and Co., 1994.

Macaulay, Catherine. *Letters on Education.* Oxford, New York: Woodstock Books, 1994. Boston: Printed by I. Thomas and E. T. Andrews, Faust's Statue, no. 45, Newbury Street, MDC.

_____. *Observations on the Reflections of the Right Hon. Edmund Burke, on the Revolution in France, In a Letter to the Right Hon. the Earl of Stanhope*. Boston: Printed by I. Thomas and E. T. Andrews, Faust's Statue, no. 45, Newbury Street, MDCCXCI, 1791.

Maier, Pauline. *The Old Revolutionaries: Political Lives in the Age of Samuel Adams*. New York: Alfred A. Knopf, 1980.

Malone, Dumas. *Jefferson and the Ordeal of Liberty*. Vol 3. Boston: Little, Brown and Company, 1962.

Maney, Jill, and Jonathan Maney. "Having It Both Ways: The Needlework Table Cover of Mercy Otis Warren." *Textiles in New England II: Four Centuries of Material Life* 24, Dublin Seminar for New England Folklife Proceedings 24 (1999): 144–60.

Massachusetts Centinel 11, no. 35 (1785).

Mather, Cotton. *Ornaments for the daughters of Zion, or, The character and happiness of a virtuous woman: in a discourse which directs the female-sex how to express the fear of God in every age and state of their life, and obtain both temporal and external blessedness*. Cambridge, Mass.: printed by S. G. and B. G. for Samuel Phillips at Boston, 1692.

McCullough, David. *John Adams*. New York: Simon & Schuster, 2001.

Mercy Otis Warren Papers, Massachusetts Historical Society.

Miller, John C. *Sam Adams: Pioneer in Propaganda*. Boston: Little, Brown and Company, 1936.

Mitchell, H. G., ed. "Reminiscences of Shays's Rebellion," *New England Magazine* (23) no. 5 (Jan. 1901): 538–42.

Mitchell, Stewart, ed. *New Letters of Abigail Adams, 1788–1801*. Boston, New York: Houghton Mifflin Company, 1947.

Moore, Frank. *Songs and Ballads of the American Revolution*. New York: D. Appleton and Company, 1856.

_____. *The Diary of the Revolution. A Centennial Volume embracing the Current Events in our Country's History from 1775 to 1781 as Described by American British, and Tory Contemporaries*. Hartford, CT: J. B. Burr, 1876.

Morison, Samuel Eliot. *Three Centuries of Harvard, 1636–1936*. Cambridge, Mass.: Harvard University Press, 1936.

_____. *Harrison Gray Otis, 1765–1848: The Urbane Federalist*. Boston, New York: Houghton Mifflin Company, 1969.

Mullet, Charles F., collected with an intro. "Some Political Writings of James Otis," *The University of Missouri Studies: A Quarterly of Research,* part 1, IV (July 1, 1929): 261–432.

Murray, Judith Sargent. *Forming a New Era in Female History: Three Essays by Judith Sargent Murray.* intr. by Bonnie Hurd Smith. Cambridge, Mass.: A Publication of the Judith Sargent Murray Society, 1999.

_____. *The Gleaner. A Miscellaneous Production. By Constantia.* Published by Act of Congress. 3 vols. Boston: Printed by I. Thomas and E. T. Andrews, 1798.

National Aegis. Worcester, Mass.: 1810.

New England Magazine. Boston: McClinctock Publishing Company, 1901.

Norton, Mary Beth. *Liberty's Daughters: The Revolutionary Experience of American Women, 1750–1800.* Boston: Little, Brown and Company, 1980.

Nylander, Jane C. *On Our Snug Fireside: Images of the New England Home, 1760–1860* New York: Alfred A. Knopf, 1993.

Otis Family Papers, Rare Book and Manuscript Library, Butler Library, Columbia University.

Otis, James, Esq. *Vindication of the Conduct of the House of Representatives of the Province of Massachusetts.* Boston: Printed by Edes and Gill on Queen-Street, 1762.

_____. "Messieurs Edes & Gill," *The Boston Gazette, and Country Journal,* (September 4, 1769): 2.

_____. "Messieurs Edes & Gill," *Boston Gazette and Country Journal,* (September 18, 1769): 2.

Otis, William A. *A Genealogical and Historical Memoir of the Otis Family in America.* Chicago: Schulkins, Inc., 1924.

Paine, Thomas. *Basic Writings of Thomas Paine: Common Sense, Rights of Man, Age of Reason.* New York: Wiley Book Company, 1942.

The Panoplist or the Christian Armory. Boston: 1807.

Parkman Family Papers and Correspondence, American Antiquarian Society.

Patterson, Stephen E. *Political Parties in Revolutionary Massachusetts.* Madison: University of Wisconsin Press, 1973.

Perkins, Edward J. American Public Finance and Financial Services, 1700–1815. Columbus: Ohio State University Press, 1994.

Proceedings of the Massachusetts Historical Society.

Pynchon, William. *The Diary of William Pynchon of Salem.* Boston, New York: Houghton Mifflin Company, 1890.

Raymond, William Odber, ed. *Winslow Papers, 1853–1923*. Printed under the auspices of the New Brunswick Historical Society. St. John, New Brunswick: The Sun Printing Company, Ltd. 1901.

Rhodehamel, John H., selected by. *Writings, George Washington*. New York: Library of America, Penguin Books, 1997.

Richards, Jeffrey H. *Mercy Otis Warren*. New York: Twayne Publishers, Prentice Hall International, 1995.

Richards, Lysander Salmon. *History of Marshfield*. Plymouth, Mass.: Memorial Press, 1901–1905.

Russell, Laura. *Laura Russell Remembers: An Old Plymouth Manuscript with Notes by Marion L. Channing*. Marion, Mass.: 1970

Salisbury Family Papers, American Antiquarian Society.

Sans Souci, alias Free and easy: or An Evening's peep into a polite circle: An intire [sic] *new entertainment*. In three acts. 2nd edition. Boston: Warden and Russell, MDCCLXXXV (1785).

Schloesser, Pauline E. *The Fair Sex: White Women and Racial Patriarchy in the Early American Republic*. New York: New York University Press, 2002.

Schmidt, Gary D. *A Passionate Usefulness: The Life and Literary Labors of Hannah Adams*. Charlottesville: University of Virginia Press, 2004.

The Seven Villages of Barnstable: Written by Its People on the Occasion of the 200th Birthday of the United States of America. Barnstable, MA: Town of Barnstable, 1976.

Shaffer, Arthur H. *The Politics of History: Writing the History of the American Revolution, 1783–1815*. Chicago: Precedent Publishing, 1975.

Shipton, Clifford K. *New England Life in the 18th Century*. Cambridge, Mass.: Belknap Press, Harvard University Press, 1963.

Sibley, John Langdon, and Clifford K. Shipton. *Biographical Sketches of Graduates of Harvard University in Cambridge, Massachusetts*, Boston: MHS, 1873.

Sigmund, Paul E., ed. *Essays on Government: The Selected Political Writings of John Locke*. New York: W. W. Norton & Company, 2005.

Silverman, Kenneth. *A Cultural History of the American Revolution: Painting, Music, Literature, and the Theatre in the Colonies and the United States from the Treaty of Paris to the Inauguration of George Washington, 1763–1789*. New York: T. Y. Crowell, 1976.

Skemp, Sheila L. *Judith Sargent Murray: A Brief Biography with Documents*. Boston: Bedford Books, 1998.

Smith, Page. *John Adams.* 2 vols. Garden City, N.Y.: Doubleday, 1962.

Smith, William Raymond. *History As Argument: Three Patriot Historians of the American Revolution.* The Hague: Mouton, 1966.

Stabile, Donald R. *The Origins of American Public Finance: Debates over Money, Debt, and Taxes in the Constitutional Era.* Westport, Conn.: Greenwood Press, 1998.

Steele, Richard, publisher. *The Ladies Library, Written by a Lady.* London: Printed for J. and R. Tonson, 1739.

Storing, Herbert J., with the assistance of Murray Dry. *The Complete Anti-Federalist.* 7 vols. Chicago: Chicago University Press, 1981.

Thacher, James. *History of the Town of Plymouth: From its First Settlement in 1620 to the Present Time with a Concise History of the Aborigines of New England, and Their Wars with the English.* Boston: March, Capen & Lyon, 1835.

Tudor, William. *The Life of James Otis: Containing also notices of some contemporary characters and events, from the year 1760 to 1775.* Boston: Wells and Lilly, 1823.

Ulrich, Laurel. *The Age of Homespun: Objects and Stories in the Creation of an American Myth.* New York: Alfred A. Knopf, 2001.

Unger, Harlow Giles. *John Hancock: Merchant King and American Patriot.* New York: John Wiley & Sons, 2000.

Van Doren, Carl. *Benjamin Franklin.* New York: Viking Press, 1938.

Waingrow, Marshall, ed. *James Boswell's Life of Johnson: An Edition of the Original Manuscript in Four Volumes,* Edinburgh: Edinburgh University Press; New Haven: Yale University Press, 1994.

Warren-Adams Letters: Being chiefly a correspondence among John Adams, Samuel Adams, and James Warren. 2 vols. Boston: Massachusetts Historical Society, 1925.

Warren, Charles. "Observations on the new Constitution, and on the federal and state conventions in Warren, Charles, Elbridge Gerry, James Warren, Mercy Warren, and Ratification of the Federal Constitution in Massachusetts." *Proceedings of the Massachusetts Historical Society 1932,* LXI (MDCCCCXXXII): 143–64.

Warren, Charles, ed. *Warren Family Letters and Papers 1763–1814.* Compiled and arranged in chronological order by Charles Warren. 2 vols. Archives of Pilgrim Hall Museum, Plymouth, Mass.

Warren, Mercy Otis. *History of the Rise, Progress and Termination of the American Revolution interspersed with Biographical, Political and Moral Observations,* edited and annotated by Lester H. Cohen. 2 vols. Indianapolis: Liberty Fund, 1994.

_____. *Poems, Dramatic and Miscellaneous.* Boston: Printed by I. Thomas and E. T. Andrews, Faust's Statue, no. 45, Newbury Street, MDCCXC (1790).

_____. *The Plays and Poems of Mercy Otis Warren.* Facsimile Reproductions compiled and with an introduction by Benjamin V. Franklin. Delmar, N.Y.: Scholars' Facsimiles & Reprints, 1980.

_____. "To a Gentleman who requested a List of those articles which Female Vanity has comprised under the Head of Necessaries," *The Royal American Magazine, or, Universal Repository of Instruction and Amusement.* Boston: Printed by and for I. Thomas, I, (June 1774): 233–34.

De Warville, J. P Brissot. *New Travels in the United States of America, 1788.* Cambridge, Mass.: Belknap Press, Harvard University Press, 1964.

Waters, John J. *The Otis Family, in Provincial and Revolutionary Massachusetts.* Chapel Hill: Institute of Early American History and Culture by North Carolina Press, 1968.

Weales, Gerald. "The Adulateur and How It Grew," *The Library Chronicle* XLIII no. 2 (Winter 1979): 103–33.

Weintraub, Stanley. *Iron Tears: America's Battle for Freedom, Britain's Quagmire: 1775–1783.* New York: Free Press, 2005.

Wells, William V. *The Life and Public Services of Samuel Adams, being a narrative of his acts and opinions, and of his agency in producing and forwarding the American Revolution; With extracts from his Correspondence, State Papers and Political Essays.* Boston: Little, Brown and Company, 1865.

Wright, Benjamin Fletcher, ed. *The Federalist By Alexander Hamilton, James Madison and John Jay.* Cambridge, Mass.: Belknap Press, Harvard University Press, 1961.

Wroth, L. Kinvin, and Hiller B. Zobel, eds. *Legal Papers of John Adams.* Cambridge, Mass.: Belknap Press, Harvard University Press, 1965.

Zagarri, Rosemarie. *A Woman's Dilemma: Mercy Otis Warren and the American Revolution.* Wheeling, Ill.: Harlan Davidson, Inc., 1995.

Acadian relocation, 22–23

Adams, Abigail: appeal to Mercy to move to Braintree, 150; attachment to John, 64, 65; bereavements of, 94, 126; and disorderly conduct of soldiers, 72; European voyage, 170, Federalist shift of, 192–94, 202–3; illness of, 238; John Adams on, 5; loneliness of, 94, 97, 123–24, 130; on Mercy's ambitions, 212; on Mercy's family life, 52, 185, 265–66; on Mercy's writing talent, 69, 110; post-war settling in Braintree, 203–4; on privations of blockade, 77; quality of friendship with Mercy, 57, 78, 233–35, 246, 262–63, 264; reliance upon Mercy during war, 76; as source of materials for *History*, 98; on Tea Act protests, 55; on Tories vs. patriots, 58; visit from Mercy's sons, 154; on women's equality, 110–12, 141

Adams, Abigail II, "Nabby," 134–35, 262, 264

Adams, Betsy, 94

Adams, Hannah, 237–38

Adams, John: Abigail's attachment to, 94, 97, 123–24, 130; and Alien and Sedition Acts, 236–37; and authorship of *The Group*, 266–67; and Boston Massacre responses, 42; on Boston port blockade, 62; on Boston Tea Party, 3, 55; on commitment to republicanism, 43, 59; critical view of Mercy's work, 217–19,
247–56, 263; and death of Nabby, 264; establishment of Warren friendship, 27; Federalism of, 190, 200, 202–3, 204, 205, 211; and first Continental Congress, 63–64, 65; on greedy materialism during war, 138–39; on Hutchinson, 46–47; inspiration from Sam Adams, 50; on intercolonial unity, 71; and James Warren, 89, 117, 200, 205, 212–13; on Jemmy, 42, 165; longing for private life, 162, 203–4, 243; and Macaulay, 47, 172–73, 204; as mentor to Mercy, 3, 4, 100, 162–63; on Mercy's father, 11; Mercy's suspicions of elitism, 192–93; and Molasses Act challenge, 25; on need for unified government, 128–29; on post-war economic woes, 186; presidential elections, 233, 242; protest against soldiers' presence, 39; reconciliation with Mercy, 264–65; republican shift of, 259; on Ruth Cunningham Otis, 39; support for Mercy's writing, 5, 56, 69, 70, 100, 151; on Warrens' desire to be together, 114; wartime role of, 130, 155, 162; and Whately letters, 50–51; and Winslow, 148, 155, 163–64; on women's intellectual abilities, 94, 111, 163, 263

Adams, John Quincy, 130, 199, 200, 259

Adams, Samuel: and Boston Massacre responses, 42; and Boston Tea

Party, 55; character of, 28; on corruption of courts, 46; on Declaratory Act's dangers, 34; Federalism
of, 209; on Hutchinson, 49–50; on
increased British military presence,
39; and James Warren, 136, 178,
190; on Jemmy, 28; on loss of rights,
61; moral critique of post-war
Boston society, 176; on need for
restraint until ready to fight, 63;
public's lack of respect for, 143;
release of Whately letters, 51; and
Stamp Act protests, 30; support for
Constitution, 197; Townshend Act
protests, 39–40; on Whigs' loss of
resolve, 43
Administration of Justice Act (1774),
60
The Adulateur (Warren, M.), 48–49
Alien and Sedition Acts (1798),
236–37, 242
Alliance (American ship), 134, 143,
149–50, 155
Allyne, Joseph (grandfather), 7
Allyne, Mary (Mrs. James Otis)
(mother), 7, 8, 12, 35
American Indians, 221, 223
American Revolution: British torching of Charlestown, 85, 86; Bunker
Hill, 79, 83, 85–86; Charleston's
fall to British, 148; Dorchester
Heights, 102–3, 106; ending of,
164, 166; James Warren's role in,
85, 87–88, 114, 118, 125, 135–36,
141–42, 161; Lexington and Concord, 73–76; Mercy as wartime
reporter, 4, 88–90, 91, 93; naval
forces, 124–25, 133, 134, 143, 149–
50, 155; in New York, 101, 122;
Nook's Hill fortification, 107;
Ploughed Hill, patriot seizure of,

91; Saratoga, 129; Trenton, 123;
Yorktown, 157
Andrews, Isaiah, 216
Antifederalists. *See*
republicans/republicanism
Arlington (Menotomy), Mas-
sachusetts, 75
Army, Continental, 92, 101, 122
Arnold, Benedict, 151

Bache, Benjamin Franklin, 237
Bernard, Francis, 23–24, 30, 36
Bill of Rights, 226, 227, 236–37
The Blockade of Boston (Burgoyne),
101
The Blockheads of Boston, 103–4
Bonhomme Richard (British ship),
149
Boston, Massachusetts: ban on live
theater in, 49; British blockade of,
60–63, 77; British occupation of,
65–66, 86–87, 90, 97–98; British
withdrawal from, 103, 106–8, 109;
patriots vs. Tories in, 4; post-
occupation ruins of, 110; post-
war materialism in, 176; refugees
from, 90; and Stamp Act, 30, 34;
Tea Act protest, 55
Boston Advertiser, 150, 151
Boston Committee, 45–46
Boston Gazette: criticism of Mercy,
177–78; Mercy's writings in, 5,
51, 69, 136; Stamp Act boycott
effects, 34
Boston Harbor, British plundering
of, 88
Boston Magazine, invitation to female
writers, 175
Boston Massacre, 42
Boston Port Act (1774), 60–62
Boston Tea Party, 3, 5, 53–56, 59

Bowdoin, James, 177, 178, 185–86, 189–90

boycotts of British goods, 29, 33, 36, 54

Braintree, Massachusetts, 71–72, 203–4

Britain, Great: Charleston's fall to, 148; debt problems of, 28–29, 35; and Jay Treaty, 19, 230, 231, 232; military buildup in colonies, 39; plundering of Boston Harbor, 88; post-Revolution tensions, 257; preparation for war, 71; treatment of espionage suspects, 151; and Treaty of Paris, 166; unrepresentative laws in colonies, 3, 24–25, 29–31, 33–34, 42, 53–55, 57–62; War of 1812, 261, 267. *See also* American Revolution; Boston; soldiers, British

Bunker Hill, Battle of, 79, 83, 85–86

Burgoyne, Gen. John, 85, 100–101, 129

Burke, Edmund, 225–26

Castle William, 57, 107

centralization of government power. *See* Federalists/Federalism

Charleston, South Carolina, fall to British, 148

Charlestown, Massachusetts, British torching of, 85, 86

Chesterfield's Letters, 140

children: births of, 26–27; first pregnancy, 22; grief over father's absence, 99; losses of, 181, 183, 224, 239, 240; Mercy's attachment to, 134; Mercy's empty nest feelings, 125, 144, 150, 169–70; and Mercy's homecoming during war, 92–93; Mercy's parental style, 34, 52–53, 113–14, 139–41; report to James on, 100; travels of, 133–34; and variolation for smallpox, 121. *See also* individual children's names

Church, Benjamin, 37, 94

civil rights. *See* rights, citizens'

Clifford Farm, 22

cloth production, domestic American, 36

Codman, John, 184, 185

Coercive (Intolerable) Acts (1774), 60–62

colonies, American: court corruption in, 45–46; heightening tensions over tea, 59–60; prelude to war, 70–71; unification against Britain, 37–39, 54, 61, 62–63, 65, 66, 71, 77, 129; unrepresentative laws in, 3, 24–25, 29–31, 33–34, 42, 53–55, 57–62. *See also* Continental Congress; economy; Massachusetts Colony; politics

Concord, Massachusetts on eve of battle, 73

Congress, U.S.: Alien and Sedition Acts, 236–37, 242; difficulties getting reimbursement from, 184, 210, 214–15; economic crisis for, 168, 174; and French tensions, 235; James Warren's refusal to serve, 185; modification of Articles of Confederation, 191

Connecticut, response to Lexington and Concord, 77

Constitution, U.S., 195, 197–98

Constitutional Convention, 191

Continental Army, 92, 101, 122

Continental Congress: Declaration of Independence, 15, 105, 109, 115, 116–17; initial meeting of, 63–64, 65; pressure on James Warren to join, 117; response to British fortifications in Boston, 65–66; wartime role of, 85, 87

Copley, John Singleton, 6, 179

Cornwallis, Gen. Charles, 157
courts, colonial, 25–26, 43, 45–46,
    49, 114
Cranch, Richard, 117
Cushing, Thomas, 50, 167–68

Dark Day, 148
Declaration of Independence, 15,
    105, 109, 116–17
Declaration of Rights and Grievances,
    66
Declaratory Act (1766), 34
The Defeat (Warren, M.), 51–52
A Defense of the Constitutions of
    Government of the United States
    (Adams, J.), 190
Democratic-Republicans. See republi-
    cans/republicanism
Dickinson, John, 35, 37, 54
diseases, infectious: in Continental
    army, 92; in occupied Boston, 86,
    90, 97, 110; smallpox epidemic, 110,
    115–16
domestic duties, women's, 5–6, 12–13,
    16–17
Dorchester Heights, patriots' taking
    of, 102–3, 106
Dotey, Edward, 7, 21
duties and taxes. See taxes and duties

East India Company, 54
economy: barter, 12; boycotts of
    British goods, 29, 33, 36, 54; cloth
    production in America, 36; com-
    modities trade among women, 36,
    154, 173–74; inflation, 127–28, 138,
    186; post-war problems, 168, 173–75,
    185–88; Stamp Act boycott effects,
    34; U.S. embargo on European
    trade, 257–58. See also taxes and
    duties

Edmund Fowle House, Watertown,
    85, 87, 93–94, 109–10
Edwards, Adm. Richard, 149
"Extempore to a young Person . . ."
    (Warren, M.), 201

family life, women's role in, 5–6,
    12–13
Federalist Papers, 198
Federalists/Federalism: attack upon
    Charles Turner, 261; and French
    Revolution, 230–32; and John
    Adams, 128–29, 190, 192–94, 200,
    202–3, 204, 211, 249–51; Mercy's
    fear of, 189, 202, 222, 240, 243; vs.
    republicans, 195–206, 230–32, 236,
    240–42; rise of, 195–206; rumors of
    New England secession, 258; and
    Sam Adams, 209; value of, 247
feminist voice, beginnings of, 106,
    110–12, 210, 228. See also women
Fort Ticonderoga, 101
France, Adams's handling of tensions
    with, 233, 235–36, 240–41
Franklin, Benjamin, 19, 29, 34, 50, 59,
    149
Freeman, Dr. James, 243
French and Indian War, 22–23
French Revolution, 213–14, 225–27,
    231, 241
Friends of Liberty, 46

Gage, Gen. Thomas: Bostonians'
    sabotage of, 63; defensive position
    post-Bunker Hill, 86; and disorderly
    conduct of soldiers, 72; and Jemmy,
    39; and Lexington and Concord
    battles, 73; takeover of Boston,
    61; tensions on eve of war, 71
General Arnold, sinking of in storm,
    133

General Court of Massachusetts, 43, 45, 49

"The Genius of America weeping..." (Warren, M.), 136–37

Gerry, Ann, 13

Gerry, Elbridge: and appointment for Winslow, 166; as Constitutional Convention delegate, 191, 195; contributions to Mercy's *History*, 229–30; and Declaration of Independence, 115; peacemaking for John Adams and Mercy, 262; political marginalization of, 197; and post-war tensions with France, 235

Graham, William, 171

grandchildren, 227, 228

Great Britain. *See* Britain, Great

Greene, Gen. Nathaniel, 75

Grenville, George, 28, 30

Gridley, John, 40

The Group (Warren, M.), 67–68, 69–70, 266–67

Hamilton, Alexander, 198, 214–15, 225, 231, 241

Hancock, John: ambitions of, 131; election for governor, 142–43; hypocrisy of, 136; insults to patriots, 142; and Jemmy's return to public eye, 164–65; and Macaulay, 172; as political adversary, 173; political maneuvers of, 167–68; retirement of, 176; "smuggling" incident, 38; support for Constitution, 197

Harvard College, 14, 16–17, 53

Henry, Patrick, 29

Hillsborough, Lord, 152

The History of England from the Accession of James to that of the Brunswick Line (Macaulay), 47, 171

History of the Colony and Province of Massachusetts-Bay (Hutchinson), 23

History of the Rise, Progress and Termination of the American Revolution (Warren, M.): general reaction to, 246–47, 259–60; vs. Hannah Adams's account, 238; James, Jr.'s role in, 242; John Adams's criticism of, 247–56, 263; John Adams's encouragement of, 4, 100; as Mercy's magnum opus, 6; Mercy's research for, 98, 130, 135, 157, 163, 229–30; public announcement of, 150, 151; publication of, 189, 243, 245–46

homes: childhood, 11; in Milton, 153, 157, 161, 174, 184, 201; in Plymouth, 4, 21, 22–23, 26

Howe, Gen. William, 83, 102–3, 106

Hutchinson, Elisha, 57

Hutchinson, Polly Watson, 57

Hutchinson, Thomas: arrival of, 23; as chief justice, 24; corruption of, 45–47, 49–51, 77; and Jemmy, 24–25, 27–28, 43; and martial law in Boston, 61–62; patriots' seizure of country home, 76–77; relocation of General Court, 43; and Stamp Act protests, 30–31; and Tea Act protests, 55, 57

Independent Chronicle, Mercy's writings in, 138

individual rights. *See* rights, citizens'

inflationary economy, 127–28, 138, 186

intercolonial solidarity. *See* unity, intercolonial

Intolerable (Coercive) Acts (1774), 60–62

Jay, John, 198, 232

Jay Treaty, 19, 230, 231, 232

Jefferson, Thomas: on Alien and Sedition Acts, 236; and embargo on European trade, 257–58; on Federalism and republicanism, 247; vs. Hamilton, 231; on Mercy's *History*, 246; presidential election, 241; and return of republicanism, 242; on rights of citizens, 61
"Jemmibullero," 29–30
Johnson, Dr. Samuel, 140
Jones, John Paul, 149

Knox, Gen. Henry, 185, 191, 213

"The Ladies Lamentation over an empty Cannister," 53–54
The Ladies of Castile (Warren, M.), 168–69
Landais, Capt. Pierre, 149
Land Bank, 28
Larkin, Ebenezer, 245
Laurens, Henry, 151
Lee, Arthur, 149, 151
Lee, Gen. Charles, 122–23
Lexington and Concord, battles of, 73–76
Liberty (Hancock's sloop), 38
Liberty Tree, 3
Lincoln, Maj. Gen. Benjamin, 161, 166
live theater, Boston ban on, 49
Lothrop, Ellen, 34, 148
Lovell, James, 141–42
Loyalists (Tories), 127, 128, 129, 130–31. *See also* Tories

Macaulay, Catharine Sawbridge: American trip, 171–72; on Constitutional debate in states, 198; death of, 227; on education for women, 228; and Hancock, 172; and John Adams, 47, 172–73, 204; and Mercy, 47–48, 66–67, 91, 124–25, 172, 177, 192; response to Burke, 226–27; at Sans Souci, 175
Mackey, Mungo, 40
Madison, James, 198, 259, 261
mandamus councilors, 67
martial law in Boston, 61–62
Massachusetts, state of, post-war economic crisis, 168, 185–88. *See also* politics; *specific towns and cities*
Massachusetts Assembly, 36, 46, 65
Massachusetts Colony: court system, 25–26, 45–46, 114; Provincial Congress, 72–73, 75–76, 85; refugees from war and occupation, 75, 90; support for Boston during blockade, 62–63. *See also* Hutchinson, Thomas; politics
Massachusetts Government Act (1774), 60
"Massachusetts Liberty Song" (Warren, M. or Church, B.), 36–37
Massachusetts Spy, Mercy's writings in, 49, 69
materialism: John Adams on American, 138–39; and Massachusetts politics, 4, 24, 173, 186; patriots' despair over, 138–39; return of in scarce times, 127–28, 136, 139, 141, 175–76
Menotomy (Arlington), Massachusetts, 75
merchant-farmer class: loss of income from Jefferson's embargo, 257; Mercy's origins in, 10, 11, 21; Otis family business expansion, 27; protest of molasses duties, 24, 25
Milton, Massachusetts, Warren's house in, 153, 157, 161, 174, 184, 201
minute men militias, 63

molasses, duties on, 28–29
Molasses Act (1733), 24
Montagu, Adm. John, 59–60
Montagu, Elizabeth, 217
Montgomery, Gen. Richard, 7, 101–2
Montgomery, Janet, 7
The Motley Assembly, 137
Murray, Judith (née Sargent), 203–4,
   228, 245
Murray, William Vans, 241

Napoleon Bonaparte, 241
National Aegis, review of Mercy's
   History in, 260
Native Americans, 221, 223
Navigation Acts (1733), 24
Navy, Continental: *Alliance,* 134,
   143, 149–50, 155; Navy Board post
   for James Warren, 125, 135–36,
   141–42, 161
Navy, Royal, 106–7, 124–25
Neponsit Hill home, 153, 157, 161,
   174, 184, 201
neutralist party, 131
newspapers: announcement of
   Mercy's work on *History,* 150, 151;
   on Boston blockade, 61; invitation
   to female writers, 175; Mercy's writ-
   ings in, 49, 69, 138; patriotic role
   of, 58; reviews of Mercy's *History*
   in, 259–60; stories against tea, 54;
   Whately letters publication, 51.
   See also *Boston Gazette*
New York, 29, 77, 101, 122
*Nicholas and Jacob Van Staphorst v.
   Winslow Warren,* 221
Nook's Hill, patriot fortification of, 107

"Observations on the New Constitution..." (Warren, M.), 195–97, 198
"Observations on the Reflections of

the Right Hon. Edmund Burk"
   (Macaulay), 226–27
Oliver, Andrew, 30, 62
"On the Death of the Hon. John
   Winthrop, Esq., L.L.D...."
   (Warren, M.), 137–38
"On the death of two lovely Sisters"
   (Warren, M.), 33
"On Winter" (Warren, M.), 22
Otis, Abigail (sister), 33
Otis, Harrison Gray (nephew), 164,
   224, 258–59
Otis, James, Jr., "Jemmy" (brother):
   appearance at war's end, 164–65;
   and chief justice appointment, 24;
   death of, 165; defection to Tories,
   41–42; education of, 11–12, 14,
   16–17; as legal advisor to family
   business, 27; and Macaulay, 47;
   mental instability of, 14, 16, 29,
   41–42, 43–44; and Mercy, 16, 26,
   33–34, 41, 44, 92, 165; political
   career of, 22, 24–28, 42, 43; portrait
   of, 15; protests against arbitrary
   government, 14, 24; rights crusades
   of, 27–31, 36, 39–41; survival of, in
   Bunker Hill battle, 85; tax protests,
   5, 29; writs of assistance challenge,
   25–26
Otis, James, Sr. (father): background
   of, 7, 8, 10; death of, 133; illness of,
   93, 121; and Jemmy's education,
   14, 17; Mercy's visit to, 64; protests
   against arbitrary government, 24
Otis, John III (grandfather), 10
Otis, Joseph (brother), 7, 11–12, 13,
   27, 174
Otis, Mary (née Allyne) (mother), 7,
   8, 12, 35
Otis, Mercy (Mrs. J. Warren). *See*
   Warren, Mercy (née Otis)

Otis, Rebecca (sister-in-law), 33
Otis, Ruth (née Cunningham) (sister-in-law), 22, 39, 164
Otis, Samuel Allyne (brother), 27, 165, 174, 175, 198–99, 265
Otis family, rebellious roots of, 5

Panoplist, review of Mercy's *History* in, 259–60
Parkman, Breck, 74–75
Parliament, British. *See* Britain, Great
patriotic values: and accusations against James Warren, 142; Federalist attack upon, 195–206; as political poison, 176–77; public's loss of, 127–28, 136, 138–39, 141, 172; Warrens as representatives of, 175, 228
patriots: vs. Hancock, 142; Mercy as patriot, 51, 58, 63, 66, 69, 105; seizure of Hutchinson's home, 76–77; solidarity pre-Revolution, 63; vs. Tories, 4, 58, 71, 126; treason charge fears for wives of, 58, 69. *See also* American Revolution
Pilgrim ancestry, 7, 21
Pitt, William, 33, 35
plays: *The Adulateur,* 48–49; *The Defeat,* 51–52; *The Group,* 67–68, 69–70, 266–67; *The Ladies of Castile,* 168–69; publication of collection, 215–17, 223, 225; *The Sack of Rome,* 179–80, 193
Ploughed Hill, patriot seizure of, 91
Plymouth, Massachusetts: family preparations for war, 73–74; homes in, 4, 21, 22–23, 26; Queen's Guards in, 71; return to living in, 201; risks of staying in during war, 76; sinking of *General Arnold,* 133; Tory/patriot split in, 126, 128

Poems, Dramatic and Miscellaneous (Warren, M.), 210, 215–17, 223, 225
poetry: "Extempore to a young Person ...," 201; "The Genius of America weeping...," 136–37; "Massachusetts Liberty Song," 36–37; "On the Death of the Hon. John Winthrop, Esq., L.L.D....," 137–38; "On the death of two lovely Sisters," 33; "On Winter," 22; overview, 6; publication of collection, 210, 215–17, 223, 225; "Simplicity," 139; "The Squabble of the Sea Nymphs...," 55–56; "A thought on the inestimable Blessing of Reason...," 42; "To a Young Gentleman, residing in France," 159; "To Fidelio," 118; "Written in Deep Affliction," 225
politics: colonial, 23–26, 72, 131–32; discouragement of women from, 5; Hancock vs. James Warren, 142–43; James Warren's marginalization, 161–62, 167–68, 173, 177–78, 185, 189, 197, 199–201, 210, 211–12; and materialism's rise, 173; Mercy's balancing with family, 90–93; Navy Board, 136; Otises in colonial, 10, 17. *See also* Federalists/Federalism; republicans/republicanism; Tories
Pownall, Thomas, 23
Prescott, Gen. William, 83
press, censorship of, 236–37
Providence, Rhode Island, 74, 75
Provincial Congress, Massachusetts, 72–73, 75–76, 85
Puritanism and patriots' values, 128
Putnam, Gen. Israel, 79

Quartering Act (1774), 60, 64
quartering of British soldiers, 37–39, 60, 71–72, 86–87, 129

ratification of Constitution, 197–98

refugees in Massachusetts, 75, 90

religion, Mercy's disapproval of
Calvinism, 13

republicans/republicanism: and censorship of press, 236–37; vs. Federalists, 195–206, 230–32, 236, 240–
42; Jefferson's defense of, 247;
John Adams's shift back to, 259;
and Madison administration, 259;
Mercy's, 188, 209, 222, 240; opposition to war with France, 235–36; and
publication difficulties for *History*,
245–46; and ratification of Constitution, 198, 199; and tyranny of Alien
and Sedition Acts, 237. *See also*
patriots

Revenue (Sugar) Act (1764), 28–29

Revere, Paul, 60, 65, 73

Revolutionary War. *See* American
Revolution

Rhode Island, 74, 75, 77, 118–19, 121

rights, citizens': abrogation of
Boston's, 60; Bill of Rights, 226,
227, 236–37; and Constitution,
196–97; Declaration of Rights
and Grievances, 66; Jefferson on,
61; Jemmy's crusades for, 27–31,
36, 39–41; post-war threats to, 190;
Sam Adams on loss of, 61

*The Rights of the British Colonies
Asserted and Proved* (Otis, J.), 29

riots against British oppression, 30, 38

Robinson, John, 40–41

Rochefoucault Liancourt, Duke de la,
225, 237

rum and molasses duties, 24–25

Russell, Rev. John, 12, 13, 14

The Sack of Rome (Warren, M.),
179–80, 193

Sans Souci, 175–76

Saratoga, Battle of, 129

Sargent, Judith (Mrs. Murray), 203–4,
228, 245

Second Continental Congress. *See*
Continental Congress

self-government for colonies, 4, 34,
50

Sever, Betsy (niece), 152

Sever, Sally (niece), 191

Sever, Sarah (née Warren) (sister-
in-law), 21

Sever, William (brother-in-law), 21

Sewall, Stephen, 24

Shays, Daniel, 187

Shays's Rebellion, 187–88, 191

Shirley, William, 17

"Simplicity" (Warren, M.), 139

smallpox epidemic, 110, 115–16

soldiers, British: atrocities by, 74–
75; on Boston conditions, 106–7;
desertions of, 86; increases in presence of, 71; quartering of, 37–39,
60, 71–72, 86–87, 129; taxes for
support of, 29

solidarity, intercolonial. *See* unity,
intercolonial

Sons of Liberty, 30, 47

spinning meetings, 36

"The Squabble of the Sea Nymphs…"
(Warren, M.), 5, 55–56

St. Clair, Gen. Arthur, 223

Stamp Act (1765), 3, 29–31, 33–34

standing army, threat of British on
American soil, 37–39, 60. *See also*
soldiers, British

states: need for more unity among,
191; objections to Constitution,
196; post-war financial burdens,
168, 174, 185–88; ratification of
Constitution, 197–98

Sugar (Revenue) Act (1764), 28–29
A Summary History of New England (Adams, H.), 237–38

taxes and duties: debt servicing motive for British, 28–29, 35; and Declaratory Act, 34; Molasses Act, 24; in post-war Massachusetts, 168, 185–88; as source of colonies' frustrations, 3–4; Stamp Act, 3, 29–31, 33–34; Sugar Act, 28–29; Tea Act, 3, 42, 53–55, 57–58, 59; Townshend Acts, 35–42; and Whiskey Rebellion, 231–32
Tea Act (1773), 3, 42, 53–55, 57–58, 59
textile production, domestic American, 36
Thomas, Ebenezer, 216
Thomas, Isaiah, 49
"A thought on the inestimable Blessing of Reason . . ." (Warren, M.), 42
Ticonderoga guns in Boston, 102
"To a Young Gentleman, residing in France" (Warren, M.), 159
"To Fidelio" (Warren, M.), 118
Tories (Loyalists): abandonment of Boston, 106–7; as close neighbors to Warrens, 71, 128; and loss of civil rights, 60; in Mercy's satires, 48; at Saratoga, 129; in Warrens' family tree, 127, 130–31; vs. Whigs in pre-Revolution Boston, 4, 37, 42–43, 53–54, 58, 71
Townshend, Charles "Champagne," 35
Townshend Acts (1768), 35–42
trade, British attempts to control American, 24–25, 54. *See also* economy
treason, patriot worries about accusations of, 39, 58, 69

"Treatise on the Immutability of Moral Truth" (Macaulay), 175
Treaty of Paris, 166
Tremont House, Milton, 153, 157, 161, 174, 184, 201
Trenton, Battle of, 123
Turner, Charles, Jr., 261

unity, intercolonial: around Boston blockade, 61, 62–63, 65, 71; and British standing army presence, 37–39; importance for victory, 63; and Lexington and Concord, 77; Mercy on, 66; over Tea Act, 54; support for New York campaign, 129

Van Staphorst, Jacob and Nicolas, 183
variolation, smallpox, 115–16, 117–18, 121, 124, 126
A Vindication of the Conduct of the House of Representatives of the Province of Massachusetts (Otis, J.), 27
Virginia, 29

Ward, Gen. Artemus, 79
War of 1812, 261, 267
Warren, Charles (son): attentiveness of, 154; birth of, 27; childhood of, 53; death of, 181, 183, 185; at Harvard, 150; illness of, 156, 167, 170, 178–79, 181; Mercy on talents of, 152; and Mercy's homecoming during war, 92; survival of storm at sea, 133–34
Warren, Dr. Joseph, 76, 85
Warren, George (son): birth of, 27; career and character of, 230; childhood of, 53; education of, 167, 169; illness and death of, 239; and

Mercy's homecoming during war, 93; Mercy's report to James on, 152; in Northampton, 181; as only son left at home, 150

Warren, Henry (son): attentiveness of, 154; birth of, 27; childhood of, 53; education of, 181; Halifax trip, 170; Hannah Winthrop on, 152–53; illness of, 155, 170; marriage of, 227; and Mercy's homecoming during war, 92; opportunity losses due to politics, 200; revival of government career, 242

Warren, James, Sr. (husband): affection for Mercy, 20–21, 85, 90, 147, 227–28; ancestry of, 21; attachment to farm and family, 114–15, 117, 167; on British Navy's departure from Boston, 107, 109; on Bunker Hill battle, 83; courtship and marriage of, 16–17, 19–21; death of, 258; on Declaration of Independence, 116; on economic conditions during war, 127; financial difficulties, 184, 210, 214; vs. Hancock, 142–43, 167–68; as high sheriff of Plymouth County, 21; on Hutchinson, 45; illnesses of, 100, 214, 215; and James, Jr.'s mental breakdown, 113; on Jefferson, 242, 257; and John Adams, 89, 117, 200, 205, 212–13; loss of state legislative position, 131–32; Mercy's separation anxiety, 64–65, 72–73, 91–92, 99, 118–19, 121; mission to Providence, 74, 75; as paymaster general, 89, 92, 109; political marginalization of, 161–62, 167–68, 173, 177–78, 185, 189, 197, 199–201, 210, 211–12; political slights against, 141–42; portrait of, 6, 84; and Provincial Congress, 72–73, 75–76, 85; republi-

canism of, 43, 105, 190; and Sam Adams, 136, 178, 190; as state legislative representative, 137, 162, 191; support for Mercy's writing, 20, 49, 69; on tax revolt in Massachusetts, 187; wartime role of, 85, 87–88, 98, 114, 118, 125, 135–36, 141–42, 161; and Washington, 88, 200; on Winslow's character, 53

Warren, James, Jr. (son): on *Alliance*, 134, 143, 149–50; birth of, 26; home from college, 100; injury of, 155–56; lack of financial support for disability, 161; mental breakdown of, 112–14; Mercy's expectations of behavior for, 52–53; recovery of, 167; as teacher, 181; veteran's pension for, 240

Warren, James, Sr. (father-in-law), 21, 22

Warren, Marcia (granddaughter), 227

Warren, Mary (née Winslow), 227

Warren, Mercy (née Otis): affection for James, 20–21, 34, 93, 118, 126, 216; on American Indians' plight, 221; anxieties about war, 64–65, 72, 74, 75, 78; appeal for patronage, 211–13; and authorship of *The Blockheads of Boston*, 103–4; on Bernard, 24; birth of, 6; on British Navy's departure from Boston, 107–8; on Bunker Hill battle, 85–86; on Constitution, 191–92, 201; courtship and marriage of, 16–17, 19–21; death of, 267–68; on Declaration of Independence, 117; descriptive portrait in her 80s, 267; domestic life of, 5–6, 12–13, 14, 26, 34, 52, 121–22, 227–28, 230; on economic issues, 127–28, 173–74, 188; education of, 11–12, 13–14; on end of war and independence, 166–67; estrangement from Adamses, 202–5, 217–19, 234, 247–56, 263; eye problems, 153, 154, 156–57, 238–39, 242; family/political obligations balancing, 90–93; fears of Federalism, 189, 202, 222, 240, 243; on French Revolution, 213–14, 241; general illnesses, 59, 77, 90–91, 98, 113, 265; on government forms, 66–67, 105–6, 195–96; on heightened British/colonial tensions, 59; on her mother, 35; on human tendency to bow to power, 211; on Hutchinson, 23, 45, 50; as inspiration to younger female writers, 228; on Intolerable Acts, 61; on James's death, 258; and Jemmy, 16, 26, 33–34, 41, 44, 92, 165; on Lexington battle, 74; loss of sister, 33; and Macaulay, 47–48, 66–67, 91, 124–25, 172, 177, 192; on Montgomery's death, 101–2; moralism of, 113–14, 128, 136–37, 139, 140–41, 143, 175, 179–80; on nadir of Revolution, 122–23; parents of, 3–11; as patriot, 51, 58, 63, 66, 69, 105; portrait of, 6; reaction to smallpox variolation, 118, 124, 126; republicanism of, 188, 209, 222, 240; and Sans Souci, 176; satirical writing risks for, 69; separation anxiety vis-a-vis James, 64–65, 72–73, 91–92, 99, 118–19, 121; on sexuality, 20; on Tories, 58, 106; on unified stance of colonies, 66; as wartime reporter, 4, 88–90, 89, 91, 93; and Washingtons, 88, 110, 217; on Whiskey Rebellion, 232; on women's role in society, 57, 67–68, 69, 76, 106, 140, 169, 229; writing anxieties of, 70, 112, 113, 163. *See also* Adams, Abigail; Adams, John; children; *History of the Rise . . . ;* plays; poetry; Warren, James, Sr. (husband)

Warren, Richard, 21

Warren, Sarah (Mrs. W. Sever) (sister-in-law), 21

Warren, Winslow (son): army career of, 221, 223–24; birth of, 26–27; character of, 53; Codman altercation, 185; death of, 224; European sojourns, 143–44, 148–49, 151–52, 153–54, 155, 170, 179, 181; financial problems of, 159, 166, 183, 184–85, 189, 221–23; Gerry's intervention for, 166; interest in Mercy's writing, 168; and John Adams, 148, 155, 163–64; lifestyle of, 134, 139–41; Mercy's attachment to, 53, 100, 143, 159, 161; and Mercy's homecoming during war, 92–93; opportunity challenges due to politics, 200, 205–6; portrait of, 160; running of family business, 98–99; visit prior to European trip, 147–48

Washington, Gen. George: change of focus to New York, 101; Dorchester fortifications, 106; on Hamilton/Jefferson squabbles, 231; and James Warren, 88, 200; and Mercy, 88, 110, 217; need for more unity among the states, 191

Washington, Martha, 88–89, 110, 177

Watertown, Massachusetts: Edmund Fowle House, 85, 87, 93–94, 109–10; as Provincial Congress HQ, 75–76, 85

weather and British evacuation of Boston, 103

West Barnstable, Massachusetts, 10–11, 17, 78

Whately letters, 50–51

Whigs, 4. *See also* republicans/
republicanism
Whiskey Rebellion, 231–32
A Widow—No Widow, 171–72
Winslow, Edward, 22, 127, 130–31,
170
Winslow, John, 23
Winslow, Mary (Mrs. H. Warren), 227
Winslow, Nathaniel Ray, 71
Winslow, Ned, 127
Winslow, Penny, 34, 58
Winslow House, 22–23
Winthrop, Hannah: on colonists'
ambivalence toward British, 129;
death of, 215; exile to Andover, 94;
on General Court's relocation, 45;
on Henry's character, 152–53; and
husband's illness, 97; on Jemmy's
mental collapse, 43; on Mercy's
access to patriotic leadership, 89;
as Mercy's friend, 34; on Mercy's
plans for *History*, 150–51; Mercy's
visits to, 38, 65; on refugees from
Lexington battle, 75

Winthrop, James, 85, 189, 227, 246
Winthrop, John, 75, 97, 137–38
Wollstonecraft, Mary, 228
women: Abigail Adams on equality
for, 110–12, 141; anonymity of, 7;
commodities trade among, 36, 154,
173–74; critique of Mercy's *History*
as sexist, 260; desirable character
of, 19–20; domestic duties, 5–6, 12–
13, 16–17; education of, 11–12, 13,
19–20, 228; feminist voice, beginnings of, 106, 110–12, 210, 228; John
Adams's veiled sexism, 94, 111, 163,
263; Mercy on societal role of, 57,
67–68, 69, 76, 106, 140, 169, 229;
Mercy's publications as recognition
for, 217
working class, 10, 28, 62
writs of assistance, excessive use
of, 24, 25, 35
"Written in Deep Affliction"
(Warren, M.), 225

Yorktown, Battle of, 157

Diary of Breck Parkman, April 27, 1775, from the Parkman Family Papers. Used by permission of the American Antiquarian Society.

Letter of Samuel Salisbury to Brother Stephen, Box 3, Folder 3, April 20, 1775, Salisbury Family Papers. Used by permission of the American Antiquarian Society.

Letter from Henry Warren to Maria Otis Colby, October 19, 1814, Gay-Otis Papers, permission by the Rare Book & Manuscript Library, Butler Library, Columbia University.

Letter from James Warren, Junior to Maria Otis Colby, May 9, 1814, Gay-Otis Papers, permission by the Rare Book & Manuscript Library, Butler Library, Columbia University.

Letter of Samuel Allyne Otis to Joseph Otis of April 10, 1785, Otis Family Papers, by permission by the Rare Book & Manuscript Library, Butler Library, Columbia University.

Abigail Adams Smith to John Quincy Adams, 28 September 1798, Adams family papers, Massachusetts Historical Society.

Sarah Cary to Henry Cary, 9 September 1814, Cary family papers III, Massachusetts Historical Society.

Hannah Winthrop to Mercy Otis Warren, 6 September 1769, Correspondence with Mercy Otis Warren, Massachusetts Historical Society.

James Warren to Mercy Otis Warren, 18 February 1793, Mercy Otis Warren papers, Massachusetts Historical Society.

Mercy Otis Warren to My dear Girl, undated, Mercy Otis Warren letterbook, pp. 113–15, Mercy Otis Warren papers, Massachusetts Historical Society.

Mercy Otis Warren to John Adams, 4 August 1814, in *Collections of the Massachusetts Historical Society* 5th ser., vol. 4 (Boston: Massachusetts Historical Society, 1878), 509–11.

Mercy Otis Warren to Catharine Macaulay, 28 September 1787, in "Elbridge Gerry, James Warren, Mercy Warren, and the Ratification of the Federal Constitution in Massachusetts," *Proceedings of the Massachusetts Historical Society*, vol. 64 (Boston: Massachusetts Historical Society, 1932), 162–63.